THE FICTIONS IN OUR CONVICTIONS

Essays on the Cultural Imagination

DENNIS PATRICK SLATTERY

Other Books by Dennis Patrick Slattery

The Idiot: Dostoevsky's Fantastic Prince. A Phenomenological Approach (1984)

William Faulkner and Modern Critical Theory. Ed. Dennis Patrick Slattery (1987)

The Wounded Body: Remembering the Markings of Flesh (2000)

Depth Psychology: Meditations in the Field. Co-edited with Lionel Corbett (2000)

Psychology at the Threshold: Selected Papers from the Proceedings of the International Conference at University of California, Santa Barbara, 2000. Coedited with Lionel Corbett (2003)

Grace in the Desert: Awakening to the Gifts of Monastic Life (2004)

Harvesting Darkness: Essays on Literature, Myth, Film and Culture (2006)

A Limbo of Shards: Essays on Memory, Myth and Metaphor (2006)

Varieties of Mythic Experience: Essays on Religion, Psyche and Culture. Co-edited with Glen Slater (2008)

Reimagining Education: Essays on Reviving the Soul of Learning. Co-edited with Jennifer Leigh Selig (2009/2019)

Day-to-Day Dante: Exploring Personal Myth Through The Divine Comedy. (2011)

Re-Ensouling Education: Essays on the Importance of the Humanities in Schooling the Soul. Co-edited with Jennifer Leigh Selig and Stephen Aizenstat (2012/2019)

Riting Myth, Mythic Writing: Plotting Your Personal Story (2012)

Creases in Culture: Essays Towards a Poetics of Depth (2014)

Our Daily Breach: Exploring Personal Myth Through Herman Melville's Moby-Dick (2015)

Bridge Work: Essays on Mythology, Literature and Psychology (2015)

A Pilgrimage Beyond Belief: Spiritual Journeys through Christian and Buddhist Monasteries of the American West (2017)

Deep Creativity: Seven Ways to Spark Your Creative Spirit. Co-authored with Deborah Anne Quibell and Jennifer Leigh Selig (2019)

Correspondence: 1927-1987 Joseph Campbell. Co-edited with Evans Lansing Smith (2019)

From War to Wonder: Recovering One's Personal Myth Through Homer's Odyssey (2019)

An Obscure Order: Reflections on Cultural Mythologies (2020)

The Way of Myth: Stories' Subtle Wisdom (2021)

Poetry

Casting the Shadows: Selected Poems (2001)
Just Below the Water Line: Selected Poems (2004)
Twisted Sky: Selected Poems (2007)
The Beauty Between Words: Selected Poetry of Dennis Patrick Slattery and Chris Paris (2010)
Feathered Ladder: Selected Poems of Dennis Patrick Slattery and Brian Landis. (2014)
Road, Frame, Window: A Poetics of Seeing. Selected Poems of Timothy Donohue, Donald Carlson and Dennis Patrick Slattery (2015)
Leaves from the World Tree: Selected Poems of Craig Deininger and Dennis Patrick Slattery (2018)

Novel

Simon's Crossing. A Novel. Co-authored with Charles Asher (2010)

Unpublished Titles

Sticky Blood: Redeeming the Violent and Violated Body in Fyodor Dostoevsky's Crime and Punishment (1982)
From Your First Mile to Your First Marathon Without Injury. Co-authored with Jerry Poole (1984)

CDs

Casting the Shadows: Selected Poems. Recorded/Mastered by Dan Canalos, Soundwaves Recordings, Huron, Ohio. (2002)
Just Below the Water Line: Selected Poems. Recorded/Mastered Dan Canalos, Graphic layout Kristen Schoewe. Soundwaves Recordings, Huron, Ohio. (2006)

THE FICTIONS IN OUR CONVICTIONS

Essays on the Cultural Imagination

———— • ————

DENNIS PATRICK SLATTERY

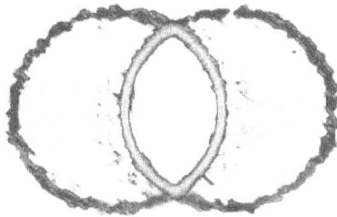

MANDORLA BOOKS
WWW.MANDORLABOOKS.COM

Front Cover Art © Can Stock Photo / PsychoShadowCover
Cover design: Jennifer Leigh Selig
Back cover photograph: Sandy Slattery

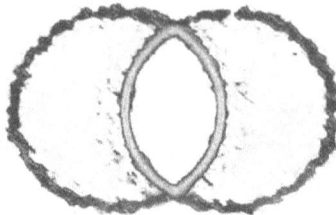

MANDORLA BOOKS
WWW.MANDORLABOOKS.COM

DEDICATION

To Sandy, my bride of 55 years, for her gifts of unconditional support and for creating a space for me to pursue a life of writing and teaching. We are *both* present in these pages.

Being human is a surprise, not a foregone conclusion. A person has the capacity to create events. Every person is a disclosure, an example of exclusiveness.

~Abraham Joshua Heschel, *I Asked for Wonder*, 72.

The intrusions of the 'mundane' become agents of the sublime. They are incorporated— 'bodied,' into the divine.

~Lynda Sexson, *Ordinarily Sacred*, 11.

...we too fail to see the mythologies that underpin our sense of who we are and the kind of universe we inhabit.

~Stephen Batchelor, *Living with the Devil: A Meditation on Good and Evil*, 4.

This is how the Koan appears in everyday life: the unanswerable questions of our lives are the greatest teachers.

~Pema Chodron, *Start Where You Are: A Guide to Compassionate Living*, 60.

Do we ever really leave our childhood home? Or rather, does our primal experience there stay with us and influence, haunt, our contemporary choices?

~James Hollis, *Hauntings: Dispelling the Ghosts Who Run Our Lives*, 33.

Strong and universal as the urge has always been to listen to a story, the urge to tell it has been stronger.

~Ruth Sawyer, *The Way of the Storyteller*, 38.

TABLE OF CONTENTS

FOREWORD

I met Dennis Patrick Slattery in the fall of 1988. I had just been hired by Incarnate Word College, now the University of the Incarnate Word. Dennis had joined the College's English Department one year before. I was in the Sociology Department.

We quickly learned that we shared many things in common: our politics tracked the same path, we both loved to read and watch movies, we both had been undergraduates at community colleges, Dennis in Ohio, and me in Kansas. The reader of this wonderful collection of essays will also learn that we have a mutual passion for trout fishing, an adventure we have nourished for three decades. We also share a passion for teaching and in Dennis's years at Incarnate Word, before he joined Pacifica Graduate Institute in 1995, he and I taught a number of interdisciplinary courses together, courses with titles like "Altaring the Image," and "Origins of Self and "Expressions of Soul." Other faculty would join us on occasion, but Dennis and I were always constant participants. Maybe I should say "mutual explorers."

We have shared other experiences as well: on the steps of the U.S. Capitol protesting an impending war, camping and hiking in Big Bend National Park, attending conferences together. We have watched our children grow into marvelous examples of adulthood, helped one another through various woundings of our bodies, and shared the joy of Christmas celebrations. In all of this, books have exchanged hands, ideas have been discussed for hours on end, and our families have meshed in rewarding ways.

So, I think I know something about what makes Dennis tick, but it doesn't arrive easily in a tight summary. After all, Dennis is a poet, a mythologist, an artist, a man who knows C.G. Jung, Joseph Campbell, and James Hillman well. I am none of those things.

Still, I know him, and I've learned from him. The reader of this volume will come to know and learn from him as well. What you will learn is the mystery of exploration, the exploration of an interior world of the human spirit. One will learn this world through stories and myth. Dennis is the master storyteller, and it is through stories that the myths that shape and guide us are revealed.

In *The Way of the Storyteller*, Ruth Sawyer writes about her book, "It is a call to go questing, an urge to follow the way of the storyteller as pilgrims followed the way of Saint James in the Middle Ages, not for riches or knowledge or power, but that each might find 'something for which his soul had cried out.' I believe it to be something that transcends method, technique—the hows and the whys. It is, in the main, spiritual experience which makes storytellers" (20).

There are three elements in Sawyer's observation that catch my attention. First, the idea that storytelling is a questing, an exploration. Second, the subject of the quest is that for which the soul cries out. Third, that this experience is spiritual in form. As one reads Dennis' collection in this book, look for evidence of all three elements coming into play. They won't be hard to find.

The collection begins with a family story, one of growing up with an alcoholic father whose rage could be all-consuming. Dennis begins here with a quest to understand this haunted past. It is not just to recite the traumas of childhood; it is his desire to see how his father's rage shaped Dennis's own soul. The story is not only of Dennis' myths, but those of his father as well, and of how time gives the soul a chance to claim redemption and heal. And, make no mistake about it, the reader will discover throughout this volume that this journey is deeply spiritual. Read what happens when Dennis goes on his three-month monastery journey and describes who comes along for the ride. That entire story is infused with spiritual themes and is beautifully told.

When Dennis and I first met, I was much the "theory guy." I had immersed myself in Karl Marx, Max Weber, and Emile Durkheim, and I tended to see society and social relations through the lens of those great classical sociologists. But I was not a storyteller. I was trying to pass on great truths. As Dennis and I spent more time together and I told him about my experiences teaching in a federal penitentiary, visiting death row in Arkansas on two occasions (the second visit coinciding with the governor commuting all fifteen death sentences), and my work in the anti-Vietnam War movement, Dennis made a simple, but profoundly impactful, observation. "You have great stories to tell," he said. "Teach by telling your stories." So, I did. Students loved it, and I enjoyed sharing my stories. It changed my teaching for the better, I believe, and I have Dennis to thank for that.

In essay #4, "A Pilgrimage from Haunting to Healing," in writing about his monastery journey, Dennis "recalled my promise to myself in planning this pilgrimage: look for nothing. Move from place to place, settle in wherever you are, submit to who and what you find there, and take careful note of what emerges on its own for contemplation…. Stay open and surrender."

I retired from UIW in May, 2021. I made the decision some three and a half semesters earlier. But, over beers, I shared with Dennis my concern that I might not have anything to do when I retired, and that was a cause for worry, as I have a history of being active. Dennis' advice to me: "Open up the space and see what fills it." Note the similarity to the advice that he gives himself in the essay: "…settle in wherever you are, submit to who and what you find there…. Stay open and surrender." In other words, give yourself space. One could easily see this as good advice not only for a journey or retirement, but wise words for one to remember all the time. And, by the way, in my retirement, I have found plenty to "fill it."

The first set of essays in this volume serve as an overview of what it is to be a scholar of myth, to grapple with Jung's question in essay #7: "What is the myth you are living?" Dennis describes this question as "one of the most important 'calls to adventure' we can embark on." I see all thirteen essays as valuable commentary in multiple ways on Jung's question.

I would also urge the reader to go deeply into the second set of essays, "Vignettes on Culture." These are op-eds that appeared in the *New Braunfels Herald-Zeitung* and the *San Antonio Express-News*. The range here is vast: our national mythic crossroads, meditation, authoritarianism, spectacle and substance, aging, friendship, and, yes, trout fishing, among others. I like these because they demonstrate that Dennis is not only an academic, but a public intellectual, unafraid to share his views on a range of topics, even if some readers may not agree with him on some topics.

Consider his response in essay #25, "Preserving Our Innocence: At What Cost?" Here he comments on the actions of a Texas state senator to presumably censor or ban some 850 books the senator considers "inappropriate." Dennis responds: "Literature that brings into consciousness topics of race, gender identity, economics, disparities of wealth and privilege, migrants, haves and have-nots, should not be purged but promoted within a context that does not breed feuds." Sane. Sensible. Responsible. A sound, reasoned voice.

Dennis tells us, "We are myth-making all the time." It also means we are continually on journeys of one kind or other. Dennis has given us a journey of many hues and shapes in this collection. So, relax, kick back, and enjoy your journey with Dennis Patrick Slattery.

Roger C. Barnes, Ph.D.
Professor Emeritus of Sociology
University of the Incarnate Word
San Antonio, Texas

INTRODUCTION

"Two folk-crafts have provided figures of speech for traditional story-telling: to spin a yarn—to weave a tale. These are good words to keep in one's mind. They provide better pictures for the real art of storytelling. . .."
~Ruth Sawyer, *The Way of the Storyteller*, 143

The series of essays in this volume do not need much of an introduction. They are quite frankly, subjects that I was drawn to over time and many to which I have returned to deepen my understanding of the themes' complexities.

Like a moth might be drawn to a flamingo because the flight holds a promise of an insight or two, so do my writings in the early morning hours lean into the darkness for inspiration. But they are also drawn to the candle I light each morning about 4:30 within a few feet from my study chair and a small gooseneck lamp. It offers a halo of light in an otherwise darkened envelope. In that cocoon of light pushing gently against the darkness, I begin the warmup of writing by an invitation of yesterday to instruct me on what wishes to be included from its multiple plotlines.

I accept the fact that part of what I remember and write down carry fictional elements in them, storied parts that contain the content of re-membrances. So yesterday already has an "as-if" quality about it.

The range of topics included in this volume mirrors what flowed in my imagination, then solidified into the words you will traverse here. In his poem, "The Guest House," Jelaluddin Balkhi Rumi suggests we be grateful for whatever guests arrive each day. I include in my guest list ideas, images, intuitions, memories, and partly formed phrases that express the creative life in me, however incompletely.

In each essay, an embryonic myth hibernates yet seeks citizenship in the world. It is birthed through imaginative midwifery. Each began with a benevolent demand, like some dreams that abrupt themselves into view long after waking. Perhaps when I am distracted when vacuuming the carpets or emptying the dish washer, or blowing leaves off the front deck, images appear out of the air for recognition and possible renewal. I stay open to oblige these presences. Hence, they are fictions of my convictions, hopes, fears, and desires.

James Hillman suggests that "Fantasy images that are the stuff and values of soul are structured by archetypes. . ... These paths are mythological; or rather, we see that fantasy flows into particular motifs (mythologems) and constellations of persons in actions (mythemes)" (*Revisioning Psychology* 23). What you will read here, then, are my "as-if" fictions. I like to think of the collaborative fictions formed in the intimacy of writer and reader.

In another poem, "On Resurrection Day," Rumi suggests that a dream is a place, and it stays in place, insistent, and demands to be interpreted. So, I write to interpret, in league for a short time with the god Hermes, the evocative divinity of Hermeneutics; so many of our stories are attempts to interpret the deep mysteries that surround us and live within us. In writing, I imagine I am awakening the dream on levels I could not have earlier imagined. Like Ivan Ilych in Tolstoy's masterpiece: in his fierce fight to remain unconscious Ilych battles his own dis-ease that eventually stirs him into consciousness. Or Ishmael, narrator of *Moby-Dick*, whose soul grows at the end of his quill to write his way to wholeness.

In the same way that I have found joy over the decades in reading, so that same joy eventually migrated into writing. Both writing and reading increase the orbit of mindfulness and of gratitude. In reading the stories of others I find folds of my own narrative that embrace my identity; they then journey out to experience the sufferings, joys, aspirations, defeats and achievements of others.

What I read into a story is largely reflective of what I extract from it that nourishes my own plotting, plodding journey to meaning, coherence and a joyful bond with others. Said another way, my personal myth entangles with theirs because I am their other and they are mine through the gift of analogy. When I discover just how much we share the same fictions, the same myths, that joy is increased, as I suspect will happen here.

Certain stories insist on being reread, like a piece of music or a work of art that insists on being experienced repeatedly because there is something else it wishes to impart to us. I love Rabbi Abraham Joshua Heschel's words on "Expectations": "There is a question that follows me wherever I turn. What is expected of me? What is demanded of me?" (*I Asked for Wonder* 85). I sense this same imperative when I read certain narratives.

Narratives need us to complete them even as they complete us; we oblige this need when we read creatively, meditatively, and deeply in unbiased expectation. Hillman is helpful here as well: "Our archetypal fictions keep their mythopoeic, their truly fictional, character beyond what we do or say about them. We can never be certain whether we imagine them, or they imagine us, . . . (*Revisioning* 151). Simply put, it takes two to entangle.

In all the articles, books, talks, courses, and interviews I have created, each expected something from me. My own growing awareness of the universal stories clinging to my partial, sometimes tattered plot, has dismantled barriers between myself and others. Reading and writing become generous acts of liberation from my own narrow-gauged aspirations and needs. In such liberation we are put in touch with a story's meaning for us now, yet always susceptible to editing to deepen an initial insight.

As Rabbi Heschel asked these questions above, and which I have included in a story's demands, I cite him once more: "Meaning is found in responding to the demand, meaning is found in serving the demand" (*I Asked for Wonder* 85). Writing is a service industry; writing is social and mythic activism; writing is a *via*, a way of seeing that develops as it deconstructs comfortable bromides.

My hope is that one or another of these chapters brings you to wonder as you discover analogies to your own story, or that you feel the inklings of the poem that has been guiding your soul. What a story finally means rests on the creative imagination evoked to complete it. Such is the power of its fictions.

That it carries a meaning that perdures and ripens for you as you continue your mythopoetic adventure to a life well-lived. This is what matters most to me in my writing—to connect with your own mystery and yours with mine.

Works Cited

Heschel, Abraham Joshua. *I Asked for Wonder: A Spiritual Anthology.* Edited and with an introduction by Samuel H. Dresner. Crossroad Publishing, 2010.

Hillman, James. *Revisioning Psychology.* HarperCollins Publishers, 1977.

Sawyer, Ruth. *The Way of the Storyteller.* Penguin Books, 1976.

PART I

WAYS BELIEFS SHAPE US

1

HEALING INTO WHOLENESS AS MYTHICAL METHOD*

"We interpret our world and ourselves through the invention of our imagination, through our fictions."
~Annie Dillard, *Living by Fiction*

I am at a place where I wish I could tell you two stories, even ten stories, but I can't. I must try to score with one story, and it will be my own. I think this theme is brilliant in congealing myth and healing. I thought recently about this idea: Myths provide the media and perhaps the mucilage, by which we coax our own stories into being and into being part of others' narratives.

Our stories are benevolent witnesses, reminding us daily who, what, and why we are. Who cannot benefit from such fresh remembering, especially when they often carry the wounds from our past that we might spend our lives being haunted by and healing from? Our stories provide a means of stepping back, as one might do with a painting they are creating, in order to see the images whole, at a distance, and so gain a perspective lost when we are too close to it.

Listen at the outset as the German poet, Rainer Maria Rilke, responds in his eighth letter to a young army poet who is struggling with his own creative process: "Just bear in mind that sickness is the means by which an organism frees itself from what is alien; so one must simply help it to

** Originally delivered to the Mythologium Conference Sponsored by the Alumni Association in Mythological Studies, Pacifica Graduate Institute, July, 2021

be sick, to have its whole sickness and to break out with it since that is the way it gets better" (*Letters to a Young Poet* 93-94). Rilke's response acts like a balm to the young man and helps him with his frustrations as a writer.

Our ability and desire to tell our own stories to others is itself a healing step toward wholeness. However, some of our stories should not be told, perhaps never uttered, for they can damage us in the telling; some discernment is necessary on our mythic journey as storytellers. In his powerful little book, *The Oldest Story in the World,* writer, filmmaker, pilgrimage leader, novelist, and cultural critic, Phil Cousineau, writes of a friend, P.J. Curtis in County Clare, Ireland who told him, "A story lives at the heart of every journey. A journey without a story told is a journey incomplete. When a story is gathered on the road and re-told on arrival can it be said that the traveler has truly made a journey home" (*Oldest* 73).

I would add that within each of our stories is a myth throbbing at its center; it too wants a place in the world, for these stories carry what we believe, value, hold dear, fear, and guide us into terrains where no stories have yet been birthed. Our stories gather our beliefs and relay them in narrative form. Where life is most awesome is often where our stories find their deepest descent into meanings that matter.

I confess at the beginning that I began this presentation twice before I settled on what I am going to present to you now. My first inclination, which I went back to with the intention of deepening my understanding of illness and wellness, was two stories: Leo Tolstoy's *The Death of Ivan Illich* and Flannery O'Connor's short story, "Revelation," which she wrote toward the end of her life. Both stories have illness and wounding as the precursor for shocking and agonizing pathways to healing. But something was not right with this safe way into and out of the topic for this mythically charged conference.

Then something or someone drew me back to read "The Prologue" to Jung's own autobiography, *Memories, Dreams, Reflections.* There he writes to us the reason for this task he set himself in the 83rd year of his life: "My life is a story of the self-realization of the unconscious. Everything in the unconscious seeks outward manifestation and the personality too desires to evolve out of its unconscious condition and to experience itself as a whole" (3). It is not a choice for Jung but part of his destiny, a quest late in life to reflect on what made him the person he is.

He continues: "Inner experiences also set their seal on the outward events that came my way and assumed importance for me in youth or later on" (5). His life quest was the daily pursuit of the grail of his inner life; that is where he found the goal of living, the clarity of meaning, and the coherence of his being.

I learned from him that to live a life, one moves forward; to understand a life, one spirals backward, into that mythic climate where memory and imagination congeal to deploy a life of meaning. Stories, you all realize, are ways to contemplate in narrative form, to grasp the deeper identity and to reevaluate what is important to one's purpose. Since not many of you know much of my personal story, I wish to tell an important aspect of my history to clarify, perhaps, for myself as well as you, where wounding pushed me into wonder and then into healing the fractured myth I was living. In this process, my destiny began to unfold with more certainty.

I sense that telling you this story will expose and establish the truth about myself through moments of mythic awareness. I will let you be the judge of the success of my task or of missing the mark in these remembrances. For narratives can capture and hold, for perhaps only a moment, the phantoms that glide through our lives, at times in regal splendor and at others in overwhelming horror. For trauma itself is an archetypal reality that can cause the soul to shudder.

To engage this story, I want to call on the figure of Asclepios who is given full measure in Edward Tick's fine study, *The Practice of Dream Healing: Bringing Ancient Greek Mysteries into Modern Medicine.* Early on he cites Joseph Campbell's insights into the genre of tragedy, where I sense that a deep wounding often involves some convolution, followed by a healing resolution and even absolution: Tragedy, Campbell observes, is "precisely the counterpart, psychologically, of the purgation of spirit effected by rite" (qtd. in *The Practice of Dream Healing* 12). I add here at the outset that such a rite is the act of writing itself. Both [tragedy and purgation] affect catharsis, writes Tick. "Where tragedy dissolves, Campbell states, myth begins. Healing is the leap out of suffering into myth" (*Dream Healing* 12).

Asclepios, a prototype of the Christ-like figure, observes Tick, "was one who healed by his art and his gentle ways, using his skill to work out the riddles of our illnesses" (*Dream Healing* 17). I therefore invite and evoke this healer whose compassionate methods feel suitable for today's occasion.

Inheriting the Wound of a Parent

I was born in 1944 in Cleveland, Ohio, the second of seven children. Two died early, one in a miscarriage, the other after one month. They were both girls. I have on several occasions in visits to Ohio, visited the grave of Mary Elizabeth, who was buried in a cemetery on Cleveland's west side. My brother and I would bring flowers and spruce up her grave site while talking to her of how we missed her presence in our family.

My brother Marty and I were born first, before my other two brothers and one sister; we lived with our parents in a dingy, dark-halled apartment building on St. Clare Avenue on Cleveland's east side. Given the history of Saint Clare who founded the Poor Sisters of Saint Clare in Assisi and who died in 1253, the street name aptly described our apartment building. Shops were below and apartments were on the second floor.

Our apartment consisted of a small kitchen, one bedroom, a living room and bathroom. The living room was converted each evening into a second bedroom for my parents. A trundle bed dropped down out of a narrow, shallow recess in the wall. Next to this recess was a curtain hiding a storage area where various family items were kept. I always feared that curtain and more specifically the haunting ghosts that my brother had convinced me were sleeping in that dark space. My brother and I shared the small bedroom beside the hall doorway.

Behind the apartment was a pock-marked gravel driveway and parking lot for the other tenants. The landlord refused to fill in the holes that formed from traffic and brutal winter snow and ice. Behind it was a patch of green that a neighbor gardened, then a narrow street that ran parallel to the railroad tracks for New York Central freight trains. We grew up playing by the train tracks with no sense of danger. It was far more interesting than the gravel driveway or the busy St. Clare Avenue in front of the building.

When I was three or four, my brother and I and our friend Butchie Morehead, who lived above his parents' dry-cleaning business, were all caught by the Cleveland Police for throwing stones at the cattle cars carrying their cargo to slaughterhouses in Chicago. The patrol car came up quietly behind us and one uniform called us over. We were taken home and handed over to our parents. I did not know then how angry I was as a child or for what reasons. I knew that our home life was not ordinary but could not grasp how it was. My parents punished us by taking away our playtime. Butchie's parents beat him badly, as we witnessed when we gathered a week later.

Downstairs of our dingy, poorly lighted hallway, with its dirty yellow and brown walls and a dark brown rubber runway that thinly covered the hallway floors, was a modest diner, Morehead Dry Cleaners, and a shoe store. We smelled food aromas from mid-morning into the evening. At the end of the hall farthest from our apartment, was our dentist, Dr. Locks' office. He loved to smoke big cigars and tell jokes when he cleaned our teeth or filled a decayed one or pulled one beyond repair.

He called us sissies when we asked for Novocain when a tooth was to be filled. I think he had a crush on my mother and so enjoyed seeing us come in for an appointment. We avoided that end of the hall unless forced down to the cul-de-sac office for what we knew would be a painful ordeal, sprinkled with cigar ash.

I knew at a young age that on the weekends my father would load up on beer and drink for most of Saturday and Sunday. I understood this as normal behavior because I did not remember anything different. It was part of the family myth that we all accepted as part of growing up. Most myths, as you know, find places for rituals to enact it; my father handled that requirement with frightening precision. I use the word "frightening" with full consciousness of its implications.

He and his two brothers were all alcoholics. His brothers did not get angry or surly when they drank, at least not to our knowledge, but my father did. We were all taught to keep the family secret hermetically sealed, lips shut tight in all conversations with our relatives and friends. Irish Catholics do not generally speak of alcoholism in their families. The alcoholic may be called a "character," which one writer has written, is code for "don't let him have the keys to the car." Alcoholics Anonymous had been founded only 20 years earlier and was not well-known. Al-Anon was not yet in existence, so alcoholism was understood as a failure of willpower, not an illness.

In 1950 my father announced that we were moving to the suburbs. We moved the very day that a two-story home next door, beyond the gravel driveway, caught fire and burned beyond repair. So, our send-off from the drab brick apartment building was fire and destruction. We moved into a two-story brick home with a single attached garage in Euclid, Ohio, part of which territory abutted the shores of Lake Erie, a polluted sewer at that time, courtesy of Industry and lax sewage treatment plants.

Our new home had three modest bedrooms and one bathroom upstairs. Attached was a one-car garage that we converted into a summer room in the spring and summer months. Then, shortly after our move, my second brother was born. I was aware that empty beer bottles had followed us to this suburban home, a luxury palace after the apartment on one of the busiest streets in the area. Decades later, when I visited the Poor Clare's church in Assisi, Italy, I always recalled her namesake just outside our apartment building, and how much we would have been thankful for her intercession in our violent home.

My father walked each workday morning to Holy Cross Catholic Church for the 6:15 Mass. He then boarded a bus outside the church and rode downtown to The Cleveland Electric Illuminating Company, where he worked in Personnel, now called Human Resources. Things were quiet during the week. But now, in his own home, and with no neighbors on the other side of the wall, he began to ramp up his alcohol consumption, alternating beers with cheap Mogen David wine on Friday evenings after dinner.

Sometimes he would not come directly home on Friday after work; instead, he detoured into Lokar's tavern at the end of our street. My sweet mother, growing more exasperated because we were waiting for his arrival before beginning to eat dinner, would ask my older brother or me to walk to the tavern, find what barstool he was perched on, however unsteadily, and tell him mom said dinner was ready. His response was most often: "Go on home—tell her I'll be along soon." Maybe…. maybe not. The longer he drank at Lokar's, the more anxious we all became because of his anger—no, rage—when he finally stumbled through the front door.

The same myth, but different rituals to accommodate the all-pervasive, all-consuming energy of alcoholism, consumed my father, another sad and helpless victim of an insatiable illness that could not be quenched. I wondered, years later—does each addiction have its own mythology through which it unleashes its insatiable thirst on all those around them? I have read that one addict directly affects or influences at least ten other people. I think that number is far too conservative.

As time passed, we all became aware of the ritual pattern his addiction insisted on: Friday evening, stop and drink or walk directly home from the bus stop and then begin drinking: Rage level: low and tolerable.

Saturday morning, early. Clean the downstairs, wash the kitchen floor, vacuum the living room. All was prep work for a day of hard drinking, either at home, or at his favorite tavern on Waterloo Road in Cleveland. That he drove the car for decades and was not pulled over for a DUI is a miracle. Rage level: needle moving towards outrage.

As we grew older, he would invite us along, giving my mother blessed relief. We would drink orange or grape NIHs and enjoy playing shuffleboard with very heavy chrome disks sliding across the sawdust surface, while Dad would sit at the bar with his cronies and get drunk. Then, the car full of smoke from his incessant smoking of Chesterfield cigarettes, we would drive home. There the fun really began, later Saturday afternoon. I pause here to reveal an observation from storyteller Clarissa Pinkola Estes: "Stories set the inner life into motion, and this is particularly important where the inner life is frightened, wedged, or cornered" (personal correspondence from Bob Wagner on a post from Richard Rohr 1/10/21). Looking back, I can feel adrenaline rush in to surround our growing fear and dread over the drama about to unfold for the hundredth time.

My father would catch second and then third gear now; he would transform from a mild, reticent man during the week, who spoke little to us, to a raging alcoholic for the rest of the weekend, or at least until Sunday afternoon, when he would desperately and pitifully attempt to sober up enough to make it to work on Monday morning. If not, my mother would call in an excuse; Roger was not feeling well, probably the flu. They all knew at his place of employment what his actual condition was.

On weekends for decades, our home became a concentration camp. By using that term, I mean it became a container that unleashed all my father's rage and unhappiness, a concentrated space from where he projected his violent interior onto us. As I look back through mirrors that are less distorted than they were then, I sense that he was enraged over the life he did not live, did not fulfill, did not risk, did not brush up against with some aspiring intentions. I believe I took this in on some unconscious level and made a pact with myself not to repeat his alcoholism nor his unlived life, which he handed down to us, unknowingly, but with fierce repetition. My intention not to repeat his life was only mildly successful.

I pause here to tell you all that writing this piece of my history, then reading it to you, is already a healing event for me. It may touch your own history and have some salvaging effect on you as well. That is my hope in even presenting this story. I see now that we were all in myth together: the myth of addiction, the myth of salvation, the myth of the journey and hundreds more; each has a power beyond measure. But we may have lived in these myths unknowingly; our family goal was to keep it secret. We tried to transplant one myth on top of another—secrecy about the traumatic life we were cocooned in, as I and my family did for decades.

The ritual pattern for the myth of addiction instilled in each of us—now three children, then a fourth, my sweet sister, who my mother once admitted, saved her life from so much oppressive male energy. Those are my words, but her sentiment. On the front lines, she had taken the full blast of my father's weekend rages full in the face; she was at times the recipient of physical abuse. Isn't that also the pattern in relationships, with or without an addiction: attack and abuse those around you who love you most? Makes perfect psychological sense in its emotional obscenity.

When my father drank heavily on weekends, he drew his sword like a mythical warrior and swung it at invisible enemies. But finding none, he turned it on those who lived in the tiny citadel with him, those who loved him. I think this wound, of being attacked by those who love you, is one of the most shaming of all; it infects those wounded with a venom of rage and resentment. So was my experience. But as I will mention soon, it caused me to begin to wonder, after decades, what was driving his behavior and his rigid refusal to admit that he had a serious dysfunction?

Fully engaged without choice in the myth he deployed on weekends, but which resonated throughout the entire week, we metabolized the emotions of shame, guilt, and anger, if not rage and fear, and honed the practice of being extremely vigilant towards the sounds downstairs on the weekends. They would erupt into yelling back and forth, plates breaking, and a loving relationship bombarded with massive detonations of disappointment. Our own beings were shaped by the addiction myth and its angry explosive expressions.

We never spoke of these horrific weekends; as we grew older, we would try to stay with friends or relatives from Friday evening to Sunday morning to escape the sandblasting of his disgust with himself and the burden of shame he carried behind him like a bag full of heavy fragments of scorn. He also burdened us with the beast that, with complete indifference, devoured him and us more completely over time.

This was our monster in the underworld that we were forced to confront without any weapons or deep understanding except disgust, shame, and fear; we carried his burden as well as our own; we ran from the rampaging chaos. In time, my older brother quit high school and joined the Navy, successfully escaping onto an aircraft carrier for four years. He never returned home.

When I was sixteen, I began working in the produce department of a large supermarket chain. I attended high school classes all week, then worked Friday evenings and all-day Saturday. Every Saturday morning, I happily escaped the house when Jim O'Rourke, a card-carrying Irish alcoholic neighbor, picked me up at 6 a.m. He pulled up in front of our house at exactly that hour in his green Buick that smelled of celery, lettuce, and produce, but celery ruled.

We drove into Cleveland to set up the produce department he managed before the store opened at 9 a.m. He then drove me home at 7:30-8 p.m. These Saturdays working all day liberated me from the chaos of the home—of course until I returned in the evening exhausted and increasingly depressed as I turned the knob of the back door to enter the rampage inside.

I think a turn occurred when what happened one evening shifted something in me. More than once, but this occasion stands out, my father, wild now and drunk, often in his underwear and barefoot, would in a wild-eyed frenzy, berate me with "You are worthless, you'll never amount to anything." Exhausted from work, I was vulnerable to these deep slivers of unworthiness. But I could not calculate them or square them with my actual life; I was paying my own tuition to a local private Catholic Marianist high school, had by now bought my own car, and did well in school. My confusion tormented me.

I nonetheless absorbed his criticism as true, for beyond the fog and ferocity, he was my father and carried that archetype for all of us, in however a wild and distorted form. I gained a profound understanding years later of the immense energy that an archetype is capable of unleashing and sustaining in the soul for decades. But at this moment I was naïve and immensely annoyed.

On one particular Saturday evening—and it is painful to admit it, but it is part of the narrative—I listened to him on the staircase berating me as I tried to walk upstairs to my room. But he was uncontrollable and relentless in his attack. In an altered state, as I reached him, I simply swung around and pushed him down the stairs. He was so drunk that he bounced down the six carpeted stairs and lay at the bottom fully awake but quiet.

He no longer verbally abused me after that incident. I had, in that one survival response to his narrative, inserted mine into his by exchanging violence for violence; the story stuck, and his verbal abuse ended. But the shame I carried at this outburst of mine for having become him in that moment, and without alcohol, shaped my sense of myself that severely ridiculed what I had been constructively doing with my life.

Before this incident, when I was thirteen or fourteen, I carried some of the demeaning effects of his illness into my body. I suffered from terrible acne, wet my bed way past the time for that activity to stop, and was anxious all the time about everything. I had successfully interiorized my father's psyche, his emotional life, and his feelings of unworthiness. The shame was an ongoing curse and extremely infectious.

I subsequently learned that shame and fear are on one side of a coin that contained resentment and rage on the other. I could not see myself as I was and became my own worst adversary. I carried the demeaning archetype deep in my body, and it became the core of a defining myth that was extremely self-absorbing and demeaning. Knowing nothing about psychology nor the power of psychological projection, I took out a subscription to this story that was annually renewed.

I had bought into his narrative at the expense of letting my own story languish in the shadows. I was miserable and became more withdrawn, even though in high school I was elected to be homeroom president and eventually student council treasurer. I was a perfect poster for a version of what Joseph Campbell has called "mythic dissociation." My interior life was split from how I lived in the world, hiding in shame but keeping it concealed and affecting a bravado posture. The energy required for such a sham was enormous. I felt constant fatigue.

I had not yet reached that place that Dan McAdams refers to in *The Stories We Live By*: "At some point in our lives we become aware of the task to create an integrative life story. Through it we come to understand who we are and how we fit into the adult world" (91). You will enjoy the fact that the chapter in which he wrote this he called "Becoming the Mythmaker." I would say it this way: at this stage in my journey, I had no perspective that I could call my own. If there was anything that might resemble a mythological perspective, it was that of illness, of pathology as normality, because it revealed to me that illness is itself a perspective.

I saw the world through the complicated context of addiction but was too naïve to give it a coherent shape or form; that is, I could not grasp it mythopoetically. I did not drink, even as a senior in high school, for fear of becoming like my father; what I was unconscious of was that I had invited or been invaded by all the salient destructive patterns of the alcoholic. In short, the booze was not the problem but a symptom of something far deeper, more spiritual, more agonizing.

The myth was having the time of its life living me, manipulating and conquering me. I felt most uncomfortable in those social situations where people talked about themselves—their favorite color, their favorite sports team, their favorite movie, their plans for a career; I realized in listening silently to them that I had no favorites, had never thought about a favorite color, much less the courage to express them. I felt like a smeared slate—not blank, just messy and confused.

Returning home from school each day was a form of patterned torture. Part of its suffering stemmed from the myth of silence the family vowed to preserve at all costs. We lived under a code of protecting and thus preserving the Family Secret. But you probably know how the power of shame can steal one's voice as well as one's desire to be seen and heard. Shame suffocates those healthy needs. It was reinforced by the stinging nettles of "not good enough" or "no good" or "you'll never amount to anything." With psychological hindsight many years later, I can look back with enormous compassion at his suffering, the suffering of my brothers and sister, and mostly of my mother, as well as my own. Remembering through an imaginal lens has its own healing qualities. But I was not yet ready for it.

The stories that have wounded us, that we carry well into adult life, have the capacity to slice us open to reveal the accumulated toxicity of a soul struggling to adapt to a narrative that had crushed my father—and was slowly steamrolling over all of us, one square inch at a time. I am trying to be very conscious here of the metaphors that have arisen to describe this narrative. C.G. Jung established that "An archetypal content expresses itself, first and foremost in metaphors" *(CW* 9, i para. 267) and we know from reading literature and poetry how effective metaphors can be in arousing and codifying our feelings.

From ages thirteen to fifteen I spent as much time as I could with a young woman in elementary school. I loved her dearly. If ever I had a Beatrice in my early life, it was she. She helped me, with her unconditional love, to begin to accept myself as someone who had value and integrity. Looking back—and that is what we do to see the larger narrative in new contexts—I see her as my first therapist. I have had four others since then.

When in 1963 I enrolled in classes at a new junior college in downtown Cleveland, the first in the state of Ohio, I was still living at home. One late morning as I was reading in the living room, my father came through the front door. I asked why he was home. His response: "They fired me." From that day forward he never drank again, but he was still in his soul life an active alcoholic. By this time my mother had discovered Al-Anon; those meetings saved her from insanity and from abandoning their marriage.

She found in that restorative organization a new set of rituals: attending meetings regularly, listening to others narrate their journey from chaos to some degree of serenity, and her relating her narrative, at once particular and universal. I accompanied her once and found it very helpful. I should have continued but didn't. She was on the road away from one myth of violence and into creating a new myth, one of recovery through discovery of the alcoholic's psychology. She gained from these meetings a sense of integrity and self-worth as well as compassion for the man she did not want to divorce. Through it she found her own myth of healing. She knew that she needed to recover from her trauma, and let our father to find his own way.

My father and she reconstituted their relationship, though he never admitted to any of us that he had an illness; he did attend AA meetings. Alcoholism is very healthy and prosperous in our family; we have a son, sober now for seventeen years and drug-free, nephews, nieces, brothers, uncles, friends, friends' parents who were or continue to actively drink.

Downside Up

Wounds are curious and fascinating human entities. Their infections and inflictions can lead to a life that seeks a different reflection of itself. They can also provoke or incite wonder. I titled a recent book I finished on Homer's epic: *From War to Wonder: Recovering Your Personal Myth Through Homer's* Odyssey. Those of you who know the lexicon of AA or Al-Anon recognize the language of recovery in the title. What haunted me as I began classes as a freshman at the junior college—and I think it was a crucial moment of awakening—is how I could be so independent, working, paying my tuition, buying my own cars and clothes, not depending on my parents for support, and at the same time feel the agonies that attended feeling worthless by someone as important as my father.

The tension between the two haunted me for years; I struggled to succeed to the point of feeling burned out most of the time. I learned in hindsight that if one does not actively seek and cultivate one's own myth, then someone or something else will lay theirs on you, like a blanket you cannot simply shake off.

I could not square this stubborn and mysterious circle. So, I declared my major in psychology to begin my own quest to understand myself and the range of influences that had shaped me to this point at twenty years old. I sought answers to the questions that initiated my pursuit to know. Even as I discovered some glimpses that satisfied my head, my heart would not buy into them. The disease was so alive in me that I could not squirm out of its clenched fist. Its grip was beyond my capacities.

I spent a good part of my life afraid, fearing failure, not measuring up, feeling inadequate. These negative feelings, I suspect now, are all symptoms of a metaphysical illness: Not Being Worthy. Always Falling Short. Doing One More Thing. Never Resting. All these plans were in the end unsuccessful attempts at engaging the myth of progress and recognition.

One course in particular, "Abnormal Psychology in Everyday Life," drew me to it. A Cleveland psychiatrist, Dr. Blake Crider, taught it magnificently and I felt the petals of persecution begin to fall from my eyes. It was a revelatory class. I did not have the language for it at the time, but I was being introduced to the psychic world of the archetypes and to primordial images that have existed from time immemorial. I felt something soothing in me, like I was in the presence of something akin to the core of life itself. My imagination caught fire at this revelation; the story I had been living in had ancient roots and encompassed something more universal than I had ever imagined. It was not all about me!

I have not mentioned that growing up, I was a voracious reader. I used to feign being sick so that I could stay home; my mother would go to the local library to check out books for herself and me; her example as an avid reader infected me as well. I would stay home for two days and read under the covers with a flashlight, my yellow plastic radio humming Nat King Cole and the McGuire Sisters, as I read the adventures of others leading fascinating lives: of horse stories, of the X-Bar-X boys having adventures on the ranch where they lived, and the surrounding areas. I loved these worlds of fiction and that has gripped me for a lifetime, courtesy of my mother's constructive example.

A pause here for a brief reflection on what I am feeling at this instant. As I tell my story, it tells me. It has its own ideas of what wants to be included. I go along for the ride. And I wonder: could our stories know what they need to express for healing to occur? Do they, as Jung said of the psyche's unconscious, have their own autonomy? That healing may take the form of growth to a deeper understanding of the plot of the narrative. Healing can and did take the form of a deepening into me. But the wounding also birthed wonder and curiosity in me to explore what mystery I was cocooned in but could not grasp on my own. I needed a guide. I also wonder if stories know that feelings must be elicited in me to bind the wound. Jung reminds us that "nothing is so infectious as affect. . ." (*CW* 18, para. 1368).

Recall how Alcoholics Anonymous began. Two men in Akron, Ohio in the 1930s, both alcoholics at first struggling alone to stop drinking and allowing the conditions for transformation to enter their disease. They then met and listened to one another's stories and felt the same story resonating in themselves. In their small community, they evoked the archetypes of trauma and healing. They recognized that listening to the dark story of the other led them into their own interior terrain, to an analogous plot in themselves, leading to their own "experience, strength, and hope."

Both Bill W. and Doctor Bob intuited that the deep layers of the soul needed to be accessed so that the archetype of transformation could have space to blossom; then an initiation could begin on solid ground: not to take a drink for twenty-four hours. That put them into the spiral of recovery that is the ground for all twelve-step recovery programs. I believe that when we listen to one another's narratives, we heal something in our communal selves as a congress of plots gather, coalesce, and benefit everyone within range. We find and feel into one of the most valuable elements of myth—that it elicits something in us as part of a shared community, a synchronicity of soul's stories that can salve long-suppurating infections.

Retreating Into Healing

I must tighten the narrative at this juncture and relate to you the mythic connection between story and healing. After moving with my family to Santa Barbara in December 1995 to begin a full-time position at Pacifica Graduate Institute, I taught for three years, followed by being awarded a sabbatical for the fall quarter. How I decided to spend it traveling to twelve monasteries, retreat centers, and one Buddhist monastery is a story for another time.

It is important to tell you as I wind this whirl of narratives down, for it involves a deeply healing experience with my father. I was to be gone on this pilgrimage for three and a half months. My wife Sandy's unconditional support for my taking this journey added greatly to my belief that this journey was necessary, unconditional, as I wrote a few years later.

I had mapped out the retreat sites to spend at least four nights in each. At the second monastery in my series of stays, a Carmelite Retreat Center in Napa Valley, in August 1998, I discovered I was the only retreatant. The older monks, mostly from Ireland, invited me to evening meals with them for the duration of my stay.

On the second or third evening, after a meal sprinkled richly with conversation, I sat by the fishpond as the sun began to recline. Next to me was my companion for the time, Rusty, a sweet German Shepherd who belonged to the Center; he accompanied me everywhere and even came to the retreat house every morning where I slept to guide me to morning Mass. He would then wait outside for me to appear to walk with me wherever I went.

As we sat together, when the birds ceased their singing and the bullfrogs would take over with their rich-throated chorus of songs, I began to write in my journal of the day that was now passing. I wrote in my journal every evening for the entire trip; it turned into a spiritual memoir eventually and was published twice in revised versions, the second of which I titled *A Pilgrimage Beyond Belief: Spiritual Journeys through Christian and Buddhist Monasteries of the American West*. Rusty and I were content to enjoy the presence of each other and the lingering daylight as a delicious calm enshrouded us to close out the serene day. I found my affection for Rusty to be so calming. I think he was a prayer on four legs.

As I recounted the day's highlights in my journal, the feelings I had being away from home, and my interior shifts of mind and feelings, my father, who had died two years earlier, appeared to me as a presence and sat on the other half of the wooden bench, to my right. At his appearance, I was and was not startled by this surprising apparition. He began to speak to me of his own addiction and as he told me *his story*, asked me to recall all the times, usually late Sunday mornings in a red-faced and blood-shot-eyed hangover, he had apologized for his reckless antics during another traumatic weekend. The term PTSD had been invented for use in clinical diagnoses for military traumas instead of the older term "shell shock," but had not yet fanned out to include the trauma of family members who survived violent conditions at the hands of an abusive relative.

I realized, however, that it appropriately applied to all of us who had survived, broken but alive, through years of violent weekends. Not just in our home but in the millions of homes in our country and around the globe. He also relayed his own shame when our local Catholic church began leaving boxes of groceries at our back door—a not-so-subtle signal that the family secret had been breached and parishioners had heard we were in need. It was not a need for food, although scarcity often accompanies homes where an addiction consumes funds that were marked for necessities.

My father spoke with such candor this last evening before I was to pack and leave in the morning for my next retreat center. When the time came, and on instinct, I emptied the passenger seat of my Ford Ranger pickup truck and placed those items into the bed of the truck that had a fiberglass lid which allowed me to use it for storage. I did this so my father could, if he so wished, have his own space to accompany me to the next ten retreat centers I had on my itinerary, or to leave when he felt the time was right. I can say to all of you without further comment he was a presence with as much reality as any other family member alive.

That evening, sitting with St. Rusty and my father—a deeper healing began, one that aroused a profound empathy in me for his shame, sense of failure, loss, and grief over the life he failed to live. The toxic contagion of that myth infected all of us who lived with him. I listened to bits and pieces of his story for the next three months and wrote down many of them. His story rested agreeably next to mine; it began to allow my narrative to open, to feel *his* suffering, not just mine. Two myths crossed on a spiritual odyssey, paused, and began to listen to one another.

In our time together, as well as subsequently, my father healed some aspects of me that I did not know I could change, alter, even reformat to accommodate a new mythos—the myth of forgiveness, the myth of tolerance, and the myth of compassion. His presence and his narrative revealed to me that I had never forgiven myself—that shame and inadequacy were still a significant spine in the book of my life. I discerned as well that I had mistreated myself with almost the same level of zeal that his tortured interior life had projected on all of us. I sensed that now was the right time to retire both destructive playbooks.

Reading the magnificent works of Pema Chodron, Thich Nhất Hanh, the Dali Lama, Al-Anon literature, as well as literary classics over the past decades allowed me to reconnect with deeper aspects of myself that still periodically require additional salve to be applied. Louise De-Salvo writes that "a healing narrative connects our experience to other experiences in our lives, and to society generally" (*Writing as a Way of Healing* 64). We can immediately see the implication here: writing our narratives, especially our painful plotlines, connects our story to other pieces of it and to others' plotlines so that a sense of coherence can be retrieved from the rubble. Then relating our writing to be witnessed, as this experience promises, adds yet another and perhaps richer sense to the story of who we are.

Healing, you all know, is like myth itself; it begins at some point, or moment of awareness of its presence, in a gradual awakening. But both continue to happen throughout our lives. I don't believe we ever fully recover from our traumas—and that is a positive element—but we can creatively construct stories that offer different ways of befriending and integrating its energy. And as far as the "reality" of my father's presence, let me disclose an idea from Tim O'Brien, author of *The Things They Carried*, recommended by one of my myth students, KK.

"Absolute occurrence is irrelevant. A thing may happen and be a total lie; another thing may not happen and be truer than the truth" (*Carried* 83). Okay, but can there be a middle ground between these two—an occurrence that is not absolute, yet happened as a true experience, with the power of an imaginal occurrence—and be more than a projection, less than an event that engages the senses?

Stories, O'Brien goes on to suggest, "are ordinarily made out of suffering" (78). The literal truth, he believes, "is ultimately to me, irrelevant. What matters is the heart truth" (81). To which I add and end with: The literal truth is history; the heart truth grows from a mythic consciousness at work on history, shaping it, to reveal what has meaning, soul life, and is now prepared to be absorbed into the larger epic plot, whose process is indeed the story of our one treasured and magnificent life.

To accept this last discovery is to be well on the road to healing by means of myth. Our wounds, when transformed into words or other forms of overt expression, enter the cosmos of *mythopoiesis,* a rich and real atmosphere, to be absorbed by those who are willing to hear their own story in another register.

I am so honored to have been able to share my story with you today.

Works Cited

Cousineau, Phil. *The Oldest Story in the World: A Mosaic of Meditations on the Secret Strength of Stories.* Sisyphus Press, 2010.

DeSalvo, Louise. *Writing as a Way of Healing: How Telling Our Stories Transforms Our Lives.* Beacon Press, 1999.

Dillard, Annie. *Living By Fiction.* Harper & Row, 1982.

Jung, C.G. *Memories, Dreams, Reflections.* Translated by Richard and Clara Winston, edited by Aniela Jaffe. Random House, 1963.

---. *The Collected Works of C.G. Jung.* Trans. R.F.C. Hull, Vol. 9,i. Princeton UP, 1971.

---. *The Collected Works of C.G. Jung.* Trans. R.F.C. Hull. Vol. 18. Princeton UP, 1980.

McAdams, Dan P. *The Stories We Live By: Personal Myth and the Making of the Self.* The Guilford Press, 1993.

O'Brien, Tim. *The Things They Carried.* Houghton Mifflin, 1990.

Rilke, Ranier Maria. *Letters to a Young Poet.* Translated by Stephen Mitchell. The Modern Library, 1984.

Tick, Edward. *The Practice of Dream Healing: Bringing Ancient Greek Mysteries into Modern Medicine.* Quest Books, 2001.

Wagner, Robert. Personal Correspondence. January 10, 2021.

2

Nodal Moments on the Spiral of Aging: The Hero's Journey*

"We are all energy and invisibility
We are all someone
We can only imagine"
~Timothy J. Donohue, "At a Graveyard by An Orchard"

Nodal Moments on the Spiral of Aging

I confess to writing this presentation months before Connie Zweig's *The Inner Work of Age* was published. I knew that I had to get my own thinking on this process out in some workable form before I read her book and, in retrospect, I am so glad I trusted this impulse. Her book became for many weeks the central focus of my early morning meditation reading and writing. I felt that my aging process took on an elegance through her insightful exploration of this rich topic.

I was both happy to see that we shared some fundamental notions on aging, especially as a spiritual form of both meditation and activism, and at times I was overwhelmed by the depth and breadth of her exploration; she consistently used individual stories from her own practice as a therapist, interviews with extraordinary people in various fields, her

* Originally delivered as a keynote presentation to a conference on *The Inner Work of Aging*, December 2nd, 2022, at Pacifica Graduate Institute. Zoom Presentation.

earlier insights into the shadows of the soul, lyrics from songs, as well as many pages suggesting corridors for meditation, perhaps in writing them out or through other forms of creative expression. So, thank you, Connie, for this epic achievement and for orchestrating this conference. As a wise Elder, your example inspires us all.

We owe Joseph Campbell a great debt as well. He offers us in his writing those archetypal situations on the hero's path in *The Hero with a Thousand Faces* (1949). We also owe the author of many books and films, Phil Cousineau, a further debt for compiling so many of Campbell's insights into this journey in his edited volume, *The Hero's Journey: Joseph Campbell on His Life and Work* (1990) and of the film that followed it. Phil also shared with me that he had laid out the circular structure with its various meetings and confrontations of the Hero's Journey and presented it to Campbell, who beamed with approval at what Phil had outlined in the template. It included some seventeen stages of the journey.

In this presentation I want to diverge a bit from these moments that Campbell so insightfully presented years ago. First, I don't believe that in the aging process there is as much fidelity to the circle—of leaving the familiar, or refusing it, confronting a series of tests as one crosses one or more thresholds, followed by finding the treasure and returning with it to where one began with a form of the elixir, the grail, or another image of the gold in the soul. Campbell referred to it as a boon, a gift; it could also be a memento of the travails of one's travels.

As I will have just crossed the border of my 78ᵗʰ birthday when I present these reflections on aging and Elderhood, I find myself looking back and ahead in my life as closer to the geometry of the spiral rather than a circle. For one reason, I do not think that in any part of my life, but especially now, I return to where I was. That "was" is gone and some other "is" has replaced it. I say this because of the feel of my life's trajectory as well as what Jung himself expressed in *Dream Analysis: Notes of the Seminar Given in 1928-30:* "One of the fundamental laws of natural development is that it moves in a spiral, and the true law of nature is always reached after the labyrinth has been travelled. . .. Psychologically you develop in a spiral, you always come over the same point where you have been before, but it is never exactly the same, it is either above or below. . .. What we are concerned with is the pattern" (*Dream Analysis* 100). I believe it is accurate to refer to James Hillman's idea of reversion in *Re-visioning Psychology* as resonating with Jung's insight.

Here Jung touches on a paradox of the aging hero's journey: we are most often folding back on something familiar, but it no longer carries in it the unfamiliar, the unknown, for between the first spiral passing and subsequent motions, history has intervened, changing the altitude and perhaps the attitude of the partly familiar, partly strange experience remembered and relived. I believe that right here, in this juncture, myth plays one of its most valuable roles in our life: to assist us in making transitions from one nodal moment to the next, serving well as a bridge, a crossing that allows us to maintain a resilience and adaptability in our unfurling progression.

I want therefore to employ the spiral as a format for the journey of aging and to reflect on my 78 years with the aid of *The Hero's Journey*, but not to get too fixed in Campbell's world so as to exclude what I have found as stations or "nodal moments" on my journey. Yet I hear echoes and refrains of my unique voyage and believe that your own passages in life are present in altered form as well. So let me start with a story, one that, like a seed, will grow throughout this presentation.

Not long ago I took my wife to a Bier Garden in New Braunfels for Saturday lunch and to enjoy live country music. After we were seated, I went up to the bar and ordered two beers. I paid for them and tipped the jar on the counter. Then I walked back to our table. Not three feet behind me was the bartender I had ordered from. He asked, with a strange smile, if I still wanted the beers I had paid for? He had them both in his hands because I had paid for them, then walked back to the table empty-handed; more importantly, I was oblivious of having left them on the counter.

He razzed me good-naturedly. This event highlighted the heroic journey in aging, which offers more frequent moments of what feels like a complete blackout. We all laughed at my failure to remember toting the drinks back to our table. I had to. It is part of the journey, to have a joke played on one when one least suspects a glitch or a gap. These gaps of forgetfulness comprise one of the most dramatic of the nodal moments I will describe. Humor can fortify us in these moments of vulnerability that is part of awakening to our current condition.

This moment is crucial, wrapped snugly in an illustration, a story. Aging has prodded both my wife Sandy and me into a new relationship with what is recollected, what is or wishes to be recalled, and, towards what often stubbornly refuses to be remembered. It also requires of both of us a renewed relationship with one another as we support and fill in the gaps of our experiences seeking expression. Together we can assemble a complete story. Whether a word, the name of a person, the terms of a vacation, or a precious incident we shared—all these that grow dim in the memory, but are still felt deeply, are markers of memories' loss.

The antidote is humor, laughter, a rousing chorus of mercy, and an attitude of compassion extended to me and to others who feel their own gaps in the sidewalk of their journey. Memory itself has its own wrinkles, weak spots, fading visions, but also the courage to express itself anyway.

If Elderhood carries any virtues, it must include the ability to laugh at one's own vulnerabilities when something from the past is to be urgently retrieved but the memory has placed it in a dead-letter office, in the top drawer, perhaps to be retrieved at 2 a.m. when one returns to bed after a bathroom break.

Campbell reminds us that the eldering journey requires one to be in constant accord with one's true nature. Biology and psychology are an intimate couple in this motion to counter the body's stiffening, its rhythms of physical discomfort, and of course an illness that announces itself absent any invitation or preparation. One does well to remain emotionally and spiritually supple, flexible even as the body stiffens and abandons some of its elasticity, its shape-shifting Protean nature.

I think we might do well in aging to develop a "spandex imagination," one that can give and take with the rise and fall of elasticity, a spandex approach to all the expansions and contractions of aging as a mythic adventure. Pliability and flexibility are virtues to be cultivated at every turn. Connie's refrain of migrating from role to soul I found comforting in navigating just this terrain as Sandy and I walk together along the bank of the swiftly flowing waters of Lethe.

The above suggests a broader adventure: to have courage, heart, to move into new landscapes, the terms of which are not immediately known; it is the landscape of aging itself—a terrain that can be terrifying as we sense something contracting, even as we contact deeper dimensions of spirit, of soul, and of purpose.

The constant in all these shifts is adaptation, even, at times, a modest or major renovation. Perhaps underneath these desires is a level of acquiescence, a recognition without morbidity, of moving closer to death. Cultivating yielding, or a giving way so one does not give up or give in, to counter despair which can gnaw at the older, yet still pulsating heart that continues to give life purpose and pleasure, offers a freedom within growing limits. Connie's term, "mortal awareness," is another helpful compass reading on the pilgrimage.

Contrary to the ego-driven knee-jerk phrase, "Surrender is not an option," aging turns that silliness around to proclaim: "Surrender is often an option, and the right one, given the terrain of circumstances that confront us." As with Dante Alighieri's own journey with the aid of his wise elder, the classical poet Virgil, one may move with some grace from an attitude of willfulness to that of willingness. After all, it is the major emotional element that separates the souls in Inferno from those more communal shades climbing together the spiral of Mount Purgatory. On their soul journey, they are purged of the imperfections that kept them from loving, as Dante describes it, "in due measure." It is a rich moment for each of the souls as they relinquish or loosen their grip on what has kept them from a purer awareness of the "Primal Love" that moves the sun and other stars in the heavens.

And so, we arrive at another paradox: the journey of aging may inspire greater regeneration in the throes of degeneration; one is part of bringing a generation to an end while simultaneously yielding to what next looms on the horizon. One is between, which in whatever format, never ceases—for the between space is an opportunity to honor something ending and something beginning, so that aging is generative as well as renewing in the face of restrictions that grow in the cells of the body. As Elders, we may help with this migration of both individuals and generations. Campbell reminds us that the hero's quest includes as part of its mystery a contest, a battle, with gravity (*The Hero's Journey* 12). But the trade-off may be a greater sensibility of *gravitas*, of a deeper sense of the soul of things and others, but not lacking in a sense of humor and play. This is a key feature of an Elder, to my mind.

Some forces new to us pull at our shoes, then our waists, then our head, with the movement generally downward; yet our energy and purpose continue to buoy us up. We can of course curse this vertical descent, but to do so, as Campbell suggests, "is that by violating the environment in which we are living, we are really cutting the energy and the source of our own living" (16). The journey of aging asks us to recognize and accommodate a new interior ecology that sustains, even composts, our lives in new ways, while it establishes a different fulcrum from which we balance elements of our new and always-evolving myth.

Aging into our double-digit higher self provides an occasion to explore, from the perspective of hindsight, how many of the ideas, beliefs, thoughts, narrowness as well as expansiveness of soul, were mine, and how many were assigned to me that I never thought to question; otherwise, I may one day learn that the myth I thought was mine to follow and cultivate belonged in fact to someone else that I accepted without question, without questing after its source. Said another way, aging into Elderhood may include reclaiming parts of our own myth that have hibernated for decades in the dark recesses of our souls.

A corollary enters here: as I feel the limited supply of energy I am given on any given day, I like to think I am becoming more discerning about how to spend it, on what, and on whom. Aging can be understood as an opening to explore where the power centers, the energy pockets in one's life are, and to interrogate whether they are still valid. I say this because where these energy centers exist is also where meaning and purpose coagulate, perhaps in a re-purposed life. These centers also prescribe for me where I am most conscious, most aware, and to reflect on whether as Jungian therapist D. Stephenson Bond calls "my patterns of adaptation" (*Living Myth* 44) are still functional. At the same time, it becomes a rich but challenging place to identify what has or is becoming cadaverous in me, and to moderate or delete these lifeless particles.

Sensing maladaptive terrains within me, as well as how I am living them out in the world, requires modification on a journey whose constant is flux. I ask myself, what do I find myself resisting, refusing, deflecting? and excavate what the motives are. For a myth that I might naively consider functionally quite well, is in fact dysfunctional, perhaps because it has a more involved and complex story to integrate into the larger narrative that shapes my identity. Calcification is the arena where I lose a give-and-take with the world; my personal myth may require some ample amounts of vinegar run through it to loosen up calcium deposits, so to reclaim some of its previous flow, and encourage greater pliability.

From the above, we can understand how being pulled down is an opportunity for a deepening in all areas of our becoming. I have found that in activities like painting, writing poetry, reading, writing, offering lectures, and writing retreats, I feel as if I have deepened what I have already done and hence feel more courage to enter new fields of exploration that call to me now. One such arena is how the relationship of beliefs, assumptions, assertions, and articles of faith shape my evolving personal myth. Both Sandy and I continue to converse about our own aging; we sense the rich paradox of losses and gains that we can name. The list continues to expand.

We are learning to respect our own declines, especially hers in this moment wherein her aging after surviving two strokes that came close to killing her challenges her memory with words that want to hide in the crevasses of her mind. She is one of the most courageous human beings I have ever met. Becoming conscious of aging is to enter a new tribe of trials that limit, and freedoms that expand what we feel called to do. Her work in Al-Anon which is her spiritual practice, and my own writing, teaching, and contributing to a larger good, even a more expansive goodness, are part of our spandex imagination in practice. What nourishes both of us is the ability to age with meaning as we explore deeper insights that complement our limitations.

Joseph Campbell plays with the image of aging in a wonderful way: "In old age, your only relationship to the world is your begging bowl, which in our culture is your bank account. That's what you've already earned, and it has to support this relatively carefree last stage of life. . . I can tell you that it is the best part of life. . .. It is a period when everything is coming up and flowering. It is very, very sweet. . .. It is a blooming" (*A Joseph Campbell Companion* 88).

The above speaks to and consciously directs moments of greater awareness that feel new to me. An important segment of this awareness is, as Campbell puts it eloquently when he relates meeting and conversing with Karlfried Graf Durckheim, "that you live the myth. That you live the divine life within you. Yourself as a vehicle; not as the final term, but as a vehicle of consciousness and life" by becoming, in Durckheim's words, "transparent to transcendence" (*The Hero's Journey* 40).

This I see as the core of mythological consciousness; such transparency is so conducive to my growing interest in the mystery of the aging journey, as I sense the soul bending more toward the transcendent as it deepens into the imminent mystery of everyday life. All, of course, within a body that has its own agenda for declining. It also allows a more accepting presence to what Connie believes, that "we can attune to our own inner guidance, remembering that we are not the Doer. We are a soul in service" (*The Inner Work of Age* 316)

Let me stay with this sense of growing awareness for a moment. I ask myself now: what is it I am becoming more aware, more conscious of? My ability to articulate them is to ask: what are my inflection points? What are my inspiration points? And what are my infraction points, where I am willing to risk stepping out of the ordinary, where I can tolerate, even relish, where my conventional boundaries of thought dissolve? These are a few of the essential questions that drive the energy of my aging quest. I also sense they are openings into a deepening sense of Elderhood, where knowledge moves from understanding and insights into the landscape of wisdom.

Wisdom is more a verb than a noun. Perhaps we can split the difference and call it a gerund, that slippery part of speech that "is derived from a verb but acts like a noun" (*Google Dictionary online*). Wisdom curves towards the application in a measured or balanced way of what has been learned, sensed, intuited, imagined to my life-in-relation to others and the generosity to share it. The imagination is often the most powerful way into service, of a grace-to-grace relation with others, while joined to the mythic knowledge gained from a life of self-reflection and self-application in the spirit of service.

As I mentioned Jung's insight earlier, that the spiral is the geometry of soul's motion as well as her emotions, I want now to add to the list some of the most prevalent "nodal moments" that arise as I continue the journey, which is one that, like a spiral, moves forward, then circles back to areas of concern, delight, and sorrow; it then moves ahead into new territory, to include the basic structures of memory and imagination. The spiral is also at the heart of a motion that seems essentially analogical and metaphoric, which is to say, mythic. It reveals "diversity in similarity and extends to the diversity of our mental character and our physical structure," writes Theodore Andrea Cook in *The Curves of Life* (4).

I would add, from my own book *Riting Myth*, that "the spiral is a sacred geometry that attends the vital motion of a life mythically lived and reflected upon; at its center is a mysterious playfulness we don't want to lose sight of in these meditations. For the play in the spiral's center space, as I have written elsewhere, is like the playfulness in our lives that promotes joy, a willingness to change and be affected by our relations with others" (31).

Perhaps the aging journey over time reveals a series of equilibriums between looking back and looking ahead. Each has its own brand and intensity of energy and angles of reception. So much of the aging hero's journey involves a recollection, a reverse motion of life. It has brought me to question: is my life now, with the great part behind me, so that I can discern many of the deeper patterns that framed it and the larger story that nourished it? The aging hero's journey includes a spiraling back to reclaim shards that had been lost or cast aside, but now loom up as important moments in the building of a life's deeper intentions.

At the same time the journey is in the form of a quest-ioning: what has been sacrificed, let go of, dismissed, or forgotten in the interests of the larger narrative working its way to the surface of time and space? I think it is valuable to name them.

At some point, they deserve some possible answers. But here is a good place to note what Campbell says at the end of *The Hero's Journey*: "I was reading in one of the Sanskrit texts recently because in your old age, my dear friends, in your free time, you go back to what fed you most in your youth and childhood" (229). He then mentions that even though he read this book before, it struck him in new and novel ways. This spiralic motion can be applied to so many venues of our aging life when we revisit where we once were and discover new perspectives, understandings, and relations. I find that the imaginative realm continues to grow richer, more complex, and textured with age. I believe that I think and reflect better now and have fewer encumbrances and worries about critical voices trying to detain my progress.

Such a motion to-and-fro opens new vistas of creativity as well as renewed courage to express it in outlets like pottery, painting, poetry, op-ed pieces on cultural moments, and presentations like this opportunity today. It has also opened new deepenings of love for myself, my wife, our sons, and their partners, their daughters, and in embracing the magnificent role of grandparent. In this role we see the longer view of multiple generations that follows us now; we want to be a presence in their lives so we will be welcome guests in their memories later when we have passed. I gain a deepening experience of my place in life's continuum because I find my home in history as one of intimacy.

To see one's own children in their children is as mysterious as it is miraculously delightful. In this stance or life position is a mythic moment, where one's life structure communes with both remembrance and anticipation, perhaps in equal measure. It encourages a fuller sense of belonging to and with the world as it is, less how I want it to be. My task is to extend this pattern as far as I dare.

What I am offering here is recognizing new rhythms of an aging life; the myth is shifting to invite additional sluices of understanding. It is also to see the rhythms of the ordinary, where one's personal myth and life's mythic structures meet and converse. Myths, both personal and collective, reveal many of the figures that comprise our inner constellation of possible stories. They should be written down and left to identify us to our family, friends, and a wider circle of people known and yet to be met.

I wake up much more often each morning with the presence of "mortal awareness," Connie's phrase. I scurry from it less now than originally. It carries with it a melancholy, an inevitability, and an acute sense of this day's value. Within its emotional blanket, I feel casually urgent. As its awareness grows, I think of creative ways to accept it, befriend it, as part of the overarching myth that must be integrated into the journey.

In doing so—slowly, to be sure—it pushes a question, like a young plant, to the surface: what have you given your life to? Is it still of such worth that I want to continue to feed that way of being and doing? Does it continue to allow me to gain joy and a sense of purpose from it? Thus far, the answers are in the affirmative. It also pushes me to question when I might retire and even what value, if any, that word carries.

I much prefer the words renovation and renewal, even re-inspire-ment to replace it as part of a spiralic consciousness and attitude. These words have life in them that gingerly step across the threshold of becoming old. In the magic motion of the spiral, I grasp how little I seem to know in the form of recollection, but what gains I like to think I have made in the realm of understanding, which at intervals offers me furtive glimpses of wisdom.

I pay attention to the more frequent uprisings of gratitude for the ordinary, for pleasure in the quotidian moment of a gift given, a gift received, in whatever form it assumes. One of the most prominent is in the form of thanks-giving, a way of gratitude that can reshape a life at any age, but in the aging journey it is especially valued. Thanks-giving draws me into an interdependence with all things, all people, even those who seem dedicated to serve as my adversaries. Learning to accept them on their terms is another way thanks-giving serves the aging journey.

When Campbell speaks of the crucifixion, he cites a letter of St. Paul to the Philippians: "For the Christ did not think the Godhead to be hung on to, but let go of. . . " (*The Hero's Journey* 229). He cites a line from Buddhism: "Life is joyful participation in the sorrows of the world.... Do you see what I mean? You get a point of view, you get—what can we call it—a nonegoistic, nonjudgmental point of view. And so go into the play and play a part" (*The Hero's Journey* 229).

Coupled with gratitude is a secondary impulse: the ability to sift through each day with a more discerning sieve, and to gauge what to hold back and what to drop through the tiny gaps in its screen. Somedays that sieve must be woven more tightly, in others with a more generous spacing. But time is not only passing but accelerating in an aging life. T.S. Eliot's J. Alfred Prufrock seems so unconcerned with time; his refrain is "For indeed there will be time. . .. And indeed, there will be time/To wonder, 'Do I dare? And 'Do I dare?'" ("The Love Song" 4). And further, "And time yet for a hundred indecisions, /And for a hundred visions and revisions, /Before the taking of a toast and tea" (4). But my aging elder responds, "Do not count on so many chances for revisions and do not wait for your tea to grow old *and* cold."

These lines from Eliot's masterpiece of a lonely hero compel this aging Elder to pause, not so much to revise but to become more aware of what has been invisible in life and to allow it a more defined visibility. Elderhood invites and even requires another register of imagination, one that is more attuned to the spiritual and imaginal life of the soul. Campbell tells us in *The Hero's Journey* that "you live the myth. You live the divine life within you. Yourself as a vehicle. . ." (40). And most especially in aging, you learn from the metaphors and analogies of others, while at the same time contributing your own rich relationships to the story of your life.

One might continue to construct new forms of expression from what has come into the imagination; it is akin to a mystical experience, a new way of seeing, to see anew through filters of what has been. To notice what lingers behind what you read, see, and experience both internally and externally. One may then sense how a mythic imagination assists in organizing and ordering the deep patterns that guide us daily.

In the final section of one of Rumi's most popular poems, "Unfold Your Own Myth," after offering us numerous stories of mythic moments in the lives of others, he takes a turn and tells us not to be satisfied with others' stories, but to unfold our own personal myth.

Elderhood Central to Aging but Not a Synonym

Rumi's exquisite poem extends the theme of Elderhood by asking: What kind of imagination makes up an Elder? Some initial notions include an imagination that reflects on the past and sees in the convex mirror of history the images birthing into the future. An Elder is perhaps a version of a special edition of a Sage, one who has learned to reflect in depth on what capacities in the past and present provide inklings for glimpses into the future. An Elder is predictive because she has noted with great particularity the patterns that have guided her over a lifetime and can express analogies seen in others and culturally over decades.

An Elder has a grasp on the long view. I think of the old Greek warrior, Nestor, who Athene has instructed Telemachus to visit to get the expansive vision of the Trojan War and its devastating aftermath. Nestor carries the history and the reflective wisdom of the past to share with Telemachus, an emblem of the promise of Greece's future.

To come into more contemporary classics, the elder in Toni Morrison's *Beloved* is the old wise sage, Baby Suggs, Holy, who carries the shame, the pain, and the suffering of her people, but who promises them hope as ninety of her people gather in the sacred space of a Clearing to hear her speak. As an Elder, she carries the collective soul of her people and liberates it from their suffocating confines of being enslaved. Their enslavement is both physical and psychological, in part a self-image, that she breaks into. Listen to her exhortation in the clearing of the woods:

"Here," she said, "in this here place, we flesh; flesh that weeps, laughs; flesh that dances on bare feet in grass. Love it. . . Love your hands! Love them. Raise them up and kiss them. . . This is flesh I'm talking about here. Flesh that needs to be loved. Feet that need to rest and to dance; backs that need support. . .. And all your inside parts, . . .you got to love them. The dark, dark liver—love it, love it, and the beat and beating heart, love that too." (*Beloved* 88)

All the images of scattered parts, shattered pieces of the home, of one's life, the scattering of children sold one by one at an auction, all congeal and coagulate here, to form a unified body—an embodied wholeness through the force of her elderly, wise, and forceful soul-presence. She coaxes the fragmented parts of those listening to reclaim their whole, embodied being through love, beginning with self-acceptance as a human being with dignity.

In this epic project of reclamation, the great racial wound of their ordeal as a people is offered a salve that begins to heal their collective shame; to suffer the hot flashes of shame is another form of being wounded, enslaved, and orphaned from oneself and one's community.

Her status as a communal Elder who assists others to risk an attitude of inner freedom engages powerful acts of generosity and love that individuals must encourage in themselves and one another if the cruelty and inhumanity of the slave traders and slaveholders—indeed of the world's suffering—are to lose their grip on them. From Morrison we learn that an Elder is a witness to suffering and to the treasure of self-liberation that hides underneath it, wanting and waiting to be witnessed, if not affirmed and celebrated.

In the frame I am suggesting above, the Elder senses the trajectory of destiny, is able as a seer to affirm to others the fate of history because of a vision of life that is possible to strive for. An Elder may see more clearly the divine working itself through the folds and creases of the human enterprise and human condition and, perhaps most importantly, can excavate the potent and poetic language to speak it. An Elder, in this sense, is in contact with the transcendent, the terrain of vision of what can be that overrides the enslaved mind to what is.

I also invited two Elders in my life to offer their reflections on Elders: Hendrika DeVries, a friend and colleague of many years who taught at Pacifica Graduate Institute and had a thriving practice as a sought-after therapist in Santa Barbara, and Reverend Barbara Child, my former creative writing teacher at Kent State University and Faculty Advisor to *The Kent Quarterly*, a literary magazine that I was general editor of for a year. Barbara has been in more recent decades a Unitarian Universalist Minister and a close friend.

For Hendrika, a senior, over against an Elder, "denotes a chronological state in years or work and study. The senior can still be a moron, especially in today's education system (Sorry, I had to throw that in 😊)".

But "the term 'Elder' holds a very different meaning. In some ways I see it closer to Kairos than Chronos." The Elder "has gained deep wisdom (Kairos wisdom) in their long-life experience, a wisdom grown out of deep experience, physical, emotional and spiritual. Elders use their wisdom to guide and teach younger people. An Elder understands the culture in which new generations must forge their identity and purpose. . . an Elder may gather knowledge and wisdom over many years and the gathering of this wisdom is not necessarily experienced as a heroic act; both may enrich the culture by bringing their learning to the community as a blessing." Hendrika then relates "a dream in which an 'Elder' came to me and taught me about death" (Personal Correspondence).

Reverend Child's response overlaps with Hendrika's and extends it. Barbara believes the difference between a senior and Elder is more a matter of connotation, not denotation: "All of us 'of a certain age' are technically seniors. And often that word is spoken in a disparaging tone."

She points out that grocery stores created a "senior hour" for shopping (I call it, to duplicate the disparaging tone, 'geezer hour'). There it's not so much that we're irritants, more that we are just the poor folks who deserve more sympathy than respect. . .. A senior is somebody that you don't want to be. Nobody envies you for being a senior. . ..

"Ah, now Elders are a different matter altogether—even though they are the very same people as seniors. In fact, the very word 'Elder' just about comes with the prefix 'wise.' . . . an Elder is either as up to speed as anybody else about technology or is someone who lives in a world where technology can have no sway because the Elder has more important things on the mind than mute buttons or chat boxes. The Elder lives in a world where ideas matter more than things. . .. An Elder is the one to go to for help with things that matter, like what to do with your life or how to manage with the deck life has already dealt you.

"Elders get honors. And deserve them. People emulate Elders, hope to do as well as when they become Elders themselves. . .. When somebody calls me an Elder, I stand up a little straighter and make ready for the gifts that are sure to follow" (Personal Correspondence).

A senior, I would add, is a pilgrim in quest of a discount—in coffee shops, McDonald's, Denny's restaurants, in stores in shopping malls, and all to the good. Show your AARP card and the passport to reduced pricing is activated. An Elder, however, carries a heritage of life, a working viable myth that can be passed on before they do. When individuals claim their successes being fortified or ratified by a wise mother, father, grandparent, for instance, they offer some simple but moving version that guided them.

In crucial ways they carry the mythic spirit of that person forward in time and place. Elders seem to have access or special admission privileges to the deeper truths in their own story, and the gift to relate it to their audience.

An Elder, I suspect, also carries a sense of the forms of things, the underlying principles of life's substances and accidents; we may say they have learned from their experiences less lessons in life, more the lesions of life and the benefits of being wounded, of integrating limitations and enlargements of life gathered in the right syntax to give them form.

My most influential mentor in graduate school, Dr. Louise Cowan, continued as my Elder for forty-five years. She shaped my imagination in so many ways; I still feel her presence when I teach, write, and think about not just literature but life itself. As an Elder, she cultivated in me a way of seeing and a particular style of imagining.

I could say so much more about her influence, but I want to end with a story of an Elder who was not so while he was alive but became a mentor after he died: my father, who suffered all the disabilities that accompanied his alcoholism. His anguish exploded each weekend on all of us growing up; our mother took the brunt of his wrath and self-loathing. Not until she discovered Al-Anon decades after the abuse began, was she guided to find the center in herself and the understanding of the illness; it was not an absence of willpower as the conventional misunderstanding was in the late 50s and early 60s.

At one point, on a spring morning my father walked into the house at 11 a.m. to announce to me, who was studying at home, that his company had just fired him. After decades working for them, they unloaded him, in part to avoid paying him the pension he deserved; they used his drinking as their excuse, although he never drank during the week at home or work. None of us really understood the devastation to our own sense of identity at the time; these defects unfolded into consciousness later for my three brothers, sister, and me.

But I don't want to dwell there. I want to describe how he appeared to me in my travels two years after he died, in 1996. I had been awarded my first sabbatical by Pacifica Graduate Institute since I began teaching. I was led to a destiny of how I was to spend this precious time off by returning to a book that fell off the shelf in San Antonio four years earlier, in 1995, when I reached for a travel guide to Ireland that my wife and I had begun to plan a trip to visit—the land of my ancestors.

The book that stuck to the Ireland tour guide was entitled: *A Guide to Monasteries and Retreat Centers in the Southwest United States.* A voice nudged me to make a pilgrimage, guided by this book. I listened, promising Sandy an Ireland trip after the sabbatical. I chose twelve monasteries, retreat centers, and Zen Buddhist centers in five states that would keep me on the road for three and a half months. I left in August and returned mid-December. Enough prelude to set the stage.

The second station of my pilgrimage was the Carmelite House of Prayer in Oakville, California, just off Route 29 north of San Francisco. I settled into this new place, where I discovered I was the only retreatant staying there this week in September, 1998. On the second day of a five-day stay, the blessed Carmelite dog, Rusty, and I were sitting in the evening by a fishpond listening to the bullfrogs begin their chorus and watching some of the Koi fish bubble to the surface. As had happened at the first monastery, I felt the presence of my father, who before he died had for a few years stopped drinking and allowed my parents to reclaim their love for one another.

As I reflected on who I was, I began to realize that so many of my father's traits had embedded themselves in my identity. This revelation was a violent shock to me, because I thought I had successfully skirted ingesting my father's toxic personality. I had cleared a space in my life for grace and instead ghastly ghosts tumbled into the silent silo of my soul. In my account of that sabbatical journey in *A Pilgrimage Beyond Belief*, I wrote, "I did not expect the presence of my alternatively enraged and reticent father to follow me on this journey, but there he was, beside me on the bench and there I was, mirroring him in attitude and design more than I had ever realized. What I thought I had avoided I had essentially become" (94).

I think at this first moment and in the remainder of the trip stretching three months into the future, my father shifted from the dispirited alcoholic to an Elder, an ancestor with a perspective I was in the right mood and disposition to learn from. When I packed my truck to leave two days later, I took all the possessions that were piled on the passenger seat and put them in the bed of the truck that had a lid so I could lock down my supplies. I made space for him in the event his plan was to accompany me through the pilgrimage. And he did. At each station on my journey, he became present, now more fully, now less so.

His desire was to put his life in perspective for me, not to elicit sympathy. When he appeared and spoke, I recorded it later. He emerged most often in the evening or early morning, even at Mass or silent time in the sanctuary. He spoke of his own rage and shame, two traits we all received graduate level tutorials in throughout our childhood and young adulthood. I learned from him about his own mother's abusive attacks on him when he was growing up. His two brothers were also active alcoholics but without the mean violence my father defaulted to on the weekends.

Throughout his confessions of anger and rage hiding a deep shame, I felt grow in me the serenity of calm which was nothing short of learning to live within love and compassion for not just him, but for my mother and my three brothers and sister. And compassion for myself after years of self-berating.

I admit that in these conversations, or more often, declarations by my father, I gained a perspective on my own emotional deficiencies and realized with a startling bolt of electricity running through me that I may have passed his patterns I inherited down to my sons. I then began to reflect more deeply on their behaviors, their emotional lives, and the generosity they needed to forge a life of self-confidence and love for their partners and children.

In his very generous and perceptive Foreword to my memoir of this sabbatical, *A Pilgrimage Beyond Belief: Spiritual Journeys Through Christian and Buddhist Monasteries of the American West,* psychologist Thomas Moore put his finger on the book's central attention: "But Dennis does tell a remarkable story within the story of his visits. As he emptied himself in one place after another, his recently deceased father became present to him, and he was able to work through mostly disturbing memories and reflect on his own role as a father. This ghostly relationship is the soul of the book" (6). Tom nailed the deeper and necessary subject of the memoir I grasped only partially it until I read his Foreword.

I leave the elders and the progress and regress of aging now. I ask the poetic utterance of William Butler Yeats to accompany me with his wonderful poem:

Among School Children

I walk through the long schoolroom questioning;
A kind old nun in white hood replies:
The children learn to cipher and to sing,
To study, reading books and history,
To cut and sew, be neat in everything
In the best modern way—the children's eyes

In momentary wonder stare upon
A sixty-year-old smiling public man

(The Collected Poems of W.B. Yeats 212-13)

An aging man, to be sure, but from my perch not an old man but an Elder.

His view is keen, his deep attention to details acute. It is the perspective that makes him so poetically wise.

Works Cited

Bond, D. Stephenson. *Living Myth: Personal Meaning as a Way of Life.* Shambhala, 1993.

Campbell, Joseph. *A Joseph Campbell Companion.* Edited by Diane K. Osbon. HarperCollins Publishers, 1995.

---. *The Hero with a Thousand Faces.* Bollingen Series XVII. Third Edition. New World Library, 2008.

---. *The Heroes' Journey: Joseph Campbell on his Life and Work.* Edited and with an Introduction by Phil Cousineau. New World Library, 2003.

Child, Reverend Barbara. Personal Communication, March 2021.

Cook, Theodore Andrea. *The Curves of Life.* 1914. Reprinted by Dover, 1979.

Devries, Hendrika. Personal Communication, April, 2021.

Donohue, Timothy. *As Close as I Can Get: Selected and New Poems.* Mandorla Books, 2022.

Eliot, T.S. *The Complete Poems and Plays: 1909-1950.* Harcourt, Brace and World, 1971. 3-7.

Jung, C.G. *Dream Analysis: Notes of the Seminar Given in 1928-1930.* Edited by William McGuire. Princeton UP, 1984.

Morrison, Toni. *Beloved.* Knopf, 1998.

Slattery, Dennis Patrick. *A Pilgrimage Beyond Belief: Spiritual Journeys Through Christian and Buddhist Monasteries of the American West.* Angelico Press, 2017.

---. *Riting Myth, Mythic Writing. Plotting Your Personal Story.* Fisher King Press, 2012.

Yeats, William Butler. *The Collected Poems of W.W. Yeats.* The Macmillan Company, 1956.

Zweig, Connie. *The Inner Work of Age: Shifting from Role to Soul.* Park Street Press, 2021.

3

Oedipus Revised, James Hillman Revisited: Mimesis, Memory, and the Shaping of a Personal Myth*

"One sees what one can best see oneself."
--C.G. Jung, *CW* 6

Myth in Story is a categorized way of pairing two basic human concerns. James Hillman reminds us in *Healing Fiction* of an important coupling of poetics and psychology: "Freud's one plot is named after a myth, Oedipus. . .. Freud's discovery of the Oedipus tragedy located psychology at the very beginning of poetics, with Aristotle's use of *mythos* in his *Poetics*. When we open that book to read in English about plot, we find that wherever 'plot' appears the original Greek word is *mythos*. Plots are myths. The basic answers to why in a story are to be discovered in myths" (11).

As I return to *Mythic Figures* to reflect on a broad range of observations James makes about fictions and figures, I want to focus on "Oedipus Revisited" to develop what resides behind the scenes. Hillman's thinking about the nature of figures and fiction implicates in profound

* Originally presented to the 6th Annual James Hillman Symposium in 2017 at The Dallas Institute of Humanities and Culture in Dallas, Texas and published in *Conversing with James Hillman: Mythic Figures*. Used by permission of The Dallas Institute.

ways Aristotle's own musings over the nature of mimesis. Hillman's own methodology might be called "mytho-mimetic." I am working with the assumption at the outset that "Oedipus Revisited" is as concerned with an archetypal way of reading as it is a series of openings into the complex poetics of Sophocles and into the intricate psyche of Oedipus. We might call this way of deep reading a form of Archetypal Activism.

As Oedipus reveals to us the complexity of a personal myth, Hillman outlines in his reading a corresponding myth of complexity by means of his rich reading by analogy. Matter and mythodology remain joined throughout his explication so that we are asked to read the essay on two levels at once: the realm of the Oedipus geography and events that lead the narrative, as well as the archetypal energy that Hillman exposes, to reveal the field activated and exposed by the plot's insistent presence as it propels us readers forward through its literal detail.

Every classic poem, even every work of art, contains an internal energy system that gives it life and vitality. Interpretation itself involves among other elements a bending or warping of the story's matter by these energies so some composite of meaning takes shape for the reader. It does so because it touches where the poem's internal energy system finds correspondences between it and the internal energy system of the reader's personal myth. Plot is the matter and action the energy that propels the matter of the plot forward. Hillman's own insights wed these two arenas or fields or grounds with such intensity that he can see in the marriage what many of us miss or only half-discern.

"The plot thickens," he writes (168). As in Sophocles' play, performed initially in Athens "sometime after 430 BCE" (27), Bernard Knox informs us in his Introduction to *The Three Theban Plays*, Hillman observes early in his essay that Mount Cithaeron harbors many moments of violence long before Oedipus met his father there in a constricted passageway. More of that in a moment. But here, we note Hillman's connecting psychoanalysis as a corresponding story to that of Oedipus. "...like Sophocles' play, like Freudian analysis, we begin to detect a repressed or forgotten clue. Again, the Oedipal imagination attracts us to its atmosphere. Our very way of pursuing the topic seeks to bring to light the buried 'real story.' And the clues are so evident" (168). I suggest here that if the plot of a story is literal action, then the "real story" comprises the arena of archetypal action and behind it, the energic field that gives it its persuasive energy.

That *way* he speaks of above is what I am calling one's personal myth, the attitude or angle or way of seeing that allows the reality of our life events to take on a certain tincture or hue, drawn from a palette of colors that shades how and what we are aware of and what we let slip by; it creates a continual tension between an aesthetics of blindness and insight. We find ourselves in Sophocles' play analogically following and interpreting Oedipus as we become him less through the plot than through the action that energizes perception itself. But more than that, we witness Hillman alternately falling into and extricating himself from the myth of Oedipus itself. Imaginal process and interpretive product congeal where three roads meet: the text itself, the text read, and the text recollected and written about. In this tri-vium, Hillman falls under the sway of the play itself as a character.

Moreover, the sphinx that Oedipus meets at the gates of Thebes is also the play's riddle that Hillman confronts; it insists on being responded to, but not just with Oedipal reasoning intent on solving a mathematical equation—one leg, two legs, three legs—but more soulfully with a mimetic imagining. Mimesis is the place of analogical making and the arena of soul making in a process that critiques and replaces the traditional roles and methodologies of psychoanalysis. More on mimesis shortly.

In a footnote to the Sphinx's riddle (169), Hillman furthers Jung's insight that "the riddle of the Sphinx was *herself*—the terrible mother-imago, which Oedipus would not take as a warning" (qtd. in fn. 20, 169). "Oedipus fell victim to his tragic fate because he thought he had answered the question. It was the Sphinx itself that he ought to have answered and not its façade" (fn. 20). Here I sense is a moment of mimesis, for there exists the surface story of the Sphinx's fascia which hides and riddles the mythic narrative below the surface that the façade offers a simulacrum or analogy of. What Hillman refers to as "the Sphinx itself" may be the archetypal energy field that gives shape to the myth but is itself formless. Poetic form is the expression of "the Sphinx itself."

In that same spirit, Hillman intends to use Sophocles' tragedy of *Oedipus Rex* as a corridor into revisioning psychology's own history, employing as one of his several launches a paragraph on the nature of fantasy from Jung's *Psychological Types*, which has served as a major cornerstone in his thought throughout his own massive and diverse explorations of soul and psychology's relation to it. Father and son meet here, on the constricted confines of the page, not to do battle but to engage in a shared insight. Jung's description is the centerpiece for all that follows in "Oedipus Revisited":

> This autonomous activity of the psyche, which can be explained neither as a reflex action to sensory stimuli nor as the executive organ of eternal ideas, is, like every vital process, a continually creative act. The psyche creates reality every day. The only expression I can use for this activity is *fantasy*. Fantasy is just as much feeling as thinking, as much intuition as sensation. There is no psychic function that, through fantasy, is not inextricably tied up with other psychic functions. . . .. It is preeminently the creative activity from which the answers to all answerable questions come; . . . where, like all psychological opposites, the inner and outer worlds are joining together in a living union. Fantasy it was and ever is which fashions the bridge between the irreconcilable claims of subject and object, introversion and extraversion. (Jung, *CW* 6, para. 78)

Using this paragraph as a guide, Hillman sets as his task a rewriting of traditional ideas underpinning psychoanalysis. His purpose, to be worked through in his Oedipus essay, is no less grand and profound as is Oedipus' search for the killer of his father, after he has convinced himself that his leaving Corinth and his supposed parents, Polybus and Merope, has been a success, never mind the man he grappled with on the narrowing road on the other side of Mount Cithaeron; no analogy formation there, of course, because Oedipus' beliefs about who his biological parents are blinds him to that event.

Hillman's re-search for the origins of psychology in mythology through the plot of Sophocles' play is also the locale for retrieving a mythic, or better, mythopoetic consciousness. This awakened way of knowing will allow him to see more, not less of Oedipus' struggling to escape his destiny, based on a false assumption: the confrontation with his father, solving and being seduced by the Sphinx, whose riddle concentrates on how many feet one stands on in three stages of one's life, the initial denial of his own woundedness, and the fatedness of his swollen feet guiding him precisely to the story that betrays his sense of success at having vanquished Apollo's oracle while revealing the true contours of his own rich destiny. As Bernard Knox points out in his discussion of Oedipus, "the Greek *oidi*, 'to swell,' is very close to '*oida*,' to know" (17). We are asked to think here of what a swollen form of knowing might look like as it relates to an inflated form of knowledge that hides the thinner truth of his plight.

By contrast, however, Hillman's journey is taken in a spirit and an attitude of openness and curiosity as well as through a belief that the Oedipus story will allow the following possibility, which he assumes correctly: "Our first aim is to unearth other relevancies for depth psychology in the Oedipus story for that is where the theater of Oedipus continues to be performed" (58). Not unlike, if I may draw an analogy of my own, here at The Dallas Institute for many years now, the theater of James Hillman continues to be performed, always with provocative and sometimes dramatic unearthings in the rich communal setting of conversations and presentations.

Now we are far enough into the play and into "Oedipus Revisited" to suggest that Hillman's methodology is a form of mimetic-mythology, a way into Oedipus and into reformatting psychology's predominant myth; it may be as well a furthering of Aristotle's notion of mimesis that the Greek philosopher gives short space to in his *Poetics*. Nonetheless, he has provoked explorations of this term that continue to the present day.

Mimesis is a Mode of Seeing Correspondences

Depth psychology may be referred to as a mimetic mythology and Oedipus himself as a relentless pursuer of his history with the same stamina and brilliance as Hillman's own pursuit of the depth psychological nature of poetics and specifically Sophocles' genius in this play and in *Oedipus at Colonus*.

As to the nature of mimesis, in one of two of his fine studies of this term in *Aristotle's Poetics* and in *The Aesthetics of Mimesis,* Stephen Halliwell relates the story he cites from Herodotus, of a man carrying a small wooden corpse around a banquet table; the verb is *mimeisthai,* which means reproduction or a copying of appearance (119). By the classical period, mimesis described several types of correspondence. Halliwell goes on to outline what he terms "metaphysical mimesis, wherein something in the visible order points to something invisible, or where a metaphor points to the invisible realm of the gods" (115-16).

In his *Timaeus,* Plato "posits a mimetic correspondence between the material and the metaphysical. . . .. Here the visible world is described as a likeness of the eternal in the mimesis of unchanging nature: the world is a *mimema* of a model and all transient shapes which come into being in the world's matter are themselves *mimemata* of eternal objects" (117). Finally, for our purposes, Aristotle in *Poetics* 25 asserts: "Since the poet, like the painter or any other image-maker, is a mimetic artist (*mimetes*), it follows that he must produce (at any one time) a mimesis of one of three things: reality past or present; things as they are said or seem to be; or things as they ought to be" (124-25).

Halliwell finds this remark extraordinary in that it liberates poetry and the visual arts from the narrowness of Plato's idea that poetry is little more than a literalistic model of a transcription of material reality, but also a "redefinition of mimesis as well as of the language of the 'image' so often associated with it; the object of the artist's mimesis not only need not be actual but may in some sense be ideal" (125). As he argues against Plato's strictures on artistic mimesis, Aristotle argues for the "independence of art from straightforward subject to standards and criteria of truth-telling and virtue; he further advances a concept of *fiction* which allows the poet's stance towards reality to be more oblique" (132-33).

Finally, another translator of the *Poetics,* S.H. Butcher, claims that there is an implicit pleasure felt in things imitated; we seem as a species to enjoy likenesses. Later in his study, he underscores that "the original that poetry imitates is human action and character in all their diverse modes of manifestation. In the drama, the poetic imitation of life attains its perfect form" (138). I believe Butcher gets closer to the implications of mimesis as I am working it: as an archetypal energy field, formless in origin but seeking form in a poetic making.

The genius of Sophocles' art successfully makes or shapes a latent energy field, by means of archetypal presences, into a formed set of images within a context of a coherent world that we as readers mimetically tap into. No less is Hillman's genius when he enters the interactive Oedipal field, gives over to it, surrenders to it, to see an emerging way to redefine psychoanalysis, a father of origin that helps to birth archetypal psychology.

Of course, the term mimesis was familiar to Hillman, who uses it throughout his writings; it is present in the Oedipus essay in a way that leads me to refer to Hillman's *mythodology* as the originating and original work of a mytho-mimetic poet of soul. I believe that in his essay, he formulates a poetic therapeutics and finds in the *Oedipus* of Sophocles, through Oedipus' attempts to escape the oracle's prophecy uttered by the inebriated man in the tavern, his own woundedness, his seeking the cure of the city, examples of a persuasive field of correspondences in which to advance a psychology that has its analogy in the character of Oedipus after his self-blinding, and, guided by his daughter Antigone, his arrival late in life into the Grove of Colonus, where he joins the ranks of the blessed ones.

James' own angle of vision is masterfully mimetic in the way he reads the play, namely, as a mythic enactment of an historical event as well as a psychic reality that both punishes and parents Oedipus: "Second, the terrible traits of the father also initiate the son into the hard lines of his own shadow. The pain of this father's failings teaches him that failing belongs to fathering" (172). Mimesis takes another step forward: through the play's action, we join in the analogy to perhaps glimpse our own wayward assumptions, which is an essential dimension of our own personal myth and our own process of awakening. Wallace Stevens' rich insight is helpful here. "Human nature is like water. It takes the shape of its container" (Quoteslyfe).

As Hillman lays out his trajectory, "continuing the line of Freud and Jung, drawing further parallels between myth and psychoanalysis" (158), I cannot help but wonder if Oedipus' own wounded search and developing awareness that he was working along correct lines but guided by wrong assumptions, does not have its analogies in making psychoanalysis aware that it is moving along reasonable lines of inquiry with false assumptions guiding its fantasies.

Assumptions themselves, whether individual or collective, carry fragments of our myth that have slipped beneath the floorboards of consciousness. A major thrust of tragedy's action is the growing sensibility, often through violence or a form of dismembering, that what has been unconscious but no less active, surfaces to be seen again or for the first time.

If so, then psychoanalysis suffers the Oedipal wound that Hillman wishes to renegotiate and realign. All early maladies track back to the absolute power of the parents, but that power is not recognized nor are the parents, as necessarily myth: "that myth hides from recognition and lies disguised in literal and secular case histories is appropriate to the very myth they teach—the tale of Oedipus, its disguises and pursuit of self-recognition" (162).

Psychoanalysis therefore gets its right in its own blindness, its own pursuit of assumptions that both undercut its theory yet advance its method. I return to Jung's words as an epigram to this essay: *"One sees what one can best see oneself."*

Oedipus, like the discipline that Hillman critiques, uses events as historical facts, but to reduce its meaning to one level (162) is to demythologize one's recollections; "all these emotions and configurations are ways in which we are remythologized." All of our emotional lives and psychological fantasies "are doors to Sophocles and Sophocles himself a door" (162). He then draws direct associations between historical events and mythic realities in the following: "Their importance rises not from historical events but by mythical happenings, that, as Sallustius said, never happened but always are, as fictions" (162).

I suggest that mimesis in one of its formats reenters the stage in close association with both metaphor and memory in what Jean-Michel Oughourlian calls "mimetic reciprocity" (xiii) in his provocative study, *The Mimetic Brain.* My sense is that history embeds myth in its temporality as myth enjoys a reputation as the inner sleeve of history, invisible but present, giving shape and order and a certain resilience to it as an invisible sleeve of a suit or a jacket offers the shape of the garment a particular fit;

it is fitting to and fits the history of an imaginal level of understanding. Myth itself is mimetic by design, memorial by necessity, and metaphorical by inclination.

What Oedipus learns of his assumed father, Polybus, who adopted him, from the drunkard spouting his own inebriated excesses in a tavern, sends Oedipus on the road, giving Corinth as wide a berth as possible, all the while following his trajectory to the place of the three roads, the moment of life trivial in its event, yet monumental in its mythic resonance.

There, because of a constriction in the road, two cannot pass one another; one must yield. But neither can. Their mutual incendiary tempers are mimetic of the road's own constriction, losing all sense of moderation, the old King and his retinue war with Oedipus, father with son, with neither having any knowledge of the other's identity. Both, Hillman writes, "Father and son shared a literalist psychology.... That is why they must 'oracularly' meet at the crossroads and act the oracle literally" (161). Both take oracles at face value; the father abandons his son, while the son flees from his assumed father (Polybus).

Both actions aim not to fulfill the oracle, yet in their escape, they rush headlong into fulfilling it. Paradox rests at the heart of this moment, for both assume that they have, each in their own way, outfoxed the future destined for them. Where literalism reigns, Sophocles suggests, there may violence detonate.

To see and hear mimetically is in Oedipus' future when his mother tells him of the story of the king's killing to calm his growing suspicion that he in fact had slain his father. It is to view or listen for the other side, for the interior, for the above or the below, for the not yet and the *what is*, if not the *what if*. As a form of mimesis, analogy is a potent form in analysis; to turn it around, analysis is a poetic form of analogizing.

Hillman's own language in his exploration, words he is fully conscious of, begin to steal into his descriptions and caveats; for example, when he reminds us that "myth hides from recognition and lies disguised in literal and secular case histories," he asserts that "*We must see this clearly*, and here again I use Oedipal heroic language" (162); further, "only through a return to the bedrock of fantasies, the myths [can] psychology as it is now conceived awaken to itself" (158). When he uses the word "inescapable," he grasps once again how it is mimetically a part of the Oedipal myth and that his assuming an "Oedipal vocabulary" makes his writing about this tragic hero a witness of his own heroic understanding. Mimetic reciprocity dons dramatic garments.

I do not believe that a clearer illustration of the power of mimesis as it remembers, restores, and analogizes the self in a creative reading or viewing of a drama or poem, is possible. Did Aristotle understand the huge implications of his statements in *Poetics,* wherein when we read and meditate deeply on poetry, we do indeed become the thing we contemplate? At the beginning of the essay, Hillman becomes aware that his vocabulary is beginning to assume the linguistic terrain of the play; he recognizes the Oedipal elements in himself through a persuasive series of discoveries in which a deeper understanding of how psychoanalysis is Oedipal in its information-gathering, its reasoned diagnoses, yet misses the soul of the client in the process.

He has appropriated the myth of Oedipus and set it down within a more soul-based interactive field in a process that mimics the action of Oedipus coming to his own identity.

I spiral back to an observation Hillman made at the beginning of his pilgrimage through the play, namely, that "Myth is the great awakener to cure our blindness" (158). Freud was one of the first to see the deep linking powers of mimesis wherein he wrote, as James cites, "The Greek myth seizes on a compulsion which everyone recognizes because he has felt traces of it in himself. Every member of the audience was once a budding Oedipus in phantasy" (qtd. on 159).

And then a reverse spiral to the essay's end: we listen to a once blind Oedipus who now, with hindsight, gains insight: "I have since recognized that the presentation of this paper is a presentation of self, of Oedipal self, of a blind man in a sick city, struggling with the Apollonic curse of his world, psychoanalysis. . . .. I did not realize at first that I was in the play, that the drama was so powerful. . . .. I did not recognize that it was I who could not hear to the heart of my own discourse. Even my asking and answering, 'Why did I come, why do I speak?' is Oedipal" (197).

The mimetic spiral closes with this recognition—Hillman's own *an-agnorisis*—a movement simultaneously of turning back to a re-cognition. The three roads of: 1. A critique of psychoanalysis; 2. The movement of drawing mimetic connections between the field and the force of the drama; and 3. The recognition that Hillman was addressing his own intention and purpose of the first re-cognition, meet in this final insight. Its brilliance can only be wondered at and, for me, on occasion, grasped as a clear-sighted vision of its possibilities.

Works Cited

Bond, Stephen. *Living Myth: Personal Meaning as a Way of Life.* Shambhala, 1993.

Butcher, S.H. *Aristotle's Theory of Poetry and Fine Art.* 3rd ed. Hill and Wang, 1902.

Halliwell, Stephen. *Aristotle's Poetics.* University of Chicago Press, 1998.

Hillman, James. *Healing Fiction.* HarperPerrennial, 1983.

---.. *Mythic Figures. The Uniform Edition of the Writings of James Hillman.* Volume 6.1. Spring Publications, 2017.

Jung, C.G. *The Collected Works of C.G. Jung.* Trans. R.F.C Hull. Vol. 6. Princeton UP, 1990.

Knox, Bernard. "Sophocles' Oedipus." *Sophocles' Oedipus Rex.* Edited by Harold Bloom. Chelsea, 1988. 5-24.

---. Editor. *The Three Theban Plays.* Trans. Robert Fagles. Penguin Books, 1984.

Oughourlian, Jean-Michel. *The Mimetic Brain.* Trans. Trevor Cribben Merrill. Michigan State UP, 2016.

4

A Pilgrimage From Haunting to Healing*

"Now we understand what a complex is, and how the present moment
is always like a lily pad floating on a vast ocean of affect."
~James Hollis
Hauntings: Dispelling the Ghosts Who Run Our Lives

Our stories are the life blood of our lives seeking meaning and coherence
as well as vibrant infrastructures of what we believe and value. In a wonderful book, *The Way of the Storyteller,* Ruth Sawyer reminds us of something that is pertinent to where we are, here in Galway, relating our stories.

Sawyer tells a story early on of the rich gifts she received from Joanna,
her Irish nurse. She remembers her saying frequently: "Tales or tunes,
ye'll find none better anywhere than what we have in Ireland." To which
Sawyer adds: "And nowhere will you find them better told or sung" (17-
18). Telling our stories, whether to dispel, deflect, or welcome our ghosts,
is as important as creating such a ritual of expression. Sawyer concludes
this vignette by recalling Joanna's traditional ending to all her stories:
"Take it and may the next one who tells it better it" (17).

---

* Originally presented at the conference "Dispelling Our Personal and Family
Ghosts" in Galway, Ireland, March 27th -April 3rd, 2023, and sponsored by the New
York Jung Society. Directed by Aryeh Maidenbaum and Diana Ruben.

Another Irish bard tells mythologist Phil Cousineau that no journey, no pilgrimage, can be complete until one tells a story about what happened (*The World's Oldest Story* 14). The story completes the voyage, the tale—like the tail of an animal, it appears at the end, for ballast and balance. It completes the animal less as an appendage, more like an appendix to a story.

So here is my story, condensed and concentrated. It relates the birth of a ghost that haunted me for decades; then something changed. But I am already getting ahead of myself. I must tell this story to complete a very painful condition that I feel more liberated from today.

Born in 1944, I grew up in Cleveland, Ohio, the second of five children. We lived in a small one-bedroom apartment on St. Clare Avenue on Cleveland's east side. At the time, only my older brother, Marty, and I lived with our parents. Early on I detected the pattern that would haunt each family member for decades. During the week my father would board a bus outside our apartment building and ride to downtown Cleveland where he worked in Personnel for the Cleveland Electric Illuminating Company. He was a quiet, shy man and spoke little at home, as I remember him.

But on the weekends, all that changed; on Friday evening he would begin loading up on beer at a tavern across from our building, then continue drinking for the better part of the weekend, at least into Sunday morning. I knew nothing else, sensed no other option, so I saw his behavior as normal; it was part of the family myth that we all accepted as part of growing up. Most myths, as you know, find places for rituals to enact them. My father handled that ritual necessity with violent precision, including shouting, sometimes howling, and occasionally hitting our mother.

He was, like his two brothers—my uncles—an alcoholic. But when *they* drank, they were not changed so radically as my father. At least that is what we believed. In our family, we were all taught to keep the family secret hermetically sealed, lips sealed tight. Years later, and in a different home in the suburbs, we began to discover boxes of groceries at our back door, courtesy of the Catholic church we belonged to and where we attended school. Apparently, someone had leaked the secret.

In 1950, my father announced we were moving to a nearby suburb, Euclid, Ohio, some four miles from our dingy apartment and the sickly-colored yellow walls of the hallways. It was a small, two-story house, with three bedrooms, one bathroom, and an attached single-car garage. Now my father had no neighbors just the other side of the apartment walls, so his drinking accelerated. His shouting in bursts of rage and shame filled the house for most of the weekend, followed by his sometimes-successful sobering up on Sunday. We did not dare invite any friends over on the weekends; we were too ashamed of his behavior to have it witnessed by classmates.

This traumatic ritual was locked in place and unloaded with alarming regularity each weekend, sometimes spilling over into Monday or Tuesday. My mother was then designated to call his company and tell them that Roger had the flu or a cold and would not be in. How hard that was for her, to be abused, then forced to lie. Of course, as we later discovered, his employer knew the actual score.

In time, a second brother was born; then, several years later, a third brother and finally, a sister, who my mother admitted one day, saved her life from all the angry male energy, with few boundaries, that saturated the home. We all found ourselves as enraged and outraged and as ashamed as our father; but not right away. Nor did make the connection that his contagious illness was now our disease.

As we grew older, I found returning home from school each day a form of patterned torture. Part of its suffering nested in the residue of anger and rage that permeated the air in the house from the previous weekend's chaos; it also stemmed from the myth of silence we all vowed to preserve at all costs. You all realize how the power of shame can steal one's voice and especially one's desire to be seen and heard. Shame unchecked and fed regularly may transform into violence to suffocate it. Shame also suffocates the healthy needs we all longed to have served in some form.

But shame was fed first; it was then reinforced by my father's stinging nettles of "not good enough" or "you're no good" or "you'll never amount to anything" that he fired at us with uncanny accuracy and frequency when he was out of control. With hindsight and some basic psychological principles under my belt, I was later able to look back with enormous compassion at his suffering, and later, my own. But not yet.

We "settled" into the chaos of the weekends, which should have been times of recovering from the work and school week but were instead occasions for riotous behavior and traumatic interludes that resonated throughout the entire week. We all became extremely vigilant on Friday and Saturday nights; we listened to the voices raised, the accusations hurled back and forth between our parents downstairs, plates breaking, and a once-loving relationship bombarded with the shrapnel of disappointment as it painfully dismantled beneath us. Our own fragile and enraged selves were continually shaped by the addiction myth and its angry ventilation.

Shrapnel, as you are aware, refers to the pieces of a bomb, shell, or bullet that has exploded. During wars, many soldiers were treated for shrapnel wounds. When people are injured or killed by bombs, many of them are penetrated by flying shrapnel—sharp, dangerous shards of metal. Shrapnel gets its name from General Henry Shrapnel of the British Army's Royal Artillery, who invented the shrapnel shell.[†]

As we grew older, we never spoke of these horrific weekends; we would try to stay with friends or relatives on these days to escape the sandblasting of his disgust with himself and the beast that, with complete indifference, devoured him and us more thoroughly over time. This was our monster in the underworld, the ghost within the tribe, that we were forced to confront without any weapons or deep understanding except disgust and anxiety. We ran from the rampaging beast. In time my older brother quit high school and joined the Navy so to successfully escape for four years. He never returned home.

A shift began when what happened one evening pivoted something in me. I later reflected that if the addict does not experience transition points in his illness, then certainly those who carry the shrapnel of his behavior do. What stood out this evening was an image of my father in his underwear, gesturing at me from a landing between two flights of stairs. He began once hurling a barrage of berating accusations at me with "you are worthless, you'll never amount to anything." It was Saturday

---

[†] https://en.wikipedia.org/wiki/Henry_Shrapnel

evening and I had just finished 11 hours of work at a supermarket and was exhausted. I was paying my own tuition to a private Catholic high school, had bought my own car, and did modestly well in school. I nonetheless absorbed his criticism for the hundredth time as a greater truth than the facts witnessed.

As I attempted to walk upstairs to my room, he accelerated his attack. In an altered state, as I reached him, I simply swung around and pushed him down the second flight of stairs without any regard for what the consequences might be. He was so drunk that he bounced down the six carpeted stairs and lay at the bottom, fully awake, but silent.

His verbal abuse ended after that incident. I had in that one survival response to his abusive attacks inserted mine into his, claiming violence for violence. I carried no honor in that victory, for I had become, in my own rage, his double. I feel right now in reading this to you, another haunting ghost join the fraternity of its kinsmen.

I clearly saw many years later that I was miles from where Dan McAdams highlights in *The Stories We Live By*: "At some point in our lives we become aware of the task to create an integrative life story. Through it we come to understand who we are and how we fit into the adult world" (91). You may enjoy the fact that the chapter in which he makes this observation is called "Becoming the Mythmaker." But when one's sense of self is so scattered and fragmented, any effort at integration remains an unlived dream.

I would say it this way: At such a wounded period of my life, I had no perspective that I could call my own. I was haunted, instead, by the viewpoint of the addiction itself, a perspective of illness. I did not drink, even as a senior in high school, for fear of becoming like my father; what I was unconscious of was that I had migrated deep into myself all the destructive patterns of the alcoholic. I had let the ghost of addiction in without any knowledge of what and who it was. More than hooked, I was haunted by the illness through the ghosts of shame and rage.

The stories that have wounded all of us in the family, perhaps our mother most of all, but that the rest of us carried into adult life, have the capacity to slice us open to reveal the accumulated toxicity of a soul struggling to adapt to a narrative that had crushed my father, and was slowly steam-rolling over all of us, one square inch and one weekend at a time.

I have tried throughout this presentation to remember how Jung had established that "an archetypal content expresses itself first and foremost in metaphors" (*CW 9*, i, par. 267). Follow the metaphors and they will lead one to the myth that undergirds their patterning.

Over time and most specifically, as I was now studying at a local junior college in Cleveland, my father came home one morning from work. I asked him if he was sick. He said no, but that the company had fired him just one year shy of his pension. From that day forward he ceased all alcohol consumption but clung to the patterns of which the alcohol was a byproduct. In time he and our mother healed their relationship; she also proved instrumental in finding him a position at the Euclid Municipal Court's office, which he kept successfully for many years before retiring.

The second chapter of this presentation was given further validity by James Hollis' observation in *Hauntings*: "The truth is unsettling: if we are to recognize the powers of the invisible world, however understood, then we have to broaden and deepen our view of our lives, continuously reassess our values, and make more difficult choices" (26).

The path to healing this haunting wounding began in a bookstore in San Antonio in 1995 as I prepared for the fall of that year to enjoy a sabbatical from a catholic university I was teaching for. As I reached for a book on Ireland in the travel section of the store, a text next door stuck to it, fell off the shelf, and landed with a thud on my left foot. This thud was the sound of a destiny that was to unfold over the next few years. It was titled: *A Guide to Monasteries and Retreat Centers in the Southwestern United States*. When I read the title, I put the Ireland book back on the shelf because this second book initiated another journey I felt compelled to follow.

With my wife's blessing, we postponed our Ireland trip. But fate intervened once again in the form of an offer to move to Santa Barbara to begin a full-time core position in Mythological Studies at Pacifica Graduate Institute, beginning winter quarter of 1996. I reshelved the monastery pilgrimage; instead, we moved that December to California. The clock for a sabbatical wound back to zero, but I had to wait only three years to apply for a sabbatical at the Institute, my first as an academic.

I began to plan for this journey early in the summer of 1998, and in August of that year, with my Ford Ranger Pickup truck packed both in the cab and in the bed that had a fiberglass lid that locked, I headed out north to Big Sur, my first monastery of the twelve selected places I would retreat at, including one Zen Buddhist monastery in northern California. I did not know that I was beginning a healing journey that would transform my life.

I felt both restless and spiritually bankrupt as my wife waved goodbye to me when I pointed the truck north for a 3.5-month sojourn that would include not only staying in retreat centers but also camping in state and national parks. I had no idea what to expect but felt the crush of this journey's necessity in my life. I vowed to keep a journal, a habit I had started years ago, to record what might be revealed on this voyage. In one of the books I had packed, the Benedictine priest, Thomas Merton, notes that "the dimensions of prayer in solitude are those of man's ordinary anguish, his self-searching, his moments of nausea at his own vanity, falsity and capacity for betrayal" (*Contemplative Prayer*).

How could he know this and speak it with such withering honesty? I pushed on, driven by the ghosts of the past that took full advantage of my vulnerable condition to carve out perches throughout my truck and in the rooms of solitude I was to inhabit.

At the second retreat center, The Carmelite House of Prayer in Napa Valley, I settled in as the only retreatant in town, a phenomenon that happened several times, as if some plan to isolate me from relying on other retreatants for refuge had been laid out in front of me. Only the German Shepherd monastery dog, Rusty, and I were there on the vast grounds. I spent evenings having dinner with the Irish priests that stewarded the House of Prayer; from them I learned the history of this magnificent estate as well as the upcoming crushing of the grapes ritual to begin that week as part of the fall harvest. What a perfect metaphor for my own feelings.

After dinner the second evening, I walked out to sit by the pond and settled into the joy of being there; the light from the hot day began to soften and cool. Strangely, I felt once more, as I did at Camaldoli Hermitage, my previous monastery, the presence of my father again, but this time he was far more pronounced. I recalled his passing just two years before. Was I here because of him? The pattern of his life at home slowly began to take form as I listened to the comforting sound of the water fountain in the middle of the pond and watched large Koi fish swimming closer to the surface. Their slow emergence into visibility mirrored my father's image rising within me.

Perhaps these powerful images surrounding my father's years of abuse at home in a distressed household had come to me now, in tranquility, to be exorcised, or at least contemplated more soberly as a past that had shaped me in many positive ways. Out of the shadows of our souls can arise the treasures that partly comprise these dark recesses. But we must, I now understand, be willing to accept them both.

How wounded we all are, I glimpsed as I sat in the cool evening air as the fish and now the chorusing bullfrogs serenaded Rusty and me on the bench next to the water's edge. But honestly, I did not like being alone with these thoughts, yet knew they were visiting me now as aggressive ghosts so I could gaze at them with less emotional upset and more compassion. I dared to let myself feel their sting, their energy, and their daring.

Vague feelings of some exorcism crossed my awareness, and I wondered if this too was going to be a crucial landscape of my interior journey. Part of me resisted heading back to the empty cottage, with all those vacant bedrooms and my imagination full of disturbing images from childhood, to face the silence of the place wherein I had cleared a space in my life for grace; instead, ghastly ghosts tumbled into the silent silo of my soul.

I then recalled my promise to myself in planning this pilgrimage: look for nothing. Move from place to place, settle in wherever you are, submit to who and what you find there, and take careful note of what emerges on its own for contemplation. Yield to everything in your path. God finds you when He needs to and visits you with what you need to hear and bear. However, it will not be more than your capacity for burdens. Stay open and surrender.

I did not expect the presence of my alternately enraged and reticent father to follow me on this journey, but here he was, beside me, on my right, sitting on the bench. And there I was, mirroring him in attitude and design more than I ever realized. What I thought I had avoided I had in essential ways, become. This recognition shocked me into thinking of our two sons and who they were becoming, and whether the same patterns were working themselves out in them. Here was a part of parenting I had never calculated, but needed to, now, in solitude.

My wife and I knew that our older son was also an alcoholic and addicted to drug use. But contrary to my father, Matt had discovered AA, along with other restaurant waiters on the River Walk of San Antonio. The six of them stopped going out to drink at 2 a.m. when the restaurants closed; instead and as a group, they began to attend early morning hour AA meetings in the city. Together, they had chosen sobriety over the scourge of their addictions. Nothing short of a miracle is adequate to describe what transformations ushered into our family. I believe my son's efforts to gain sobriety and a spiritual life healed his mother and me as well.

But this pilgrimage had shaped itself into a descent that I did not know I had the courage to own. It was turning into a voyage that included facing demons—those ghosts with graduate degrees—by entering some infernal pockets of my past. The journey's energy had taken on its own life, its own motives, and its own constructive rhythms.

I now faced a choice: to truncate this trip and leave, head home, and spend the rest of the sabbatical on chores around the house to keep me busy, distracted and unaffected by such visitations. But some feeling of destiny overrode and deleted my desire to choose retreating from the retreat. Resignation stepped in to overpower my restlessness and loneliness.

That feeling of loneliness increased as I walked slowly back to the empty cottage in the gathering dark stillness of a lovely fall evening. I looked hopefully to see if another retreatant had perhaps arrived and parked close to my truck, but there it sat by itself under the tree, appearing as solitary and forlorn as I felt. I resolved to stay another day, to break the trip down into edible pieces to digest so as not to be overwhelmed with what had just entered my thoughts.

I knew I could drive home in two days, but some felt sense deep within me resisted acting on this delicious and yet malnourished temptation. Instead, I put my journey in God's hands and prayed that He show me the path. Doing so instantly calmed me; a feeling of relief crept over me, offering the resolve I craved to enjoy the solitude of a quiet and isolated night. But I did not relish this specter emerging from the deep again—yet I knew it would.

I continued to read Thomas Merton on *Contemplative Prayer*. "The monk searches not only his own heart; he plunges deep into the heart of that world of which he remains a part, although he seems to have 'left it'" (18). When I read this, I thought of my father's voice, his actions, his tormented life as an alcoholic, a disease that had a thick crust and very populated line running throughout my family of Irish Catholics.

He had now visited me powerfully and vividly at both retreat centers, waiting, perhaps, to be witnessed further, or even noticed, by me. Perhaps in this deep silence, his voice, so scarcely heard when he was sober, now sought out a conversation. I hoped that I could garner the forgiveness in me to oblige his insistence.

My last morning at the Carmelite Retreat House of Prayer passed quickly and I found myself packing the truck the next morning. My father had expressed an interest in accompanying me on the rest of my pilgrimage. He was so earnest that as I packed the truck, I emptied the passenger seat for him. His presence was palpable and strangely comforting. I gave my faithful disciple, Rusty, a big hug, thought for a moment of dognapping him, but felt better about it when I realized he would be needed by other retreatants also seeking solace in his companionship.

Since I had three days between monasteries, I drove north where I found a campground near the ocean, pitched my tent, and settled in for two nights. It was Sunday afternoon when I set up camp; by evening I was the only one inhabiting the entire park. As I sat in my chair enjoying the heat of a fire I had started, I felt I was not alone.

My father had once more decided to pay me a visit. Apparently, he still had more to say, and I was much more accepting of his desire to speak about the past, which was already beginning to heal decades of abusive behavior.

He haunted me in a constructive way by questioning how I may have been a harmful father to my sons in ways I was unconscious of. Wounds from the father inherited by his sons seemed as old as humanity itself, and I was to relive some of the wounds inflicted throughout my childhood and adolescence. Sitting by me close to the campfire, he revealed how his deep depression was passed on to me, along with the shame and anger that were its constant cohorts.

Yet there was something devotional to the life of the spirit that my father also passed on to me, and which, with its negative features, I had passed as a paternal package, on to my sons. Violence and the sacred— were these inevitable partners? What a revelation while sitting by the fire as it fired hot embers against the stones that encircled it, to recognize that as a parent I had unconsciously repeated, modified, and exaggerated both the sins and the sanctities of my parent.

I had carried the illusion that I was liberated from his influence, only to discover I had been repeating them in my own style, which did not hide the bare reality of the repetition. Perhaps this ghostly truth was the most painful of all on my pilgrimage.

As the embers in the fire began to settle down into a serene, heated glow, I realized how the shame and anger I had felt for so long had their own heated radiance as haunting energies in my own emotional life and that they had found likely hosts in my sons' own behaviors as well as the positive, genius parts of them that I so admired.

More visits were to come in my 3.5 months on the road, but the haunting father had, even this early, transformed into a healing presence.

I end with an insight from one of my favorite and inspiring writers, the Buddhist nun Pema Chodron. She opened another corridor to the themes of this rich and provocative conference. In *Start Where You Are* she describes the basic notion of *lojong* meditation practice (mind training in theory and practice): "that we can make friends with what we reject, what we see as 'bad' in ourselves and in other people. At the same time, we could learn to be generous with what we cherish, what we see as 'good.' If we begin to live in this way, something in us that may have been buried for a long time begins to ripen. . . this something is called *bodhi-chitta*, or awakened heart" (6-7). Such a friendship is achieved, even partially, with great effort and willing surrender. A relation in which ghosts can become guests and hauntings can find their own core of healing and remembering can be a fine territory for renewal.

I wanted to share with you my pilgrimage from haunting by violence, shame, and inadequacy to the place of a more awakened healed heart, which continues to ripen, scars and all. I am grateful to you all for listening to my story and the feelings that propelled it forward.

Works Cited

Chodron, Pema. *Start Where You Are: A Guide to Compassionate Living.* Shambhala, 2001.

Cousineau, Phil. *The Oldest Story in the World: A Mosaic of Meditations on the Secret Strength of Stories.* Sisyphus Press, 2010.

Hollis, James. *Hauntings: Dispelling the Ghosts Who Run Our Lives.* Chiron Publications, 2015.

Jung, C.G. *The Collected Works of C.G. Jung.* Translated by R.F.C. Hull. Vol. 9, ii. Princeton UP, 1971.

Merton, Thomas. *Contemplative Prayer.* Image Books, 1971.

McAdams, Dan. P. *The Stories We Live By: Personal Myths and the Making of the Self.* The Guilford Press, 1993.

Sawyer, Ruth. *The Way of the Storyteller.* Penguin Books, 1990.

Shrapnel, Henry. https://en.wikipedia.org/wiki/Henry_Shrapnel

5

BELIEF, FAITH, AND THE WORLD OF AS-IF: "I WANT TO BELIEVE"*

Recently my wife and I began rewatching *The X Files* on Hulu. It had been decades since we were mesmerized by this startling and ground-breaking series. Created by the visionary Chris Carter, each show in its multiple seasons is ostensibly about extraterrestrials, occult phenomena, the unexplained, the mysterious, and other earthly events that defy the logical categories of making sense of what is loosely called reality. All true. But underneath these excursions into the mysteries of both earthly and galactic figures and events is the deeper motif of *belief.*

You might recall the two characters that carry the series. Fox Mulder (David Duchovny) is an FBI agent who has been allowed to set up a one-person branch of inquiry into unexplained phenomena. His office is in the basement of the FBI building in Washington D.C.; it has no windows, its tiny size is suffocating, and yet it works for this underground mole who delights in cases which stubbornly stand outside the boundaries of logical analysis. A poster on his wall tells it all: "I Want to Believe." The words gather at the bottom of an image of a flying saucer.

To essentially spy on him, the Bureau assigns a medical doctor and agent, Dana Scully (Gillian Anderson) to ostensibly assist Fox, but in fact

---

* Originally presented to the Washington, D.C. Friends of Jung in a four-part course on "The Mythology of Belief: Exploring Multiple Faces of What We Believe and How They Shape Our Personal Myth."

she's tasked with reporting regularly on his activities. Over time, Scully begins to comprehend that Fox is on to something, but she is cautious and intrudes her words of caution and skepticism to his cases and their inexplicable nature. For she is the figure of the skeptical scientist of logic and hard facts. They are what constitute reality for her and she sees Mulder's cases through those prisms. This masculine-feminine dyad is far more effective together than separately.

He, in turn, is the more intuitive, imaginal, and even mystical imagination who can sense something invisible through the visible phenomena he chases across the United States. His terrain is the underworld of the normative visible reality that shellacks over the phenomenal world. But in this strange alliance, they need and complement one another's visions of the real and the beliefs that lead them through their respective interpretations, their distinct mythologies, that give form and shape to their respective fields. They mutually guide and correct one another's approaches to the reality of the unexplained, two myths fostering a compact of cooperation. Their separate beliefs about reality find nexus points with each case they explore.

Through the influences of several sources, I want to explore the realms of belief, faith, and the "as-if" worlds that serve as boundaries for each. In addition, I am fascinated by how beliefs and articles of faith can, over time, morph into facts, into secure and fixed realities that an individual or a nation can begin to accept as the real. It is part of the dilemma and the tribalism we are ensconced in today. The results of such warring visions of reality have led, as you know, to real violence and to efforts to dismantle the shared mythology we have all participated in, to whatever degree, that has been in place for our two-hundred-year history.

Here I would like to pose a few questions that have grown out of my explorations to date; the list is not inclusive but does give the flavor of the areas I want to pursue.

- What beliefs do you display to create an "as-if" version of certainty about the nature of reality?
- What beliefs do you use as bricks and mortar to build walls around what you fear, despise, dislike, and feel alienated from?

- Do your beliefs help you to regard uncertainty and a lack of grounding as constants in your life?
- How do you make the distinctions and then place them into specific categories of faith and belief? What criteria do you implement for what you believe in and what you have faith in?

Not long ago, I wrote an op-ed piece for our local newspaper, the *Herald-Zeitung,* in which I flipped the more popular "Seeing is Believing," to "Believing is Seeing." I was spurred on by recognizing how the battle over beliefs today seems to have passed a boiling point: news shows, opinion pieces, and other forms of communication are all intent on showing us one position or another, while demeaning its opposite and those who support what we don't, so we might succumb to believing it. Without simplifying the horrors of global conflicts, one constant seems clear: they are all fought primarily for the same reason—a clash of beliefs. The thinking goes something like this: "We don't agree with your beliefs so we will set out to silence what threatens our belief system." Acts of violence have become more pronounced and frequent as a consequence.

The underlying assumption or belief is that I am right, and you are wrong. Because I believe this version/vision of what constitutes reality and you do not, I will attempt to silence you to eliminate the gnawing discomfort of hearing ideas, attitudes, and assertions that contradict mine. The fundamental flaw wriggling around in this stance is that often what I believe or what you believe cannot ever be proven as an air-tight and iron-clad position or perspective. The fantasy, however, is that what I muster to "prove my point," or "point of view" can also be manipulated to fabricate the veracity of my perspective.

But let's tack at this juncture into the realm of faith and its relation to beliefs. At times they seem to be used as synonyms, but I think not. May they be gradations of truths that we accept *as if* they were true? Possibly. In "A Psychological Approach to the Trinity," C.G. Jung brings us to the moment of faith: "Religion is a 'revealed' way of salvation. Its ideas are products of a pre-conscious knowledge which, always and everywhere, expresses itself in symbols. Even if our intellect does not grasp them, they still work, because our unconscious acknowledges them as exponents of universal psychic facts. For this reason, *faith is enough*—if it is there" (*CW* 11, para. 293, my emphasis).

Lamentably, today's ethos of rationality divorces us from accepting symbols as valid ways of knowing and, further, believing. For Jung, connecting with the dogma of the Trinity as a valid belief came about only when he envisioned it through the archetype, "with the *consensus omnium* . . . that I was able to establish any relationship with the dogma at all" (para. 294). The archetypal reality was his corridor into the dogma; nothing in the rational realm would allow him to gain intimacy with it.

But "a knowledge of the universal background was sufficient to give me the courage to treat 'that which is believed always, everywhere, by everybody' as a psychological fact which extends far beyond the confines of Christianity, and to approach it as an object of scientific study, as a *phenomenon* pure and simple. . . (para. 294). So, what congeals towards the end of this chapter on the Trinity is faith, belief, psychological facts, and universally agreed on doctrines that have been believed in for over two thousand years by countless millions of people.

I want to take his radical conclusion a step further, for it begins to push faith and belief into the same conversation. Those who have believed this doctrine with such massive numbers and millennia have comprehended the "symbolum" which "possesses the highest degree of actuality. . . as a valid statement concerning those things which one cannot see with the eyes or touch with the hands. It is this fact that needs to be understood. . ." (para. 294), for we are limited to the metaphysical truth, which is man-made. But then Jung's keyword: "unless." "Unless the unbiddable gift of faith lifts us beyond all dubiety and all uneasy investigation. It is dangerous if these matters are only objects of belief; for where there is belief there is doubt, and the fiercer and naïver the belief the more devastating the doubt once it begins to dawn" (*CW* 11, para. 294).

Faith in his discussion lifts one beyond mere beliefs to a realm where doubt is not present; it places us within the transcendent nature of divinity, or the divine and of the gods. Faith, we also delineate, is a gift, something freely given, not sought after; it also opens a much larger discussion of the nature of being human than mere belief can attend to. Faith captures the symbolic realm where belief may not. He writes in the next section, "Transformation Symbolism in the Mass," that the Catholic ritual of the Mass and its symbols would "be profoundly alien to man were it not rooted in the human psyche" (*CW* 11, par. 339); if true, then similar patterns would be evident throughout human history.

Faces of Faith

Not all beliefs or articles of faith are created equal or believed in equally. They too have valences; such is also true of what we know or claim to know. For example, what I place my faith in can be altered, enhanced, modified, or dismantled by life events that confirm or weaken what I have chosen, or maintain through habit, of what my faith is.

In this section I am guided by two books from very different authors who write eloquently on belief and faith. The more recent text is by T.M. Luhrmann, *How God Becomes Real: Kindling the Presence of Invisible Others* (2020). The other is authored by a very popular Benedictine Brother, David Steindl-Rast, *Gratefulness, The Heart of Prayer* (1984).

I am intrigued by Luhrmann's term, "Faith Frame," which she contrasts with beliefs: "I use the word 'faith' here, because belief is a promiscuous word. 'Belief' refers to any kind of claim, intuitive or deliberative, that there might be an invisible spirit. By 'faith' I mean a sustained, intentional deliberative commitment to the idea that there are invisible beings who are involved in human lives in helpful ways" (*How God* 21). Faith is more focused and rests on a "mode of thinking and interpreting, a set of expectations and memories, in which god and spirits matter" (22).

I would use the phrase "personal myth" to describe such a way of being present in and towards the world; it includes invisible presences as realities that comprise one's *as-if* world. Both faith and beliefs are used for the same fundamental purpose: to help individuals shape their lives into meaningful and purposeful identities.

Often individuals will construct such a frame spurred by fear—of the unknown, of certain images of the afterlife, of a general anxiety, or a way to assuage the gnawing sense of uncertainty—in order to ground themselves in a world of plausibility. Let's stay with this rich metaphor of a frame for a few more minutes, for it is a structure (noun) and an action (verb). In another context, in a volume of co-authored poetry, I mused on what a frame is and want to include some of those notions here.

I considered that poetry itself is a form of linguistic and aesthetic framing of the world through its particularities. It persuaded me to think of the way in which poetry frames the world. It forces me to think further about how windows to the world have power. The power resides in the frame the window glass clings to. A sheet of glass with no frame is relatively useless because it's so fragile and vulnerable, but a frame without a sheet of glass loses its potency. Frames remain faithful to the world view they both structure and contain through the boundary they establish. Frames both bound and beatify one piece of the world's arena; the frame attends to its shaping (*Road* 84).

A frame is also a fidelity. It is faithful to a way of understanding one thing and everything at once. Poetics may then be an aesthetic act of framing the world into a worldview. Its optional optics are infinite (84). The work area or space in which frames are constructed is the imagination itself in its making and shaping power. The Irish poet W.B. Yeats called this space "the foul rag and bone shop of the heart" (qtd. in *The Rag and Bone Shop of the Heart* xvii) The heart, not the head, is the organ that organ-izes a frame's construction, as Luhrmann speaks of one's faith as a frame. With the heart at its center, it is assured an embodiment that perhaps did not exist before.

I suggest further that a frame is a way that one's faith has shape and coherence; it may include an attitude, a belief, a feeling, an insight, a prejudice, an ignorance, a moral certitude, an aspiration, an arresting vision, and even a complete, compelling apprehension of the relationship between what is visible and what is invisible, but nonetheless sensed. Without a frame of any kind or substance, we would move through each day as-if in a fog; everything would remain opaque and blurry with no clarity of vision. All would run together in a lava flow of unclarity. Frames thus form our vision, for good or ill (*Road* 84-85).

Our habitual patterns in life that no longer benefit us consist of frames that remain stuck in place, stubbornly rebuffing our efforts to give up their space and influence. As with poetry, and even the arts generally, if taken to heart, can offer us new frames by revealing to us what frames are folly as well as discerning those whose shelf-life has long expired.

Now to connect these observations back to Luhrmann's fine study: "When people act within a faith frame, they engage an ontological attitude in which they act as-if something were true—that there is an invisible person who loves them or judges them or is willing to protect them" (*How God* 23), even as they realize that this faith sits in an as-if field.

I understand this faith frame as a guiding mythology, one that, in the words of the popular mythologist Joseph Campbell, can move an individual to a place where they become transparent to transcendence: "The life of a mythology derives from the vitality of its symbols as metaphors delivering, not simply the idea, but a sense of actual participation in such a realization of transcendence, infinity, and abundance" (*The Inner Reaches of Outer Space* xx).

His understanding of myth coincides at this juncture with the faith frame developed by Luhrmann. A sense of an ontological reality is part of both Campbell and Luhrmann's understandings of faith. Contrasted with it is what Luhrmann calls a "reality frame" (23), which is different from a "play-frame," both of which are not divorced from the faith frame. I would ask at this juncture: how are these two areas different? List and describe three particulars of what you believe in. List and describe three particulars of what you have faith in. I think it is worth considering how you might respond, and it might assist in making further distinctions between these two fundamental, archetypal realms of our being.

I very much like the word "kindling" in the subtitle of Luhrmann's book. It suggests dry, even volatile matter, just waiting for the arrival of something to ignite it. Kindling is fuel promising and expecting a fire, ready to happen. How might kindling catch fire to bring forward invisible presences? I understand the word as a synonym for faith or for the presence of faith's power to ignite the presence of invisible others or the spark of God's divinity within. Luhrmann may say it best: "Faith is about being able to keep gods and spirits somehow viable even when the crops rot, the child dies, and the war ends in dust and blood. . ... Faith is about having trust that the world is good, safe, and beautiful—a world in which justice is triumphant, enemies are still thwarted, and you can thrill at the delicate beauty of the day" (*How God* 26).

Imposition is the way into such a frame of reference, which I understand as a frame of reverence. What each of us reveres is what we pour the most faith into. I say this because in our own personal mythology, what we reverence in life is what we reference in life with great regularity. Doing so offers our lives a coherence and a confluence through a series of faith influences. We impose a world of hope on the realities we face each day.

Luhrmann's intentions in this book are many, but the following particularly stands out for me: the faith frame is to be worked at daily, without interruption so "that people learn to pay attention so that they kindle that sense of realness, so that the play-like faith frame comes to seem more like the everyday and gods and spirits feel alive" (*How God* 24).

The last idea I want to present before moving to Brother David's penetrating distinctions between belief and faith, is what Luhrmann calls "paracosms" that concentrate on the narratives that engage us in our faith; without stories, the world we are developing here can quickly turn to conceptual statements rather than imaginal experiences. "A paracosm is a private-but-shared imagined world, typically created by children. . . .. The term also describes the world-making that, for example, besotted Tolkien fans engage with Middle-earth. When people can experience their faith as vividly as Tolkien fans experience Middle-earth, their gods feel more present to them" (*How Gods* 25-26).

I want to highlight her phrase, "feel more present to them." Stories have the power to create, as cultural humanist Robert Armstrong develops it, "affective presences," in which another world becomes as feelingly present as the one we move through each day (*The Power of Presence* 47). In addition, it is not an object but carries its own subjective aura, its personhood, that conveys analogous experiences of our own or pushes our own imaginal boundaries beyond their comfort zones, into invisible realms. The details, the particularities, and the artistry of selecting language that most forcefully conveys the world being created nourish the soul of the reader or listener.

Luhrmann cites James Woods who refers to these details as the "'thisness' of literature. . . .. 'Thisness' is the detail that 'centers our attention with its concretion'. . .. Literature differs from life in that life is amorphously full of detail, and rarely directs us toward it, whereas literature teaches us to notice—to notice the way my mother, say, often wipes her lips just before kissing me" (26).

She then turns—and I am grateful for this hinge—to the realm of myth in her discussion of paracosms—which I further understand as an entire cosmos with its own poetic logic and force that resonates in the heart of the listener/reader. Luhrmann cites the classicist Sarah Iles Johnston who asserts that myths "are stories told again and again, stories whose meanings come to depend on what those who hear them already know about the characters" (27). Johnston goes on to suggest "that in some ways just telling the myths made their content feel more real. . ... The ancient Greek poets and historians regularly used kennings [phrases whose meaning depends on the listener's knowledge of the myth] that immersed the listener in a mythic world, even if only for a moment" (qtd. in *How God* 27). Another world is made present "affectively" as Armstrong describes it.

The poet was a weaver, not just of words but of worlds, and is to this day. In the imaginal cosmos of stories, all poets create a world in which one could address gods and mortals in the same story, which engenders and encourages "a relationship, a copresence, a sense of sameness . . . so that the audience felt "that they were living amongst the gods and heroes, even if as lesser participants, as Johnston affirms (*How Gods* 28).

In short, the artist or poet could create a mimetically believable world in which the plot of the story I am reading on the outside finds deep analogies in my own interior world of fictions, fabrications, identities, and realities, giving the latter shape, form, and coherence. The external story I read or listen to resonates with the interior mythic realm of my developing soul.

Stories are, indeed, like myths, "transport vehicles" in Joseph Campbell's phrase, by which we can for a time see double and experience a double narrative—the one crafted for my attention and the one unfolding within the cloistered confines of my personal interior world where all my beliefs lodge. By means of the story, I can expand and deepen my own understanding, question, or strengthen my beliefs and reorder, if necessary, the terms of my personal myth.

When Joseph Campbell, mythologist and storyteller, developed his own connections between myth and story, he claimed, rightly, that "the metaphorical languages of both mythology and metaphysics are not denotative of actual worlds or gods, but rather connote levels and entities within the person touched by them" (*Thou Art That* 6-7). Our stories are reflective of the identity from which they spring, the individual, in their own tongue. Story itself is a metaphorical expression of a world we perceive and a world we live within us. So analogical thinking is central to mythic consciousness.

I should mention how centrally important the power of analogy is for Jung when he writes in *Aion*: ". . . analogy formation is a law which to a large extent governs the life of the psyche, . . ." (*CW* 9, ii, para. 414).

Brother David's book, *Gratefulness, The Heart of Prayer: An Approach to Life in Fullness,* has influenced my own thinking as well as my faith for years. He illustrates how what we know can begin from the outside in or the inside out, for faith itself "is an inner attitude" (123). What I glean from his observations is that learning to live gratefully enhances how we can learn to live faithfully, when the heart awakens to the inter-webbing of both the external and internal worlds we inhabit, which webbing continues in our relationships with the social world we journey through daily.

Furthermore, I appreciate his breakdown of the idea that mysticism is a special way of knowing allowed only to mystics, a separate breed of humanity. Rather, his assertion is that "we are all mystics" (*Gratefulness* 86), so we should not shy away from that trait, gift, or ability, for "every human being is a special kind of mystic, so that each of us is to experience God in his own unique way" (86). We each experience at various moments a quickened excitement at being alive, being attuned, being present in abundant ways, and feeling joy with pleasurable frequency. These are precious creative moments that instill or incite gratefulness.

He encourages us to "keep a courageous trust in life; not inner breakthroughs" (88). His attitude leads me to sense that faith is not a collection of religious beliefs. In my own experience as a Christian and a Catholic, I have found that clinging to beliefs suffocates the more dynamic qualities of faith. One might ask oneself: What do I trust most deeply? Where do I most often place my faith in my life? What surprises me on any given day? What brings me to wonder, to be curious, to yearn to know more or to explore? Brother David looks historically to the early disciples and notices that faith was comprised of "a courageous trust in Jesus and His good news" (89). But to engage this trust, one must risk something, put something on the line, and trust that courage will be gifted in this venture.

One seminal moment in this in this frame, he claims, "is the courage to accept myself as the person I am. Self-acceptance rests on self-forgiveness" (91). To accept myself "as given is in itself a form of gratefulness" (92). By implication, I believe it is a moment of gracefulness, of allowing the mysterious energy of grace to enter one's lived sense of self. In that last sentence you hear "I believe," for belief is a stepping stone to faith's presence and influence. I believe myself towards faith; this pilgrimage is based on trust and courage, for both are active in the journey towards faith-fulness.

The poet Rainer Maria Rilke's poem "Sometimes a Man Stands Up During Supper" distinguishes between two individuals, one encouraged by and who acts on faith by standing up during supper and walking toward a church in the East that calls him, while the other kind of individual seems to lack the courage to venture forth because he has forgotten the church. While Rilke was writing in a particular historical period that emphasized the male figure, we can be certain that women most certainly stand-up during supper as well.

There are several ways to read this poem; my angle is that it reveals two different responses to the call of faith, of destiny, and of the courage needed for the journey we are each called uniquely to participate in, to shape and to sculpt. They are both called to accept and to embrace the grace of a summons. From it, we might imagine this poem asking each of us: What does any given moment in my life call for? What am I being called to fulfill, to continue to give meaning to my unlived life by heeding the call? Am I willing to be interrupted, even intercepted, in the simple act of eating, to reach out for another form of nourishment that could sustain the sacredness that incubates within me?

I also want to voice what Brother David says about the act of walking, given the poem we have just encountered; the first man does not hesitate. He gets up in the middle of a meal and walks out and toward, while the second man remains within the confines of his possessions and suffers perhaps not a physical but a spiritual heart attack. Perhaps his preoccupation with the utensils used for meals blinded or deafened him to his unique calling.

Brother David rightfully claims that when we walk, we risk falling at every step. To walk is an act of faith. Just watch a toddler assembling the courage to get up off all fours as she risks both verticality and locomotion on two legs. The infant exhibits enormous courage in standing up for itself and walking on half the legs it used to crawl. The compensation is uprightness. The risk is falling back on to all-fours.

The infant illustrates that walking is risky business; each step placed in the air, then down on stable ground is a missed fall, a save from a fall; that is how we make progress in the world. "Every day we take the risk of falling; walking is a constant losing and finding balance" (*Gratefulness* 95). Walking is a heart-felt action. When we walk, our entire being is at risk. I think we take steps to fix something, to achieve something; we give ourselves over, in complete surrender, to the risks of walking with its attendant possibility of falling

When we are very young it is risky business; when we are old, we return to the risks of walking and the dangers of falling, snapping a hip, breaking an arm, for our strength is far less a cure for falling. Perhaps coming to terms with our mortal limits and balance is a sign of wisdom's knocking.

I like Brother David's connection of heart-work to walking. "The heart stands for the self. I find myself when I find the courage to be myself, for the heart stands for the point of encounter with self, others, and God. When I find my heart, I find the courage to walk" for "the heart is my center of gravity" (96). When we put one leg out in the air in walking, we must let go of having two legs on the ground at the same instant. If both are on the ground at the same instant, chances our progress is end-stopped. We must begin the motion of free-fall, which takes courage.

To make this point of uncertainty as part of walking, think of a time when you put your foot down, only to find that the ground you thought was there to catch you was absent or slanted or otherwise threw you into uncertainty. Perhaps you stepped off a curb and did not take the drop from the curb to the street into your calculation. For an instant, as I have done, I felt instant panic because the certain world was pulled out from under me.

Now I had to make immediate adjustments so as not to fall into traffic or the hard street surface or into a ditch. I think these moments of spirit test our faith with insistent conviction. "God asks us to walk," writes Brother David, "a constant losing and finding our balance. I must be willing to lose my balance. Faith is the act of making fools of ourselves wisely, like dancers" (95). When we put our foot down, we may be calling out someone's behavior. But progress demands that we put the other foot up, not down.

Perhaps the second man in Rilke's poem was too frightened of making a fool of himself, so he chose to remain insulated and shielded from the risk of faith that spurred the first man to get up during a meal to satisfy another hunger deep in his spirit. "Fear clings; faith lets go. . .. And so, as faith grows weaker, we clutch our beliefs more and more tightly, more and more rigidly" (*Gratefulness* 97).

I pose this question here: What feeling or affect attends each of the following statements? "I believe that. . .." and "I have faith that. . .." Do they feel different? Do they lead you to different reflections? Trust your heart here. For Brother David, faith transports us to the level of the unbelievable. "Trust takes me beyond belief" (101). But then he flips things for a moment: "Beliefs can never replace the experience of live faith, but they can help us keep it alive" (102).

He goes on to observe that from the primal sources of faith our beliefs spring, not the other way around. Thus, we learn that there is not a Grand Canyon between our faith and our beliefs; they are wedded in our heart. But faith is the origin, the source, and the genesis of our beliefs. One does not cancel the other out; in fact, they complement one another.

"The courage of gratefulness and the courage of faith are one and the same movement of the heart, a gesture of trust. . ." (105). Faith is the teacher, asking us every day to live within the heart's fidelity. Doing so places us in a perpetual field of gratitude, which disallows fear and clinging and natural responses to our weakness, which we acknowledge and then liberate ourselves from. Such is the gift of every human life.

And on that affirming note, I will end this series of speculations, conjectures, and wondering wanderings with the hope that some of their meanderings ring true for you.

Works Cited

Armstrong, Robert Plant. *The Powers of Presence: Consciousness, Myth, and Affecting Presence.* University of Pennsylvania Press, 1981.

Campbell, Joseph. *Thou Art That: Transforming Religious Metaphor.* Edited by Eugene Kennedy. New World Library, 2001.

Donohue, Timothy, Donald Carlson, and Dennis Patrick Slattery. *Road, Frame, Window: A Poetics of Seeing. Selected Poems.* Mandorla Books, 2015.

Jung, C.G. *The Collected Works of C G. Jung.* Trans. R.F.C. Hull. Vol. 11. Princeton UP, 1977.

---. *The Collected Works of C.G. Jung.* Trans. R.F.C. Hull. Vol. 9ii. Princeton UP, 1968.

Luhrmann, T.M. *How God Becomes Real: Kindling the Presence of Invisible Others.* Princeton UP, 2020.

Slattery, Dennis Patrick. "Believing is Seeing." *The Herald-Zeitung.* October 24, 2019. 4A.

---. *A Pilgrimage Beyond Belief: Spiritual Journeys Through Christian and Buddhist Monasteries of the American West.* Angelico Press, 2017.

---. "Poetry as Frame and as Form." *Road, Frame, Window: A Poetics of Seeing. Selected Poems of Timothy Donohue, Donald Carlson, and Dennis Patrick Slattery.* Mandorla Books, 2015. 83-88.

Steindl-Rast, Brother David. *Gratefulness, the Heart of Prayer: An Approach to Life in Fullness.* Paulist Press, 1984.

Yeats, William Butler. "The Circus Animals' Desertion" in *A Rag and Bone Shop of the Heart.* Edited by Robert Bly, James Hillman, and Michael Meade. HarperCollins, 1992. xvii.

6

---•---

PREJUDICES, ASSUMPTIONS, AND THE FACTS THAT SHAPE THEM*

Connected with our beliefs based on facts are the arenas, attitudes, and dispositions that comprise our prejudices and assumptions. In the last paragraph of *Freud and Psychoanalysis,* C.G. Jung writes: "The contrast between Freud and myself goes back to essential differences in our basic assumptions. Assumptions are unavoidable, and this being so it is wrong to pretend that we have no assumptions. That is why I have dealt with fundamental questions; with these as a starting point, the manifold and detailed differences between Freud's views and my own can best be understood" (*CW* 4, para. 784).

What we assume, if not acknowledge as an assumption, can morph over time into a fact. If an assumption has its ground in some fact or semblance of a belief, then it does not require much slippage for it to compete with other, even contradictory, facts. I sense that an assumption can arise out of an analogy to a fact we know, from which we venture further, to a fact we may surmise, and then to a fact we can assume.

Our assumptions are important elements in our myth-making abilities. I pose a few questions at this stage:

- What are two of my strongest assumptions?
- What do they serve in my life?
- Are they indeed necessary and unavoidable?

---

* Originally presented to the Austin Friends of Jung in a lecture and workshop, "The Mythology of Belief" September 24th-25th, 2021.

- Where do my assumptions, as transport vehicles (Joseph Campbell's term for metaphors), carry me?
- Do these assumptions open me to the world more broadly, or constrict what I am able to understand and integrate?

Hans Vaihinger's influential book cited by both C.G. Jung and James Hillman is *The Philosophy of As-If: A System of the Theoretical, Practical and Religious Fictions of Mankind*. I choose this metaphor of Campbell's to speak of metaphors as "as-if" fictions. Metaphors allow me to metabolize what I comprehend as related to facts, but not quite. It is worth entertaining that we are always seeing through a metaphor, an as-if fiction. We are always seeing by means of a myth. Myths are ways or avenues by which we can think/imagine/remember something or someone.

Vaihinger suggests that often what we struggle to comprehend is too complex, too nuanced, for us to grasp in its entirety. Complexity slows down our understanding. Thought may then employ an artifice to understand something, but in the process, it may provisionally select a few characteristics and neglect a number of others in order to arrive at a comprehensive view of something. And yes, this can easily lead to stereotyping: people take one or two elements or qualities of a person, candidate/leader/neighbor, and base an entire judgment on them. I sense that myths are often formed in just this way—through an as-if system building. We might look closely at how our own prejudices are feeding the definition or description.

Vaihinger continues: "Provisional assumptions should be accompanied by a consciousness that they do not correspond to reality and that they *deliberately substitute a fraction of reality for the complete causes and facts*" (*Philosophy* 20). I am interested here in how the psyche constructs elaborate fictions to give shape and form to the world's events, both in the interior as well as the exterior of an individual or an entire nation. In addition, Vaihinger's assertion above opens the groaning iron door to the construction of prejudices—a way of pre-judging—by selecting some facts and deleting others. Here one then can effectively sculpt reality to conform to a set of beliefs that bolster and support one's personal myth. In just such a movement, ideologies are shaped.

How does my behavior, my opinions, beliefs, doubts, assumptions, uncertainties, and thought patterns allow me to uncover these fictions? Vaihinger draws a distinction between a hypothesis and a fiction, which we engage in all the time. For example, he proposes, some assume a period in mankind's history when language did not exist. Some claim this is a reasonable hypothesis. Some claim it is a reasonable fiction. And others claim that "because some constructs are devoid of reality, they are to be regarded as devoid of utility" (22).

A fiction can appear false on the outside yet true on the inside in the psychological life of the individual; it can take the form of an assumption, a prejudice, a hunch, or a gut feeling: "I just know."

Jung gives us a version of this "as-if" quality in human experience when he relates in his chapter on "Synchronicity: An Acausal Connecting Phenomena," the story of a woman who, at the moment of her husband's death, experienced the presence of a flock of birds, "which occasioned a vague fear" in her (*CW* 8, para. 850). Jung observes that "there is an obvious simultaneity between the flock of birds, in its traditional meaning, and the death of her husband"; he suggests "the psychic state. . . appears to be dependent on the external event" (*CW* 8, para. 850).

The deceased man's wife's psyche "is nevertheless involved in so far as the birds settled on her house and were observed by her. . . . For this reason, it seems to me probable that her unconscious was in fact constellated. The flock of birds has, as such, a traditional mantic significance. This is also apparent in the woman's own interpretation, and it therefore looks *as if* the birds represented an unconscious premonition of death" (*CW* 8, para. 850). The world of as-if is founded in part on a reasonable assumption and an actual external event—a fact, if you will.

In a culture where there is scant belief in an unconscious, such an example above would be greeted with great skepticism. Is, then, synchronicity based in part on fictions, created to get at some deeper truth of the psyche's intimate relation with matter, with events, and with the stories that form around events in the physical world? These fictions can be useful, Vaihinger suggests, to format some useful constructs (*Philosophy* 23).

At the heart of Vaihinger's exploration, and closer to our concerns here, is the power of the analogical. It pervades and shapes our "as-if" field of meaning and purpose. These fictions "may be called symbolic or analogical. They are closely related to poetic similes as well as to myth" (*Philosophy* 27). I want to move from his theories in a moment; however, I sense that something basic, germane, and core to the workings of consciousness and unconsciousness is pushing to the surface here, to say nothing of the way in which assumptions and prejudices are formed.

Thus, in these analogical fictions, "the mechanism of thinking is as follows: A new intuition is apperceived by an ideational construct in which there is a similar relationship, an analogous proportion to that existing in the observed series of perceptions. In such cases relationships constitute the apperceiving power. This is also the formal origin of poetry" (27). His thinking leads me to conjecture that we do not build our infrastructure of what we consider our reality exclusively out of facts, but out of fictions as well.

Recall Jung's sense of analogy, which he offers in his conviction that "sooner or later nuclear physics and the psychology of the unconscious will draw closer together as both of them, independently of one another and from opposite directions, push forward into transcendental territory, the one with the concept of the atom, the other with that of the archetype" (*CW* 9ii, para. 412). He freely admits that the comparison (the analogy) he is proposing is of "an extremely hypothetical nature," but he bravely pushes on: "Psyche cannot be totally different from matter, for how otherwise could it not move matter? And matter cannot be alien to psyche, for how else could matter produce psyche? Psyche and matter exist in one and the same world, and each partakes of the other. . .. This, like the events I call synchronistic, points to a profound harmony between all forms of existence" (*CW* 9ii, para. 413), followed immediately in the next paragraph by this assertion: ". . . analogy formation is a law which to a large extent governs the life of the psyche, . . . (*CW* 9ii, para. 414).

My hope is that the as-if quality of the psyche reveals how, in creating comparisons between different matters and thoughts, prejudices, assumptions, opinions, and the like, they find their fertile soil. Metaphors, for instance, are what allow me to metabolize what I comprehend. What we loosely call reality is at heart an as-if fiction that allows me to sort out the events in my life and shape them into meaningful experiences. Here is what myths offer: a way, a via, a method, or a mythology for sorting out through a fiction, through a story. So that all our thinking, imagining, fantasizing "is the apperception of one thing through another," as Vaihinger writes (*Philosophy* 29).

I would then ask: Do I hold a particular belief, prejudice, or assumption because it keeps securely in place a fantasy I have invented, situated, groomed, and nourished over weeks or decades? What might happen if I interrupted that belief-fed fantasy? How might I begin to unlearn it or modify it? Blow its flame out? Replace it with one closer to my current life? Or turn its energy in another direction? Dan McAdams reminds us, "Our stories need to be flexible and resilient. They need to be able to change, grow, and develop as we ourselves change. . .. We must seek credibility in our life stories" (*The Stories We Live By* 111).

Underneath all the above discussion resonates how we are all creatives—we are constantly regime-building or compassion-building or shield and sword-building within the edifice of our own psychological, embodied, and spiritual life. We are myth-making all the time. Allow me one more example.

Under a section entitled "The Story of the Universe," Phil Cousineau tells this narrative in *The Oldest Story in the World*. He relates a talk by the world-famous explorer of gorilla behavior, Jane Goodall. where she tells a story of coming on a group of chimpanzees performing rhythmic dances, backflips, leaps from foot-to-foot, and even throwing rocks at the waterfall. She crawled close enough to the chimps to see the hair standing on their arms when they stared at the waterfall.

Years later, in 2003, Phil writes, "I heard her delve deeper into the story, at the Commonwealth Club, in San Francisco. 'If they had this spoken language,' she said, 'if they could sit down and talk about the feelings of what must be something akin to awe and wonder that triggers these amazing displays, then that might turn to one of the early human religions, the animistic religion, worship of water and sun and moon and elements that they couldn't understand. But that leads me on to my belief that there is a great spiritual power out there, and it's a spiritual power from which I believe that I can draw strength'" (*The Oldest Story in the World* 22).

I first want to state that we create stories both to narrate what we believe and to codify it. But let's look at the progression that Goodall gives us a window into:

- Initially she witnesses firsthand something taking place in the world.

- The event draws her fascination, cultivated over many years working with chimps in the wild.

- She then draws a relationship from the event she witnesses to what it might mean, a kind of as-if fiction, so to make sense and meaning from it, or at least begin this imaginal venture.

- She discovers an analogy to form this event into what might be a meaningful experience both for the chimps and for her. It is a way to commune with and to connect with them through a shared moment as well as a shared story.

- She then forms an "If. . .then" model or hypothesis, based on what she witnessed, to interpret what she saw, a story here as a form of interpretation. We tell stories in order to narrate a moment in our lives into a framed meaning. Stories are mythopoetic ways of interpreting what we perceive, imagine, fantasize, and make-up, either over time or on the spot.

- She then shapes what she saw and how she thought about it into a conjecture, a "perhaps" moment, that the chimps were worshipping what they could not understand—as she interprets it—and interprets it as perhaps a moment when religion was collectively born in them.

- This hypothesis, conjecture, hunch, or assumption leads her to a belief that there is a great spiritual power out there. (Perhaps within us as well, but she does not address that.)

- She then furthers her belief by leaning on the first belief to help with her second belief, in order to draw strength from it.

- Thus, she moves from witnessing an event to fostering a set of beliefs that "package" or make a "meaning of wholeness" for her. The events witnessed are "suited up" in the fabric of a conjecture, a "what-if-then" fiction.

- Her personal myth is working both on her perception and on her hermeneutic, her way or manner of seeing, even a style of seeing that leads to a shaped belief.
- The structure appears as a spiralic feedback loop; a belief that lets her see more. (It is also possible to foreclose on other ways of seeing.)
- All the above makes *me* believe that mimesis is at the origin of mythmaking and shaping—by the power of analogy I presented earlier. Mimesis is an imitation, a re-presentation of an action by analogy.
- Where we shape the events in our lives into meaningful experiences by way of corridors that are mythic, or mythopoetic, is to shape a myth into a coherent form.
- Coherence is also at the heart of such an enterprise and an end to be desired.
- We engage this template all the time, as creative mythmakers.

Cousineau then adds: the oldest story is the first one that evoked awe and wonder. He shares P.J. Curtis of County Clare's insight: a story lives at the heart of every journey. A journey without a story told is a journey incomplete; when a story is gathered on the road and re-told on arrival, can it be said that the traveler has truly arrived home (*The Oldest Story* 21).

The progression reveals how we perceive, then judge what we have seen, then form a story of it, then conjecture about the story, followed by asking and answering what it might mean for others and myself. Then we remain open to what connections we sense are present. At the core is the creative act of mythmaking, myth-shaping, story-making as forms of interpretation, of interpenetration—giving our experiences a soul life, or discovering in our experiences the voice of soul.

Assumptions that Frame Me

Within the self swirl dozens, if not hundreds, of assumptions that help to frame as well as form our way of experiencing and modulating our world. Within assumptions, the self-world dialogue can burrow into solitude, take a vertical turn underground, and speak in whispers rather than fully-voiced utterances. Assumptions shape the sense of our world in an "as-if" mode of perception. What I assume about myself and others I then think and behave "as-if" it were true.

These same assumptions have an expiration date stamped on them that we may have overlooked. Even so, they can still exert strong pulls on us, structuring our styles of awareness guided or coerced by our personal myth. Further, these same assumptions may reveal where our perceptions are distorted, excessive, deficient, a bit twisted, and where we are deformed in our knowing. They may, at the same time, reveal the most interesting qualities about us. As carriers, or cargo holds for the fantasies we harbor, we in turn protect and feed them regularly because their importance underscores how we define our essential self.

At one point they were conscious beliefs that over time have become shop-worn and paralyzed into knee-jerk modes of thought and action. They can put us to sleep when we are trying to awaken. Assumptions witness how we imagine the world, even if we are only partly conscious of the process.

Riting Meditation: A Positive Assumption

Describe an assumption that helps to get you out of bed in the morning. This assumption gives you energy and a purpose for getting up and plunging into your day with enthusiasm. For instance: "Today will have meaning for me," or "I can make a difference today" or "I may discover something new today." The assumption you choose to write about is constructive, beneficent, and challenges you as a person to participate in the world in an engaged way.

Riting Meditation: A Negative Assumption

Describe an assumption that arrests you, or curtails your life or holds you back, or takes the arresting form of an albatross around your neck, constantly pulling you down by constricting your options for understanding or tolerance. For instance, "I am unable to do X and have always been unable to do it" or "when I see X, I will not be able to express myself with confidence or adequately." This assumption still guides you but in a destructive way; to date you have not been able to rid yourself of it or to integrate it to lessen its power (*Riting Myth, Mythic Writing* 14-15).

Formation of Prejudices

Many of you know Robert Johnson's fine little book, *Owning Your Own Shadow*. Do our prejudices originate there, in the darker recesses of what we would be more comfortable foisting onto others?

The meaning of prejudice—to cause "injury, physical harm"—arises in the mid-14th century, as does the legal sense of "detriment or damage caused by the violation of a legal right." The meaning "preconceived opinion" (especially but not necessarily unfavorable) is from late 14th century in English; now usually "decision formed without due examination of the facts or arguments necessary to a just and impartial decision" (www.etymology.com). "To terminate with extreme prejudice," meaning to "kill" is by 1972, its most current sense.

Many meanings gather around the above history of the word. I am focusing though on "preconceived opinion." It connotes a view that one forms with only a tenuous connection to reality. Prejudices can certainly protect us from facing what might be distasteful.

Johnson relates the intriguing story of the origin of the term "bogey man." It derives, he writes, from old India, wherein each village chose a man to be the "bogey." We might substitute the word "scapegoat," which derived from the Hebrew tradition. At the end of the year, he was ritually slaughtered to carry the evil deeds of the community with him, thus purging them of the transgressive nature of their behavior (*Shadow* 33). In appreciation of his impending "service" to the community, he was treated royally while he lived by having all his desires satisfied by the tribe.

We can readily think of examples in our own day where this same mythic enactment is ritualized in law, custom, attitudes, institutional prejudices, and conventional wisdom. But today we seem to have entered a terrain where a prejudice, say, against what appears to be a legitimate and fraud-free election, is created simply out of someone claiming "fraud" and enough people accepting this prejudice that it slowly morphs into a "reality" for many. The prejudice becomes, over time, a belief, "as if" it was based on a fact or a concrete historical event.

Prejudices are very effective in creating and sustaining tribal thought and behavior because prejudices label without knowing, or knowing fully, or knowing the truth over against a deception. Often, we tend to fill in what we don't know with assumptions, stereotypes, ways of grouping and collecting others into a mass audience, with few differences or distinctions. I think that prejudices also flourish in the darkness of a fearful life or are created to generate fear and loathing.

Such a way of shaping our reality is a powerful psychological method of keeping the Other at a distance by maintaining a sense of purity about us, away from the shadow that roils beneath the floorboards. Prejudices seem to carry their own mythic energy and signify an archetypal behavior that is a universal human trait. They may grow in the soil of too much or too little imagination, or a third possibility, a false relationship between imagination and reality, one that is distorted, excessive, or anemic.

In prejudice, the soul aligns itself with an image that is in a questionable equilibrium with a shared common sense of things. It may then create or manufacture its own reality to coincide with its own *idea* of reality. Cultural observer and critic Brooke Gladstone reminds us, "Reality is what forms after we filter, arrange, and prioritize those facts and marinate them in our values and traditions. Reality is personal" (*The Trouble with Reality* 2).

Dispelling prejudices rests on a new level of awareness and a generous accommodation: I am willing to accommodate this reality without agreeing with it or attacking it. I wonder at this juncture whether a prejudice we hold can allow us to see more, not less? I say this because a prejudice does not have to be a negative judgment. One might harbor a strong prejudice towards learning, towards resiliency, towards remaining flexible within life's ambiguities.

I wonder, too, what prejudices might compensate, hide, veil, or substitute for in the realm of beliefs. Does prejudice, for instance, give greater authority to a belief I hold? Or does the belief I hold become more real in the world when it is incarnated as a prejudice? Perhaps it finally rests on the level of awareness and sense of honesty one cultivates in their quotidian worldview.

Jung believed that only when something goes awry in consciousness is a compensatory move stirred, for something is amiss or exaggerated, and "because only a faulty consciousness can call forth a countermove on the part of the unconscious" (*CW* 10, para. 448). So, prejudices and dealing with them means that some other compensatory symbols of order are necessary to be integrated into unconsciousness; it requires an individual act of realization, of understanding and moral evaluation.

"Small and hidden is the door that leads inward, and the entrance is barred by countless prejudices, mistaken assumptions, and fears. Always one wishes to hear of grand political and economic schemes. . .. Therefore, it sounds grotesque when anyone speaks of hidden doors, dreams, and a world within" (*CW* 10, para. 328). Jung calls it a vapid idealism disconnected from everything real (para. 328). He wrote in 1928 that the normal person acts out his psychic disturbances socially and politically in the form of mass psychoses like wars and revolutions (*CW* 10, para. 470).

So it is that prejudices, hatreds, bigotry, and scapegoating are various ways of coping, with an atrophied imagination, when faced with psychic forces breaking into consciousness from the unconscious; to suppress them, one turns to individuals and groups to take on the devastating psychic power of these underground forces because their conscious level is not adequate to stem the acceleration of such disturbing and uncontrollable psychic forces.

In another context, Jung writes of the shadow "as a moral problem that challenges the whole ego-personality, for no one can become conscious of the shadow without considerable moral effort" (*CW* 9ii, para. 14). I think we can add prejudices to this insight. The question raised here: is then the shadow the source of prejudices that the individual or a nation or a tribe has persuaded themselves that the source of their prejudice is anchored in facts, in history, and not in a fantasy in the psyche that has been confused with and so fused with some version of reality selected to support and buttress prejudicial thinking and behavior? I pose the following for writing meditations:

- How does this experience of the shadow situate us in the Underworld as a territory that can promote change?
- Write out a prejudice that you hold dear and resist relinquishing.
- Can what we are prejudiced toward be a shadow of our own psyche's refusal to face?
- Does our personal pathology gather itself in the crux of energy of our pre-judices?
- Judicious, judicial, pre-judicial are implicated in the word "prejudice"; something coming before something that blocks, offends, retards, or arrests the second thing.
- Are our prejudices expressions of our own frustrations of justice?
- Is what we discriminate toward a vessel that carries our psychic shadows?
- What is created and what is destroyed within the mythology of our prejudices?
- Prejudice, discrimination: are they forms that hatred nests in?
- Dis-cord, dis-taste, dis-satisfaction, dis-temper, dis-gruntled, dis-qualified, dis-integrate, dis-avow, dis-own, dis-ease. Dis- as negation, as repudiation. Reflect on this list of "dis" words.
- Is prejudice a form or expression of hopelessness in us?
- Do our prejudices mock diversity and plurality?
- Are our prejudices a perversion of divine presence?
- Is there some attribute in our soul that is calcified, stuck, coagulated into an immovable bolus through the hardening of negative prejudices:
- "They are all like that."
- "They will not, cannot change."
- "They don't conform to my belief system of reality."
- "They are not as good as me."
- "I do not, nor do I need to, understand them."
- "They are an inferior form of me."
- "*They* need to change—not me."

Offering some reflective writing on any of the above will allow our prejudices to surface. Then we can decide if they are worth clinging to; or perhaps letting them go will open more space within for a deeper compassion towards oneself and others to grow. That is my hope.

Works Cited

Cousineau, Phil. *The Oldest Story in the World: A Mosaic of Meditations on the Secret Strength of Stories.* Sisyphus Press, 2010.

Gladstone, Brooke. *The Trouble with Reality: A Rumination on Moral Panic in Our Time.* Workman Publishing, 2017.

Johnson, Robert. *Owning Your Own Shadow.* HarperSanFrancisco, 1991.

Jung, C.G. *The Collected Works of C.G. Jung.* Trans. R.F.C. Hull. Vol. 4. Princeton UP, 1979.

---. *The Collected Works of C.G. Jung.* Trans. R.F.C Hull. Vol. 8. Princeton UP, 1969.

---. *The Collected Works of C.G. Jung.* Trans. R.F.C. Hull. Vol. 10. Princeton UP, 1970.

---. *The Collected Works of C.G. Jung.* Trans. R.F.C Hull Vol. 9i, Princeton UP, 1971.

---. *The Collected Works of C.G. Jung.* Translated by R.F.C. Hull, Vol. 9,ii, Princeton UP, 1970.

McAdams, Dan P. *The Stories We Live By: Personal Myths and the Making of the Self.* The Guilford Press, 1993.

Prejudice. www.etymology.com

Slattery, Dennis Patrick. *Riting Myth, Mythic Writing: Plotting Your Personal Story.* Fisher King Press, 2012.

Vaihinger, Hans. *The Philosophy of 'As-If': A System of the Theoretical, Practical, and Religious Fictions of Mankind.* Trans. C.K. Ogden. Routledge & Kegan Paul, Ltd., 1968.

7

THE JOURNEY FROM INCOHERENCE TO COHERENCE: DISCOVERING A LIFE OF PURPOSE

How puzzling it is to any of us when we cannot understand something we read or that's said to us or that we stumble across. When we bump against incoherence in our life events, it may be sufficient to disorient us on our path. Depending of course on the severity of the incoherence, we can be knocked from our horse and find ourselves lying backside up on a road that, on reflection, we realize is no longer the correct terrain for us. Such a flash of understanding can be a moment of dramatic transformation, for it makes clear to us the path we should no longer pursue.

We may then awaken, to a transitional place, as the poet Dante did at the genesis of his classic epic journey—between coherence and incoherence. Here is how he begins his comic epic, *The Divine Comedy,* enjoying its 700-year anniversary. The poet-pilgrim describes a journey not unlike anyone of ours when we find our lives deepening into, and perhaps even careening towards incoherence:

> When I had journeyed half of our life's way,
> I found myself within a shadowed forest,
> For I had lost the path that does not stray (*Inferno* I, ll. 1-3).

But what, we might ask, is "the path that does not stray"? That is the path that encourages or gives our life coherence. I suggest at this juncture my own prejudice: a coherent life is far more valuable than a happy life. But that we will leave for a further conversation. And how far is it to journey "half of our life's way"? Can I be 23, 46, 55, 78? Where is the halfway point in one's life? We can certainly say that we can't fully know; on the other hand, yes, we can. When we admit to ourselves: I have been doing or thinking or believing X for my entire life. Now, I want to change; that is the half-way point for us, regardless of chronological age. It is closer to one's psychological, spiritual, or emotional maturity, therefore far more relevant.

But let's stay with Dante on his epic journey a bit longer. For he has accepted the call to adventure, the call to venture into the mysterious arena of poetic language, in order to give a form and shape to his experience, with us as fellow pilgrims readers:

Ah, it is hard to speak of what it was,
That savage forest, dense and difficult,
Which even in recall renews my fear:
So bitter—death is hardly more severe! (*Inferno* I, ll. 4-7).

The question that might occur to you at this juncture, whether or not you have ever read a word of the poem until now, is what journey are we actually speaking about? The physical journey through *Inferno, Purgatorio,* and *Paradiso*—places that all of us have encountered in our lives, or the remembrance of it wherein the words he chooses to relate his story is the adventure we each enter to discover or create suitable analogies to our own stories? From Dante's own road of trials, we sense in our imagination an intimacy with our own road of struggles, which is essential for any meaningful transformation of a life from incoherence to coherence. From them, we can learn some possible effective options for conversion.

Now we are entertaining three stories: Dante's adventures, his recollecting and retelling them, and our stories that travel with his so we can learn something about our own epic narrative. We read or listen to his story from the outside in and from the inside out. And what he relates are the terms of his own mythic life that resonate often with our own as well as diverge from ours. Both are valid and valuable. One more passage from Dante's beginning adventure before we leave it:

But to retell the good discovered there,
I'll also tell the other things I saw.
I cannot clearly say how I had entered
The wood; I was so full of sleep just at
The point where I abandoned the true path *(Inferno* I: ll. 8-12).

From a poetic point of view, Dante's reflection reveals what dropping out of a coherent life into one of fog, haze, and a blurred sense of one's path looks and feels like. Who has not fallen asleep to their own life, their own purpose, and their own meaning, much less to their own responsibilities to others and to themselves? It is akin to losing consciousness and falling into ignorance and oblivion, a hideout. When we become oblivious to something, someone, or some path we are on, they immediately hide from us.

Dante's poem offers an opportunity to regain our life's balance because it renders new ways of rediscovering our path through the metaphors and symbols of his journey. I think of metaphors as imaginal equilibrating images that touch the soul in us, shake us loose to find perhaps another attitude toward our life's circumstances. In his essay, "On Psychic Energy" *(CW* 8, paras. 1-130), C.G. Jung offers a series of insights into the hero that implicates a poetic response to disequilibrium. He describes how, "as early as 1912, I pointed out that my conception of a general life instinct, named libido, takes the place of the conception of 'psychic energy'..." *(CW* 8, para. 56). To which he adds some pages later, "The hero is the symbolical exponent of libido" *(CW* 8, para. 68). When psyche becomes too one-sided, some significant shift in attitude is necessary to bring it into a healthy equilibrium in its polarities.

The metaphorical and symbolic nature of Dante's deep dive into the process of individuation in his *Commedia* is at the same time an unfolding of his own myth. Through their particularities, they inflect archetypal situations and conditions to aid us in discovering ways to rebalance what has become dissociated within us. He writes of them as "mythical fantasies." "They arise," he suggests "and present themselves as images or chains of ideas that force their way out of the unconscious, and when they are recounted, they often have the character of connected episodes resembling mythical dramas" *(CW* 8, para.71). I want then, to think of

Dante's journey, recollected and reflected on mythopoetically, to be our guide into our own tangled journey.

Regaining consciousness through meditation, reflection, and entering an honest appraisal of what our life's worth has become, is a necessary moment or moments on the path. Otherwise, we move through our lives without direction, all of which can lead us to journeying in circles when we believe we are making progress. Traveling in circles without direction and reflection or any memory of where we have been form a pattern of movements that describes the souls in *Inferno*.

Dante runs the risk of just such futile motion because he has fallen out of his personal myth. He cannot go it alone; he needs a guide, a mentor, preferably one sanctioned by a more-than-human power, which is exactly when Beatrice Portinari, whom he loved as a youth, petitions the Blessed Virgin Mary to send Dante a mentor to guide him; she assents and sends to the medieval poet the classical poet, Virgil, who also wrote one of the greatest epic stories of a figure in exile, Aeneas. He escapes the burning towers of Troy as the Trojan War ends and sets out with figures of his household gods as well as his father, Anchises, and his son, Ascanius, to wander, then to be directed to enter the underworld, and finally to found the new city amongst the seven hills, Rome.

Early in Book III, "Sea Wanderings and Strange Meetings," Aeneas recalls how "Our minds were turned by auguries of heaven/To exile in far quarters of the world" (*Aeneid* ll. 5-6). Virgil's poem as well as its author together guide Dante on the largest portion of his exilic journey.

Such a rich image is Virgil's description: to leave a place and a life that has been invaded and destroyed, and to set out for a promised land—the Roman empire, which Aeneas will be instrumental in founding. While we do not have to leave a burning city in order to abandon a life of incoherence where meaning is no longer present or satisfying, and to be willing to risk, nonetheless, exile may be part of our imagination as we seek a new home out of the rubble of a life in disarray.

Another illustration now to help us along the path from incoherence to coherence: C.G. Jung's "Foreword to the Fourth Swiss Edition" of *Symbols of Transformation* (*CW* 5, xxiv). This volume proved to be a transitional one for him. Its contents were to occupy him for the next few decades. But that is not why I bring it up here.

For when he finished this volume, a question stared him in the face: What it means to live with a myth, and what it means to live without one. He then quotes an unidentified Church Father who claimed that a myth "is what is believed always, everywhere, by everybody" (*CW* 5, xxiv). He draws from this definition that it is a rare exception for a man "who thinks he can live without myth, or outside it. . .. He is like one uprooted, having no true link either with the past, or with the ancestral life which continues within him" (*CW* 5, xxiv), or with society at large.

Let's pause here: What is it to live within a myth? Dante, whom we met earlier, had fallen out of his culture's myth, which was in essence the powerful presence and teachings of the Catholic Church, the prevailing mythos in Western Europe in the Middle Ages. Whether we agree with that myth or not, it gave people a clear frame and context by which to live their lives. In short, it gave their lives a coherent set of values, beliefs, and behaviors that were often performed as rituals, like the Mass as well as the seven sacraments. Together they offered stability and sustenance in a world beset by diseases, wars, and internal strife, all of which happen within each of us. But many have no frame of reference by which to negotiate them.

The next question to consider might be framed as such: What is it to live outside a myth, or when we fall out of a vital mythology that gives life purpose and meaning as well as a "right attitude"? a term Jung uses in another volume. While it is true that a myth's shelf life can expire so that it needs revitalization, re-editing, and revisioning, which is where an effective mentor can be a huge asset, we each nonetheless need a myth to live by. Therefore, let's return to Jung's description that we initiated above.

One who tries to live outside a myth, Jung suggests, winds up living "in a subjective mania of his own devising, which he believes to be the newly discovered truth" (*CW* 5, xxiv). Reason is often rejected in favor of fantasies that spring up, like the fruits of a rhizome growing horizontally underground. But Jung believed that "myth had a meaning which I was sure to miss if I lived outside it in the haze of my own speculations. I was driven to ask myself: 'what is the myth you are living?'" (*CW* 5, xxiv). He had no ready response to that question, a fundamental human question that we all must ask as we grow in self-reflection and self-definition. Such a question often is the catalyst for beginning a quest.

I believe the question Jung poses to himself above is one of the most important "calls to adventure" we can embark on. To refuse this call to the myth we are living is to end-stop our development because it will not grow deep into where the roots of our myth reside. Then, when we need a stabilizing force in our lives at times of immense crisis—loss of income, job, spouse, lover, family, prestige, purpose—where can we turn or return to? Let's return to Jung for some insight here.

He finally is forced to "admit that I was not living with a myth, or even in a myth, but rather in an uncertain cloud of theoretical possibilities which I was beginning to regard with increasing distrust. I did not know that I was living a myth, and even if I had known it, I would not have known what sort of myth was ordering my life without my knowledge" (*CW* 5, xxv). That's a huge personal admission and it signals an inner crisis that he must resolve for both personal and professional reasons. He grasped that the myth he needed to discover would offer his life meaning both consciously and unconsciously.

And a greater call to adventure: to begin an internal quest to discover the contours of his own myth and then, to see the workings of that myth in the world, almost as a subset of this original quest that begins a new journey. To quest is to pose the question, not about what is needed to be purchased but the meanings that need to be pursued for a life of wholeness, if not joy.

- Like: what is my life's meaning at this stage?
- Who is living my life: me or others?
- Have I adopted another's myth as a way not to have to suffer into knowing my own?
- What stories do I tell myself and what stories are told about me such that I could catch glimmers of my personal myth?
- What seems to be a force or forces that draft incoherence in my life?
- Where is this incoherence located? In my habits, thoughts, language?
- In the way I treat others?

- In the way I treat myself?
- What significant control do I have in and over my life such that change could become a real possibility?
- What powers or forces may I begin to recognize that inflects my life in ways that I find uncomfortable or downright repulsive?
- What forces or presences in my life can I call on to transform the questionable life I am in or to pick up bits and pieces of the myth that has shattered through neglect?

Jung again: "So, in the most natural way, I took it upon myself to get to know 'my' myth, and I regarded this as the task of tasks, for—so I told myself—how could I, when treating my patients, make due allowance for the personal factor, for my personal equation, which is yet so necessary for a knowledge of the other person, if I was unconscious? I simply had to know what unconscious or preconscious myth was forming me, from what rhizome I sprang" (*CW* 5, xxv). Without this knowledge, he concludes at the end of the "Foreword," he can never grasp "the soul that is ill" (*CW* 5, xxvi).

He has reached that stage of consciousness where he understands the necessity of crossing the threshold from a state of incoherence of his own myth to questing after its source in the deepest part of himself, the terrain where the myth resides as a force of coherence. He has identified in the above language where the inner crisis is and what must be done first to engage it and then to learn from it. Incidentally, he worked and reworked this volume for over thirty-seven years. One of its most fascinating chapters is entitled "The Origin of the Hero" (*CW* 5, paras. 251-299).

Now Jung as person and as therapist begins the road back, where, in the years he has worked on the large universal themes of this seminal volume, he returns to his "normal" life and profession, carrying the world in which he questioned whether he was living in a myth. Now he negotiates coming to terms with the living "rhizome" that is his myth, growing horizontally underground, and sending up sprigs and roots to flower above ground, in the conscious world we all share.

I find it astonishing that the four-page "Foreword" I have cited frequently carries the stages of the hero's journey, all in the service of a marvelous transformation of consciousness, which seems to be at the nub of individuation, that is, of becoming the whole and complete person one is destined to be.

Okay, so what is Jung's myth? A fair question given the above. Never at a loss for words, Jung fills up 359 pages laying out his myth in *Memories, Dreams, Reflections*. This magnificent memoir is an aesthetic meditation on the power of myth in our lives as well as a brilliant rendering of a coherent life.

He tells us in the Prologue: "My life is a story of the self-realization of the unconscious. Everything in the unconscious seeks outward manifestation, and the personality too desires to evolve out of its unconscious conditions and to experience itself as a whole" (*MDR* 3). He goes on to assert: "Myth is more individual and expresses life more precisely than does science. . ... Thus, it is that I have now undertaken, in my eighty-third year [1958] to tell my personal myth. I can only make direct statements, only 'tell stories.' Whether or not the stories are 'true' is not the problem. The only question is whether what I tell is *my* fable, *my* truth" (*MDR* 3).

If anyone is just beginning to read Jung's massive collection of writings, I would encourage them to begin with this autobiography; in it, he lays out the development of his personal myth in delicious details, anecdotes, and narratives that will captivate any reader. One will hear and feel resonances of one's own narrative through Jung's deeply mythical story.

Works Cited

Alighieri, Dante. *The Divine Comedy*. Trans. Allen Mandelbaum. Introduction by Eugenio Montale and Notes by Peter Armour. Alfred A Knopf. 1991.

Jung, C.G. "On Psychic Energy." Trans. R.F.C. Hull. *The Collected Works of C.G. Jung*. Vol. 8. Princeton UP, 1960. 3-66.

---. *The Collected Works of C.G. Jung*. Trans. R.F.C. Hull. Vol. 5. Princeton UP, 1967.

---. *Memories, Dreams, Reflections*. Trans. Richard and Clara Winston. Random House, 1963.

Virgil. *The Aeneid*. Trans. Robert Fitzgerald. Random House, 1983.

8

"ACTIVE LOVE": FATHER ZOSIMA IN DOSTOEVSKY'S *THE BROTHERS KARAMAZOV**

"Strive to love your neighbor actively and indefatigably. Insofar as you advance in love you will grow surer of the reality of God and of the immortality of your soul."
~Father Zosima to Madame Khokhlakov in *The Brothers Karamazov*

Introduction

One of the great works of literature that has long instructed its readers in the areas of teaching and learning by a master teacher is the Russian writer Fyodor Dostoevsky's last and perhaps most profound work, *The Brothers Karamazov*, completed in 1881, just months before its author died at the age of 60. It is the last of a series of five novels written over decades after its author was released from a Siberian prison camp where he spent several years after being convicted of participating in a reading of a radical pamphlet the Russian authorities found seditious.

Emerging from the frozen tundra and a term of extreme suffering that revived violent epileptic seizures originating when he was only 20

* Originally published in *What is a Teacher? Remembering the Soul of Education Through Classic Literature*, edited by Dr. Claudia Allums. Reprinted here by permission of The Dallas Institute of Humanities and Culture Publications.

years old, Dostoevsky suffered them for the rest of his life. Nonetheless, one of Russia's greatest writers, though having published and gained a mixed notoriety with earlier works, was poised to create his greatest poetic expressions. He began with *Crime and Punishment* (1866), followed by *The Idiot* (1868), *The Possessed* (1873), *A Raw Youth* (1875), and finally *The Brothers Karamazov* (1880), agreed on by most as encompassing his greatest psychological, spiritual, and poetic insights.

Central to the action of *The Brothers* is a teacher; more specifically, the elder, Father Zosima referred to in the Russian Orthodox religion as an "elder," a holy man. The Russian word is *staretz* or *starets*. His place in teaching was one that bridged both spiritual advisor and wisdom guide. He administered to both the soul and to the embodied intellect; he aided those who sought him out by offering advice, spiritual direction, and the necessity of ethical responsibility.

In another context he might be considered a shaman, a holy man, who heals the deep wounds of his people and leads them towards their collective destiny. Zosima in this same light is a spiritual beacon for all who come into his purview seeking instruction or pretending to. As an elder he reveals the collective memory of his people, guides their spiritual pilgrimage, and instructs them in ways that aid their direction, purpose, and quest for their full identity.

Finally, Zosima reminds his people of the myth that they have engaged and engages them as a kind of identity compass. Just as with an individual, so an entire people can become amnesiac of their identity—mythic, personal, collective—and thereby lose their direction and coherence. An elder like Zosima, then, acts as a guardian, remembering and reminding his people of their uniqueness, their value, and their purpose as citizens, and in this novel, as students seeking what is true for them within their shared mythos.

Following on what I wrote above, Dostoevsky suggests that a figure like Father Zosima serves others as a paradigm of the teacher because learning itself is, among other characteristics, a spiritual action of the soul as much as it is an intellectual exercise of the mind. In fact, there is good reason to suppose that Zosima is the paradigm of the good teacher because he understands deeply that active love is a form of eros and eros is what promotes and cultivates relationship. Eros as active love is what binds and cultivates affection between the student and his/her teacher, the student and teacher with the content of what is to be studied and understood, and the wisdom that accrues from such an enterprise in the classroom and beyond.

Active love is the mucilage, the adhesive, binding one to another in community as well as the individual to one's teacher and the teacher to both the material to be grasped and the students to be loved so that the deepest form of learning becomes possible. Father Zosima's presence as a spiritual conduit to deep learning witnesses that erotic love must be present to deepen the relationship between student, teacher, and material. Active love, then, is a way of knowing, of perceiving, and of understanding. Loveless learning is no learning at all. Love of learning may be the most rewarding and sustained consequence of the teacher's presence and persuasive influence.

Dostoevsky's powerful character reveals that learning in the right spirit is as crucial as the content of that action. Less is Zosima promoting a religion than he is an impulse of the soul's own spiritual growth to be informed and ultimately transformed by what one learns. He also understands that one consequence of transformative learning is a greater sense of freedom, both personal and collective. Learning without freedom produces knowledge without wisdom. Learning without love produces information, not transformation.

We will notice, in addition, that this awakening or midwifing students into their own imaginative involvement with what is to be learned, worked imaginally, then transformed into something beyond itself, is at the same time a re-birthing of the student into both a higher and deeper level of understanding, one so powerful as to transform their lives. Learning then takes on a spiritual dimension as it elevates the student beyond a preoccupation with literal facts to a more universally shared participation in what lies invisibly behind or below the facts, as well as what these facts, ideas, or images lead to: an understanding of the original formative principles that undergird them.

But none of the above can happen, or even be approached within the bounds of what could be achieved, if the teacher has lost the eros of learning. In other words, the loving relationship between learner and material must be alive and animated through passion if the student is going to be infected and inspired by such a dramatic presence. We might even think of this relationship as a form of spiritual contagion, for it is in the spirit of love itself that not only a deeper learning prevails but also that joy deep within the soul attends it. Note how far beyond "teaching for the test" or "accountability" we are, though these forms of measurement have merit. Not engaging the spirit of the student, his/her divine calling, yields only a shallow form of knowing.

One cannot measure the quickening of excitement or the flush of enthusiasm that attends a breakthrough in the student because of the alchemy of the passionate teacher in love with both the students under his/her responsibility as well as the eros attending the teacher's relationship with what one believes, knows, and offers in instruction. It is precisely the active love of the teacher for the above that quickens one's imaginative involvement in the material that is always double-sided: its literal, concrete objective reality and the analogical resonances or haunting echoes that it elicits in both student and teacher. Demoting the former in the service of the latter is a form of mythic bankruptcy in the entire enterprise of education.

A teacher like Zosima, in tune with the spiritual dimension of learning, can reveal how the act of learning is double: it engages the kind of objective knowledge of which the curriculum is constituted as well as the action of insight wherein the material is transformed as it enters the imaginative field of the learner, transformed because the imagination acts on it to make it one's own.

This latter movement is a spiritual act of love; a teacher who does not participate in this level of understanding keeps the material within the bounds of the first level only. Moreover, such an active love is as well an embodied form of compassion, compassion for one's students who suffer their own limitations, distortions, challenges, life circumstances, all of which can keep them enslaved to their personal conditions and unable to learn deeply.

When the teacher is driven, inspired, motivated, and made vulnerable and porous by the material as a way of cultivating a fuller and more authentic life, and then carries that sense of relationship to his/her students, a stronger bond of erotic knowing, or a knowing-in-relationship guided by the principle of analogy, is forged in the smithy of the classroom and beyond; but it must be ignited in the classroom through a model, a form, a presence of a teacher in love, active and unconditional, by what one has been called to—a vocative presence that touches the interior landscape of the student. Without this dynamic actively present, material appears and remains closer to inert and uninteresting matter than an active embodied presence of value. Data-processing becomes a pale simulacrum or an alternative hunting-gathering form of acquisition of information rather than a transformation of consciousness itself.

What informs a teacher like Father Zosima is the form of his memories as they coalesce into a worldview, a body of faith, and a commitment to being responsible for all, lived out in his fierce heart-attention to everyone who comes into his vision to teach, to instruct, and to be instructed by. Only a teacher fully present and available to learn can effectively teach others. One's heart must be disposed to being wounded; only then does it carry the largesse in love for one to be a contagious teacher. Educator Parker J. Palmer writes that "a knowledge that springs from love may require us to change, even sacrifice for the sake of what we know" (*To Know as We Are Known* 9).

The Story

The story of *The Brothers Karamazov* focuses primarily on the one family named in the title. It is comprised of the old patriarch, Fyodor Pavlovich Karamazov, and his sons: Dimitri, the oldest and in competition with his lecherous father, Fyodor, for the love of a young woman. Next is Ivan, a fierce intellectual repulsed by a world that in its creation allows the innocent to suffer; then Alexey, also called Alyosha, a young monk under the tutelage of Father Zosima, who serves as a scribe for the elder's homilies and conversations. The novel builds to the murder of the father under the cloak of treachery. Dmitri is charged with the killing, but as the novel unfolds it becomes clear that he is innocent and that the bastard son, Smerdyakov, influenced by the intellectual half-brother Ivan, interprets his half-brother's teachings as confirmation that old Feodor should be killed.

The reader senses that the whole family, except for the youngest son, is implicated in a terrible crime. The youngest son, Alexey, drawn to the monastery and the monastic life, introduces his teacher; through Alexey's voice we hear much of what Father Zosima offers to those who will listen to him.

Ivan eventually disintegrates under the burden of his tormented imagination. His half-brother, Smerdyakov, is eventually arrested and tried for murdering his father, and Dmitri is set free. The action also includes the sudden death of old Zosima and his rapidly corrupting and putrid-smelling corpse, which inspires a scandal amid accusations that such corruption of his body is proof that the old monk was not as holy as he wished to appear.

At Zosima's funeral Alyosha experiences in a dream state a transformative moment of death and rebirth and through them discerns that he must follow his mentor's instructions to leave the church and enter the world, marry, and teach. The novel concludes with Alexey carrying in his soul the image of his mentor's active human love, teaching a group of young boys who represent, as a composite, the future of Russia.

Father Zosima

Perhaps the most evident quality of a teacher like Father Zosima is that he loves: 1. unconditionally; 2. selflessly; 3. everyone without condemning any; 4. in hope; 5. generously. These qualities of active love allow him to see beyond others' limits, prejudices, and habits that are not conducive to learning because he discerns the fundamental distortions and limitations of their souls. In addition, he combines both masculine and feminine traits that comprise a wholeness of approach, a generosity of receptivity, and a critical awareness of deficiencies. In this regard, an image that fits here is that of a midwife rather than a facilitator, or worse, a classroom manager.

As midwife, Zosima helps to birth ideas, images, and insights in his fledgling students, motivating them by responses of largesse rather than negative criticism. His active love allows him to be critical without demeaning another. His aim is to awaken the dormant life of the student who, when roused by the intangible but palpable love of learning, is well on his or her way to becoming a midwife of one's own ideas as a self-motivated learner. For is it not part of the responsibility of any teacher to awaken the life of learning as a love of learning? In this regard, active love of the teacher is a love by the spirit of the student to engage learning as a continuous project as well as learning as a waystation towards wisdom informed by self-knowledge.

Several scenes in the novel where Father Zosima engages members of the larger community reveal the nature of an inspired and effective teacher. The first, the one in which Alexey brings his father and brothers to the elder to help settle a family dispute, reveals Father Zosima teaching and interacting with many of the "types" of students that teachers see every day. But his teaching begins with who he is, as we see in the careful descriptions early in the scene.

In appearance, Father Zosima is unimpressive: he "was a short, bent, little man, with very weak legs" (32) and appeared older than his 65 years because of his illness. "His face was very thin and covered with a network of fine wrinkles, particularly numerous about his eyes, which were small, light-colored, quick, and shining like two bright points. . .. His pointed beard was small and scanty, and his lips, which smiled frequently, were as thin as two threads. His nose was not long, but sharp, like a bird's beak" (32). So diminutive and yet so powerful in his frailty is this teacher. His strength and force are clearly not enshrouded in his physical appearance but in his speech and manner of presence. His is the physiognomy of a bird, with eyes that glow in their ability to penetrate deep into his audience's authenticity or its absence.

His demeanor carries an atmosphere of affection, of openness, and vulnerability, one that would hardly threaten those who visit him. A sociability attends his presence; his whole attitude suggests that far from being above others, if anything, he is beneath them in size and gesture, a way of under-standing others by standing beneath them, giving him an angle of vision perhaps not available to others. This sense of unconditional openness is a quality of the active love that attends all his dealings with others who seek him out. His fundamental understanding of others is that each is suffering in his/her own way.

Likewise, the furniture in his cell was old and wrinkled, well-worn and faded to match its occupant. Its wide array of various objects suggests an eclectic person's domicile. When he is visited early in the novel, he has them sit "in a row along the opposite wall on four mahogany chairs, covered with shabby black leather" (32), perhaps in imitation of a classroom. He himself sits "on a very old-fashioned mahogany sofa, covered with leather" (32). Around the small cell that shares its inhabitant's well-worn face, are variously arranged "two pots of flowers in a window, and many holy pictures in the corner. Before one very huge, very ancient icon of the Virgin, a lamp was burning": Near it were two other holy pictures in shining settings, and, next to them, carved cherubims, china eggs, a Catholic cross of ivory with a Mater Dolorosa embracing it, and several foreign engravings from the great Italian artists of past centuries. Next to these costly and artistic engravings were several of the roughest Russian prints of saints, martyrs, prelates and so on, such as are sold for a few farthings at all the fairs. On the other walls were portraits of Russian bishops, past and present (*Brothers* 32).

What one notices is the range of materials that include sacred and secular images, expensive and modest items exhibiting a range of values, natural and artistic objects, as well as Eastern and Western objects of veneration. Far from being other-worldly, Zosima is rather multi-worldly; his cell reflects an eclectic, multi-cultural and polyvalent imagination. While a specialist of the soul, his avenues into learning are poly-theistic and temporally varied. As a teacher of individuals and groups, he has a rich vein of resources to pull from, a sign of a life-long learner himself.

His cell is an analogy of his own imagination in the world, unashamed of what is worn through and at ease among both elegant expensive objects as well as "rough" sacred images. As imaginal space, Zosima's cell is a microcosm of the world's large characteristics in both time and space.

We can understand further his cell as a *temenos,* a sacred space, like the classroom itself. It indicates that setting has a responsible and critical place in the act of learning, humanizing, and promoting learning, or alienating and retarding them by muting their sacred and human nature.

That we first encounter the old priest greeting guests in his cell, with its worn but comfortable furniture, suggests a quality of his teaching throughout the novel as both a social and spiritual practice. Engaging others through what he will call "active love" weds social interaction with spiritual largesse that represents a pillar of his pedagogy captured in the insight that each person is responsible for all others. According to Father Zosima's example, in the human act of teaching and learning, no barriers should exist, though that does not exile disagreements.

Zosima patterns both his disposition towards others and his teaching on unconditional love as a way of both knowing and being. Without a deep and nonrestrictive love for the student, he believes he is incapable of being either effective or persuasive. Such a love is mirrored in his attraction to the world at large, captured in the almost flea-market portrait of his cell's possessions.

Moreover, what Zosima reveals in this initial appearance with the visitors who have found seats in his cell is his hospitality. He treats all who enter his living space with reverence and respect, much as one would engage honored guests. As a teacher, Zosima's disposition is one of a welcoming presence wherein a host/guest relationship is established to create an atmosphere and an energy favorable to learning. The compassionate teacher consciously creates an atmosphere so that those willing to be instructed and to participate in the conversation that grows from it will be porous, open, and receptive to entertaining both the matter and the manner of instruction.

While Zosima is a holy man interested in the well-being, if not the transformation on earth of each person, what he teaches are fundamental insights on leading an authentic life in great freedom, a task hardly divorced from any good teacher's repertoire. The receptive teacher exhibits a fundamental goodness and care, if not compassion, for those who seek his/her tutelage. Moreover, while he is nourished by the teachings of Christ in the New Testament, he is not intent on "converting" anyone to a creed or a calling; those intangibles must spring from within the fertile soil and soul of the learner.

What is crucial for any teacher's success as an effective guide is a fundamental sense of abundance, of a generous spirit of both inquisitiveness as well as the ability to impart that abundance of knowing, and of seeking, to one's charges at a level that they can grasp, meditate on, push further, and integrate, even metabolize in their own way and in accord with their own needs and appetites.

Further, as Father Zosima gains his own authority from the wisdom tradition of the Gospels, his lesson plan is not to foist his authority's origin on others. Rather, another sign of his effective teaching is to instill in his students a creative and sustained hunger for each to seek his/her own authority, for only then does one cross the threshold from being only a student, to being a student-teacher to oneself, based on an authentic power of authority that far from being tyrannous to oneself and others, actually liberates each to find his/her own path, his/her own personal philosophy or set of guides. But learning in community is not to be ignored or deflected, for the relationship between learners enriches the enterprise.

A large part of this authority-seeking and attaining rests in the tension created between the objective form of knowing that is so visible in education's menu, with the unseen realm of imagining, processing, shaping, and contouring that information into a formed and transformative experience. In this way, the effective teacher passes his/her own venue for gaining authority on to the students. Learning, without integrating what one has grasped organically into one's deepest places of being, is closer to mechanical rote acquisition, a data processing of the most mundane variety.

I would say it this way: through the inspiration of an effective teacher like Zosima, students hunger for aspiration wherein they yearn not to be a copy of the teacher, which is a form of idolatry, but to become an analogy of the teacher in recognizing their own style of learning, of self-reflecting, and in grasping the form of what learning leads them toward: a sense of their own being. Both teaching and learning, then, are ontological acts of understanding in relation with others.

Father Zosima as Paradigm of the Inspired Teacher

In the novel, Father Zosima confronts, converses with, and even converts a variety of students that are common in any classroom. As we locate a few of these "types" of students, ones any teacher will recognize immediately, we can witness the way Zosima responds to each of them with an acumen that reveals how the inspired teacher is not dissuaded from one's own authority. Perhaps old Fyodor Karamazov is the most cogent example of the unruly student who may act the buffoon, or the class clown, to avoid being touched by instruction. Underneath the buffoonish behavior is an individual who not only deflects being changed but who never enters the imaginative space of the classroom the teacher is eager to create.

Zosima's guiding principle in all he does is recollected later in the novel: active human love. Just before his death, he remembers his own childhood and what guided him—the stories of the gospels that cultivated his sense of purpose and his attitude toward all others. "'Brothers,'" he tells his fellow monks in his cell, "'Love a man even in his sin; for that is the semblance of Divine Love and is the highest love on earth. Love all God's creation, the whole and every grain of sand in it. Love every leaf, every ray of God's light. Love the animals, love the plants, love everything. If you love everything, you will perceive the divine mystery in things. Once you perceive it, you will begin to comprehend it better every day'" (298).

In sum, these observations constitute Zosima's attitude towards all who enter his cell and guide him in his dealings even with those most recalcitrant to his efforts. Love, for him, is a way of seeing and a manner of knowing; love penetrates beneath the veneer of others' behavior. Love allows him to see the essence of a person beneath his/her surface words and actions. Being unconditional, his love allows him a freedom in knowing denied to many.

Teaching the Unruly

We know the unruly student quickly in a new class of students. Often, he/she sits in the back of the classroom and may initially try to hide. Under the guise of humor or silliness, this student's motive is often to undermine the teacher's intentions and instruction, to keep the teacher off balance and perhaps even unfocused; such a student narcissistically demands a great deal of attention.

The unruly student wants to avoid contact with anything that might shift his/her perspective, attitude, point of view, or convictions. S/he is inhospitable and as unnerving as a bad guest in one's home. Such a student's disrespect for the enterprise of teaching and learning may have many historical influences, but the teacher, not knowing their case history, must deal with this student both publicly in the classroom and most likely in private through parent-teacher conferences and direct counseling.

In the classroom, the teacher's task is not to have his/her intentions sabotaged by the "class clown" who may harbor malicious intents, ones that the student may be unconscious of, which makes this brand of non-learner keenly obstructive to the enterprise of teaching and learning. Fyodor Karamazov, as I have mentioned, falls into this category of student when he visits the old monk in his cell.

Early in the novel, accompanied by his son Ivan and friends Miusov and Maximov, Fyodor arrives at the monastery to visit the old monk. Fyodor is excited, even giddy with anticipation as they seek out the elder's cell, which is set apart from the rest of the monastery by a short distance. As they enter the grounds, Fyodor Pavlovich makes much of the fact that they are all to be on their best behavior: "'And believe me, we've all given our word to behave properly here...'" (29) he reminds his colleagues.

Miusov follows up quickly and addresses old Fyodor: "'But, look here, Fyodor Pavlovich, you said just now that we had given our word to behave properly. Remember it. I advise you to control yourself. But, if you begin to play the fool, I don't intend to be associated with you here. . .. You see what a man he is'—he turned to the monk—'I'm afraid to go among decent people with him'" (29). The old monk referred to is their guide to the elder's cell, the contents of which have been described above.

As they enter, Father Zosima emerges from his bedroom. In the cell already are two monks: Father Librarian and Father Paissy. A novice and Alexey Karamazov accompany Zosima from the bedroom to the living room of his cell. Almost immediately Zosima bows low to the guests and asks for their blessing in a ritual of hospitality and humility. Each in turn receives a blessing from the elder even as Fyodor launches his buffoonish behavior. As Miusov bows to Zosima and moves to sit down, "Fyodor Pavlovich did the same, mimicking Miusov like an ape. As Alyosha watches his father's antics and his brother Ivan's refusal to embrace the elder, he flushes in shame: His forebodings were coming true" (32).

As they converse, Fyodor apologizes for the lateness of his eldest son, Dmitri. In the process, he refers to Zosima as "sacred elder," which makes his son Alexey shudder. He knows his father and his feigned humility. Such a slight mockery of Zosima opens the door to a string of verbal antics that pulls all attention to Fyodor's unruly manner: "'But there! I always say the wrong thing. Your reverence,' he cried, with sudden pathos, 'you behold before you a real buffoon! I introduce myself as such. It's an old habit, alas! And if I sometimes talk nonsense out of place it's with an object, with the object of making myself agreeable. One must be agreeable, mustn't one?'" (33). Father Zosima's response is silence laced with a scrutinizing curiosity. Old Fyodor takes this as a signal to continue his clownish ways.

"'Great Elder! Forgive me, the last thing about Diderot's christening I made up just now. . .. I made it up to add piquancy. I play the fool, Pyotr Alexandrovich, to make myself agreeable. Though I really don't know myself sometimes, what I do it for'" (34). The narrator remarks that for many decades only the greatest reverence for the monk's cell had been displayed, "so that the buffoonery shown by Fyodor Pavlovich, the lack of reverence for the place he was in, amazed and bewildered the spectators, or at least some of them. The monks, with unchanged countenances, waited, with earnest attention, to hear what the elder would say…'" (35).

Teachers know this moment, when the unruly student makes his/her move in deflecting the purpose of learning that all students, ideally, are present to engage. How the teacher responds to the disruptive student can set the tone for all subsequent outbursts.

But old Fyodor is only warming up at this point. Next, he attempts to control all parts of their meeting: "'Great elder, speak! Do I annoy you by my vivacity?' Fyodor Pavlovich cried suddenly, clutching the arms of his chair in both hands, as though ready to leap up from it if the answer was unfavorable" (35). Instead of responding in kind, Zosima moves to calm Fyodor and to relieve him of his stress. "'Do not trouble. Make yourself quite at home. And above all, do not be so ashamed of yourself, for that is at the root of it all'" (35), he addresses the roused old man.

Excited and wound up in himself, however, Fyodor is not ready to heed this advice; he doubles his momentum: "'Do you know, blessed father, you'd better not invite me to be my natural self. Don't risk it. . .. I will not go so far as that myself. I warn you for your own sake. . ... but as for you, holy being, let me tell you, I am brimming over with ecstasy'" (35), even as he continues to mock him with epithets that ridicule the elder's sacred demeanor.

Now hurling out of control and accelerating his aggressive and disruptive presence, he stands and with mock reverence proclaims: "'Blessed be the womb that bare thee, and the paps that gave thee suck—the paps especially. When you said just now, 'Don't be so ashamed of yourself for that is at the root of it all,' you pierced right through me by that remark, and read me to the core. . ... If I had only been sure that everyone would accept me as the kindest and wisest of men, oh, Lord, what a good man I should have been then!'" (36). The genius of Zosima's response is that he does not attack in kind the unruly student before him; rather, he observes with a dispassionate objectivity the origin of his buffoonery but in the spirit of hospitality, not hostility.

That observation begins to disarm the old man, whose response after it is at first both condescending and mocking, then settles into a recognition of the truth claim of the elder. It seems that at this moment a turn takes place in the old man, who seems to begin to move to understanding himself. He has not, however, lost all sediments of his mocking nature.

When the elder again addresses old Fyodor Pavlovitch Karamazov's clever manner of mixing sincerity wrapped in mockery, Zosima responds to his question raised just after the above citation: "'What must I do to gain eternal life?'" (36) by reminding old Karamazov of what he already recognizes: "'You have known for a long time what you must do. You have sense enough: don't give way to drunkenness and incontinence of speech; don't give way to sensual lust; and above all to the love of money'" (36). Zosima discerns what infections reside in the soul of the lecherous man; his teaching then is more prescriptive and invites Fyodor to remember what he already knows.

Memory itself, certainly at this juncture, is the locale of learning, which may be seen as an act of remembering what we already know but have forgotten. Perhaps learning itself is a perpetual imaginative act of recollection that the effective teacher inspires in one's students. Zosima himself teaches through the narrative authority of the New Testament. It is his guiding text and lodestar that directs him in all he says and does in both attitude and in his angle of understanding.

Whatever work, inspiration, or person one chooses, it seems imperative for any teacher to have a ground, a substantial anchor that one can return to, be nourished and fortified by, in order to reclaim an authority that can be worn down by the unruly student. For many of us who teach, it is the imago of a former teacher who shaped us further into who we are.

In this respect, the effective teacher, among other strategies, engages the students in acts of remembering, which includes here the imaginative act of recollection rather than the mechanical act of memorization of material, so that not data-retrieval but purpose and meaning can slowly emerge in the material meditated on in new ways. Teaching as recollection involves an act of imagination; it can lead often to learning as renewal of what one had known but forgotten. It must be remembered anew.

Teaching the Vulnerable

Soon thereafter, Zosima leaves his cell and addresses the group of peasant women who have gathered like a chorus of students, we might say, each seeking some insight and wisdom from the old monk. Each of them is vulnerable, wounded, possessed, or poverty-stricken; all of them are frightened and uncertain of their futures. The vulnerable students we teach have great difficulty concentrating, have home lives that are wretched, violent, and abusive, and struggle simply to arrive at school regularly. They are often easy prey for other students and often have difficulty fitting in, of being accepted, and so remain along the edges and margins of the school population. As such, they need attention and care that goes beyond the needs of those more ably equipped to handle the demands of the school, the social structure, and learning itself.

Father Zosima engages several of them directly, but not before listening to them with complete attention. Zosima places his hand on one woman possessed and howling in his presence and blesses her: "and she was at once soothed and quieted" (39). Such a gift of being able to be attentive, to listen closely and with full attention to the other, is a crucial quality of good teaching: absorbed listening. For how else can the teacher interested in the welfare and learning capacity of one's students further those aptitudes if one is not able to be attentive to their limits, their vulnerabilities, their needs, and, in the case of these women, their afflictions? Zosima understands that effective teaching spreads out to include one's ability to listen with full attention, which I understand as an act of generosity and respect for the other, to better calibrate what and how one responds to where the learner is.

Such an attitude towards one's more fragile students is a special form of active love; he does not take responsibility for what they can or cannot do; rather, he instills in them a sense of worth and value so that they can serve themselves with integrity and nobility. Listening with unconditional attention to the other allows the student to become fully present to what he/she understands and expresses. Listening is a form of teaching because of what it allows the other to be present to. To listen with attention is to witness an active love of learning on the part of the student as well as to assess where further instruction may be most fruitfully deployed.

As Zosima mingles with the women, attending to them one at a time, the narrator offers: "There is silent and long-suffering sorrow to be met with among the peasantries. It withdraws into itself and is still. But there is also a grief that breaks out, and from that minute it bursts into tears and finds vent in wailing. . .. Lamentations comfort only by lacerating the heart still more" (40). Active love in Zosima's response reveals itself in compassion; he blesses and listens to them, asking questions, offering an emotional forum for them to express themselves.

With afflicted students, such a response is best suited for private meetings, not public displays, although there is a sustained value in Zosima's being intimate with each woman so that the others can witness his active love manifested in the attitude of care. He understands that "lamentations spring out from the constant craving to reopen the wound" (40).

While he believes that even the vulnerable, wounded, and afflicted students can learn, they must be given the feeling of solid ground beneath them through the love of the teacher by means of compassion. Father

Zosima's demeanor is always calm, his voice modulated, not to invite excitement but rather to promote a soothing calm to lessen the anguish in his charges who seek from him solace and advice. Such a demeanor is accompanied by an authentic curiosity to know each woman's individual stories and to give each of them an audience to relate it.

One of the women had lost many of her children and had just buried her young son, Nikita, who was only three years old. He was her last. Now she grieves for them all, but especially for Nikita: "He seems always standing before me. He never leaves me. He has withered my heart. I look at his little clothes, his little shirt, his little boots, and I wail" (40). What happens next as Zosima listens to her is a lesson for teachers who may feel that a pat or stock response might be the best way of dealing with a student's crisis or affliction.

Zosima first relates to the grieving mother a story about an old saint in "olden times" who came upon a grieving mother like her in the Temple. He told her not to weep, for her little one was now an angel in God's kingdom: "'Therefore,' said the saint, 'thou too, oh mother, rejoice and weep not, for thy little one is with the Lord in the fellowship of the angels'" (41).

Zosima tells her that is what the old saint, who as a holy man could not express himself falsely on this tender subject, believed to be true. But Zosima turns the saint's words to the mother in a dramatic way: "'Therefore you too, mother, know that your little one is surely before the throne of God, is rejoicing and happy, and praying to God for you, and *therefore weep*, but rejoice'" (41, my italics). He has heard her deeply at this moment, so that Zosima alters the old saint's advice not to weep to allow her to weep. He transforms the sage advice of the saint to accommodate this woman in her circumstance under these unique conditions. His compassion has eclipsed the older story; the older story needed an emotional face-lift, a redesign to fit the actual experience of Nikita's mother's grief.

When teaching those most vulnerable, no stock response will do; only actively loving this woman in her grief will bring her any solace, for she is inhabiting the living world of the son's absence, not the heavenly world of angels that he may now call home. Then Zosima takes this suffering woman's situation one step further.

He sees before his eyes, in an imaginal moment of recollection, an analogy to the Biblical story of Rachel. "'It is Rachel of old,' said the elder, 'weeping for her children, and will not be comforted because they are not. . .. Be not comforted. Consolation is not what you need. Weep and be not consoled, but weep. Only every time you weep, be sure to remember that your little son is one of the angels of God, that he looks down from there at you and sees you and rejoices at your tears…'" (41-42).

Zosima reveals by way of a poetic insight in the figure of Rachel how the teacher may allow who is being instructed to respond not as one would think one should, but more authentically, more intimately with the actual experience one suffers. The analogy with the Biblical figure of Rachel, however, gives the grieving woman's experience a more vast and divine context.

This level of authenticity students detect intuitively and know what teachers they can trust and which they might be less forthcoming in their presence. Such an amazing instance of compassionate pedagogy is revealed at this moment of instruction by analogy. Here the teacher does not attempt to fix or cure the grieving mother, nor does he leave her to suffocate in her grief. What he achieves in his act of loving her in her grief is placing her suffering into another narrative context, into an older, more ancient story, while respecting her right and need to grieve and to shun consolation.

It is a brilliant moment: Zosima sees her suffering in the remembered context of the Biblical figure, then encourages the suffering mother not to be consoled, not to be denied her loss. He then provides that grief a new space as well as a spiritual vision that modifies or allows for another imagining of the suffering. Here his teaching is an act of love and generosity without sentimentality, without *a fix* attached to it. It now has an alternate image to be experienced by a more sacred imagination that allows the grieving mother to find in her suffering an image that gives it another life while simultaneously placing her in a new context of a wider human narrative. Healing can now grow in a more welcoming soil.

Two worlds coalesce here: the living reality of her grief in the present and a rich analogous story for her to hang on to as she remembers it, and through it, to the memory of her son as an angel; the earthly combines with the spiritual realm in the imagination. Active love binds the two in mutual sympathy. Educator Parker J. Palmer, in sympathy with just such a kind of teaching, writes that "the act of knowing is an act of love, the act of entering and embracing the reality of the other, of allowing the other to enter an embrace our own" (*To Know* 8). In such a community building, we are all members of one body. He continues: "Our knowing becomes a way of reweaving that community's bonds" (8).

Zosima guides her to an image of faith that can indeed *console* but not *erase* her great loss as it gains an alternative imaginative form. Teaching here on several levels is based on remembrance— "be sure to remember"—as a way into integrating her suffering. Of course, the grieving mother is free to choose this alternate narrative or simply cling to the one she has inhabited; the theme, however, is not lost: learning involves fundamental and profound choices, a freedom to engage an alternative image than the one that has sustained and at times incarcerated the intellectual and emotional life of one so the individual suffers a paralysis of the will in exchange for not having a supple enough presence to what afflicts, in this case, the woman who grieves.

Teaching the Proud

The proud student may be the most difficult to teach because of his/her self-absorption, an excessive self-love, which leaves little room for learning. The proud student tends to think that he/she has the answers already and needs little else from others—be they teachers or students. They will often rest in their own knowledge as containing all knowledge and so are in their imaginations resistant to anything new that might challenge or topple their own epistemological edifice, their own tower of knowledge.

When their proud disposition is wed to sentimentality, as is the case with the wealthy woman who visits Father Zosima, then a double plate of armor for learning is firmly worn to deflect anything that would detect their vulnerability, for their pride is a shield for their vulnerability. Zosima's active love as compassion, however, is a formidable way of penetrating through such insular pride.

As a counter to this authentic and compelling moment, Zosima turns finally to Madame Hoklhakov, "a sentimental society lady of genuinely good disposition in many respects" (44), a woman who has returned to Father Zosima after having recently been in his audience. She embodies another iteration of the vulnerable student, as I mentioned, but a much more formidable one because of the power of pride to hide and protect her fragile nature. Thus, she appears after the vulnerable students Zosima addressed and cared for above.

She suffers, she claims, from an inability to love the people though she wishes to and believes she must; she gushes to the old monk in feigned helplessness, not unlike old Fyodor Karamazov earlier. In some ways, she is another iteration of the old buffoon even in her adolescent anguish. She greets Zosima "ecstatically" (44). She tells him that she has been deeply touched watching the elder care for the other women, but her emotional excess is the face of pride as she attempts to seduce Zosima with it. In contrast to his authentic active love, her love is a sentimental gush of empty emotion: "'I love the people myself. I want to love them. And who could help loving them, our splendid Russian people, so simple in their greatness'" (45).

We remember old Fyodor Karamazov, who can both mock and attempt to seduce simultaneously. We can understand her as the kind of student whose pride takes the form of devotion, but it is a ploy to gain the upper hand where her own pride masters the teacher. "'Forgive me! I am suffering!' And in a rush of fervent feeling, she clasped her hands before him" (47). Zosima discerns the childish quality of such a student and is careful not to be caught in its manipulative net.

Admitting to her teacher that she suffers from lack of faith, she inquires of Zosima what he thinks of her now. The elder does not reprimand but rather encourages her to engage in authentic love of others: "'If you attain to perfect self-forgetfulness in the love of your neighbor, then you will believe without doubt, and no doubt can possibly enter your soul'" (48). What task could require more from a person steeped in pride than to become self-forgetful?

Later in the novel, Zosima comments on the arduous process of love: first, one must be vigilant in love that "'your image be a seemly one'" (298), for to be careless about one's actions, especially in the presence of a child: "'you may not know it but you may have sown an evil seed in him and it may grow, and all because you were not careful before the child, because you did not foster in yourself a careful, actively benevolent love'" (298). He continues to instruct his fellow monks on how: "'Brothers, love is a teacher; but one must know how to acquire it, for it is hard to acquire, it is dearly bought, it is won slowly by long labor. . . . Everyone can love occasionally, even the wicked can'" (298).

Such an abiding belief in both the difficulty of benevolent love as well as the long struggle to acquire it causes Zosima not to abandon anyone, whatever kind or condition of student who approaches him. Thus, in his conversation with the young Lise's mother, he appeals to her inflated sentimental notions of suffering and offers an antibody—authentic active love lived in self-forgetfulness. He ends by encouraging her to avoid all forms of falsehood, "'especially falseness to yourself. Watch over your own deceitfulness and look into it every hour, every minute'" (49).

Never ceasing to love even the most self-involved of his charges, the generous spirit of Zosima does not shy away from the fundamental flaw exhibited by the student, but instead has the skill to turn it by suggesting that one be vigilant about one's own motives in constant acts of self-reflection. The work is to be done by her, not him.

No sentimentality attends the noble and difficult work of coming to love without conditions. Honesty and forthrightness, coupled with a generous spirit and an attitude of reverence for the suffering of others, scripts Father Zosima's discerning teaching. He observes what is noble and redeemable in his students; they do not need answers or cures so much as direction and guidance; then the responsibility rests directly with them, not with the teacher, although both remain integral parts of the journey.

Knowing who one is teaching is as crucial as the subject matter being presented. Blaming the teacher for the student's failure to learn is both short-sighted and too convenient; it also deflects responsibility away from the student onto the shoulders of the teacher. Zosima reveals the value of keeping the student engaged in the process of learning and keeping the competence of the student approximate to the demands of learning. He also understands that without the proper disposition towards love itself, only a superficial level of learning will be achieved.

Finally, when Madame Hoklhakov seems to open authentically to Father Zosima, she confesses her fear of the afterlife, that "enigma" (47) that causes her great anguish. Her suffering stems not from lack of faith in God but in the terror she experiences toward the unknown, so she seeks a cure from the elder. He responds that "'I quite believe in the sincerity of your suffering'" (47) but makes no effort to cure her of this uncertainty. Rather than descend to her level, he insists she struggle to attain his "'by the experience of active love. Strive to love your neighbor actively and indefatigably'" (48).

Zosima's love for her continues to peel back the layers of her pride until she reaches a point of full disclosure: she cannot love humanity to such an extent that she is willing to help to relieve the suffering of the wounded and diseased because they might not show her the requisite gratitude she believes must come from such service. Her pride keeps her at the center of attention and concern, yet she desires to love selflessly. Such is the crux of her suffering. She finally admits: "'...if anything could dissipate my active love to humanity, it would be ingratitude. In short, I am a hired servant, I expect my payment at once—that is, praise, and the repayment of love with love. Otherwise, I am incapable of loving anyone'" (48). Her deep-seated pride reveals at this point a lack of courage and generosity as well as an unwillingness or inability to liberate herself from self-absorption.

Rather than respond directly to her plight, Zosima's genius rests in the fact that he tells her a story: "'It's just the same story a doctor once told me,' 'observed the elder'" (48). He understands the power of narrative to address the suffering or dis-ease before him because by its indirection and its analogical nature, it carries the point he wishes to make while attributing it to another. His craft is not unlike the one Dostoevsky uses in writing this novel. The crux of the story distinguishes between the kind of abstract love one harbors for humanity in general versus the active love of helping a single individual, a theme that Ivan Karamazov will intensify in his own belief system.

Father Zosima's story has a profound effect on Madame Hoklhakov. "'You have revealed me to myself. You have seen through me and explained me to myself!'" (49), to which Zosima responds: "'Are you speaking the truth? Well, now, after such an admission, I believe that you are sincere and good at heart. If you do not attain happiness, always remember that you are on the right road, and try not to leave it. Above all, avoid falsehood, every kind of falsehood, especially falseness to yourself'" (49). As a generous teacher, he has not ridiculed her once but has struck home to the essential core of her pride and suggested the hard work needed to overcome her egocentricity. As readers, we witness in this crucial scene active love embodied and its benevolent effects on the most hardened and proud heart of a student struggling to shed one's childish ways and paralyzing self-preoccupation.

His teaching has instilled in her hope of change and firmness of purpose in her ability to love with greater munificence without need of repayment. Now she has a narrative to fall back on, to remember, to reflect on, as well as the more conceptual nature of Zosima's insights; the two together create a much more potent form of teaching and learning than either one in isolation could achieve.

Teaching the Unbeliever

Although we do not want—and perhaps *should* not want—to surrender to this notion, as another of Father Zosima's lessons shows, not all students open themselves to learning despite the best teacher's efforts. One of the most difficult barriers for a teacher to break through is the despair that comes from unbelief, caused by a calcified imagination held hostage to a concept or an attitude with no other possibilities on the student's horizon. This kind of unbelief poses a particular challenge for the most seasoned mentor. Such is Zosima's experience with the tormented but brilliant Ivan Karamazov, author of "The Grand Inquisitor" prose poem that he reads to his brother Alexey.

In the scene in Zosima's cell, Ivan and Father Zosima state their respective positions on the nature of virtue and what forces sustain virtue's presence. Zosima argues from his unconditional belief in the power of active love to soften the heart's hardness to make one more malleable to be instructed: what can harden the heart of our students is the absence of hope, of a futility of even continuing to try to achieve what they feel is beyond them, coupled with their own sense of lack of self-love brought on by their conditioning and life situations.

As a non-believer of God's creation, one which historically includes horrendous suffering of the innocent, Ivan rejects such a world and the character of a God who would allow such senseless brutality. Ivan lives with a pessimism that paralyzes him. He wrestles with how one can hope in such a world or believe in God's goodness with such suffering that seems a part of its innate nature.

How, then, might the student who has grown cynical and hopeless about his/her own situation in life, be coaxed into belief, even into enthusiasm for learning as well as a hope that such an endeavor could affect and even transform their imaginative life and their image of a more positive future despite surroundings or influences that continue to erode such a posture? Rewards and punishments would seem simply to perpetuate the same round of success and failure so oppressive in its repetition.

Father Zosima's meeting with Ivan in his cell soon revolves around two systems of belief, two different imaginations about the nature of creation and the nature and place of love within it. Zosima's task is to shift Ivan's thinking from a mechanical response to transgressions into a more organic one based on the historical reality of Christ's actions as embodiments of active love. Hope and belief, Zosima suggests in this conversation, are what active love seeds, inseminates, and brings to fruition.

He observes to Ivan that if evildoing is punished only by a knee-jerk chastisement spoken of just now…"'which embitters the heart'" (55) but is no real deterrent because it does not soften the heart "'which lies in the recognition of sin by conscience'" (55), then no genuine change is forthcoming. Taken most broadly, no teaching or learning occurs without some formative boundaries or parameters. The freedom that the teacher imparts to the student in order to encourage a variety of ways of knowing cannot happen in boundless space.

In his argument, Zosima fastens his conviction to the recognition of one who transgresses the law, that he has violated something essential to the community. By contrast, Ivan argues that "'there is no law of nature that men should love mankind'" but virtue under any color exists only "'because men have believed in immortality'" (60). To Zosima's questioning of his belief, Ivan rejoins: "'Yes. That is my contention. There is no virtue if there is no immortality'" (60). He will in fact admit to his brother Alexey later that "'Christ-like love for men is a miracle impossible on earth'" (218). Zosima has no rebuttal for Ivan's argument; instead, he sees through and beneath it to something dark in Ivan's soul and addresses it.

The perceptive and loving teacher can address his/her student with the truth of the other's nature in such a way that the student becomes aware of him/herself with a depth and penetration previously unavailable. The despair and sense of sterile limits that a student may suffer is an expression of a form of nihilism—a profound sense of helplessness and hopelessness, which Ivan suffers intensely. What the teacher's task includes is an effort to bring the student to believe in him/herself as a starting point, for without this foundation, no transformation may be possible. I believe Ivan carries this same sense of non-belief in himself.

Conceptual thinking has alienated Ivan from himself and Zosima detects just such cleavage in his soul. He tells him, without rancor or malice: "'in your despair, you, too, divert yourself with magazine articles, and discussions in society, though you don't believe your own arguments, and with an aching heart mock at them inwardly. . ... That question you have not answered, and it is your great grief, for it clamors for an answer'" (61). Nonbelief is wedded to despair and a cynical or even disruptive behavior may stem directly from such darkness.

We witness a different moment of learning in their exchange. Mentoring includes at times not teaching the material of a discipline when the student recoils from it or remains indifferent to it. These are student choices, not the teachers. But such a situation of resistance can be transformed by the discerning teacher who can grasp the internal workings of the imagination of the student to such a degree that s/he is able to assist making the student known to him/herself, a knowledge or awareness that one may possess only minimally.

In the moment above, Zosima reveals to Ivan where his suffering is most active and, by implication, where in him the sacred may co-inhabit with it: "'But thank the Creator who had given you a lofty heart capable of such suffering; of thinking and seeking higher things, for our dwelling is in the heavens. God grant that your heart will attain the answer on

earth, and may God bless your path'" (61). Zosima has turned Ivan's re-
bellion into a moment of gracious acceptance of who and what he is and
what grace may be needed to use his gifts for nobler ends.

Zosima's language encourages Ivan to believe first in himself, then
to hope in himself. His style is direct, loving, and supportive; he does not
condemn Ivan for who he is, but he does offer him another way of imagining himself, perhaps even another way of reordering his values, including the most basic one of self-worth. This scene is one of the potent
witnesses to the quality of compassion embodied in Zosima's response
to Ivan's intellectual recalcitrance.

In his conversation with Ivan, he is more attuned to making the latter
feel seen and heard, not dismissed as a strange fellow with even stranger
ideas. In addition, Zosima never makes the mistake of personalizing the
argument, even when he comments on the condition of Ivan's heart. He
brings both Ivan's heart as well as *heart* into the conversation explicitly so
that his student may take heart, even begin to feel a change of heart.

Only loving the student can bring about such a profound change and
with it, a sense of hope. Hope must be seeded and grow from within, not
because of outer circumstances. The imagination, not external surroundings being changed (when that is not possible) is the seat of conversion
where the attitude of the student can be transformed by the teacher who
makes clear repeatedly that the student is worthy of being taught and able
to be changed by the learning.

Active love frames the moment when the student internalizes such a
belief and makes it his/her own. Learning with affection can instill hope
when the student begins to believe that s/he is worthy of learning.
Zosima has instructed Ivan through love; however, it did not become
mired in Ivan's ideas but in the condition of his suffering heart. Here, as
with other illustrations above, we detect a pattern: learning's most vulnerable region may be where one is most deeply wounded, afflicted, disoriented, and dismembered or hopeless. At this juncture is an opening
for change that, without such a soft, porous space in the soul, learning
might not be invited in, however revelatory it may be.

Teaching the Willing

As Zosima's death draws closer, Alexey is stirred by his words to go into the world, marry and teach: "'Remember that, young man. When it is God's will to call me, leave the monastery. Go away for good'" (67). Alexey is terrified of both losing his mentor and leaving the place of his instruction, yet this too is part of the learning process: uncoupling from the mentor and carrying his wisdom in memory is to risk losing one's moorings and place of safety where the challenges demand little of one's capacities. I sense that separating from one's central sources of instruction can certainly be terrifying but necessary so that one does not live a life by following a path already conveniently laid out by another. To do so is to live once again another's life while foregoing one's own.

Finding one's own path as one transitions from student to teacher, guided by the wisdom of an ancestor, in this case his monastic mentor, both completes as well as extends Alexey's process of learning. The perceptive teacher can fathom the inchoate teacher in his student and knows that giving birth to that teacher within the folds of the student requires that the mentor step aside, as Virgil, for instance, does for Dante in the last Cantos of *Purgatorio* in his *Commedia*. Out of active love, even as the good teacher instills in the student a way of learning and coming to know that is not a Xerox of the teacher's way but an illustration of how learning can be engaged and furthered according to one's own style.

Zosima's wisdom and courage are contained in the words above as his instructions usher Alexey out into the world to follow his own teaching path guided by *pamiat,* the Russian word for memory which includes the memory of ancestors, what is most important that will sustain one. Learning itself is an act of memory and teaching is an art form in service to such recollections.

We could say that Alexey Karamazov grows in love and courage because he has been seeded by the words of Father Zosima in the chapter, "Notes of the Life in God of the Elder Zosima." He has also served as the elder's scribe and in recording his words, they enter him deeply to infuse in his soul the power of active love's presence. He instills in his student not only knowledge but an attitude toward life. Any learning, it seems, is analogical by its nature and design. Thus, for example, when

Zosima is told by his doctor after a physical examination that he will live "'for months and years too,'" Zosima exclaims to him: "'Why reckon the days? One day is enough for a man to know all happiness. My dear ones, why do we quarrel, try to outshine each other and keep grudges against each other? Let's go straight into the garden, walk, and play there, love, appreciate, and kiss each other, and glorify life'" (268).

Active love is an attitude of acceptance and remembrance, the latter of which we will note in a moment. Zosima's words cultivate a feeling of acceptance for one another in all one's limitations and imperfections. Active love that he espouses in both word and deed is one that exhibits tolerance, patience, eliminating self-torment, and the suffering of others.

Moreover, Zosima instructs those who gather around him, including of course Alexey, to remember "'those precious memories'" of childhood, "'for there are no memories more precious than those of early childhood in one's first home. And that is almost always so if there is any love and harmony in the family at all. Indeed, precious memories may remain even of a bad home, if only the heart knows how to find what is precious'" (269). Even in the worst home, there is something to retrieve, to treasure, and to grow from. But there is an attitude, a way of seeing that Zosima suggests is at the heart of active love.

The strength of Zosima's way of knowing in love emphasizes the cultivation of a perspective, a point of view, that far transcends the content of learning but does place the student in a particular disposition to learn. Part of its success rests with the degree of freedom the student allows him/herself; active love is a love of freedom, of self-courage, not allowing shame or failure or external limits to override what the student is capable of if given the sense of courage by his/her teacher.

Alexey takes these words in and, at Zosima's death, gathers them into a revelation that is a gift. But he has done the work needed to have this visitation and the courage to act on it. Such is the initial goal of active love, one that does not encourage self-laceration or self-molestation.

In life, Zosima's refrain is embodied in the following affirmation: "'Love one another, Fathers,'" said Father Zosima, as far as Alexey could remember afterwards. "'Love God's people. Because we have come here and shut ourselves within these walls, we are no holier than those that are outside. . ... When he realizes that he is not only worse than others, but that he is responsible to all men for all and everything, for all human sins, general and individual, only then the aim of our seclusion is attained'" (148-49).

In his cell close to death, Zosima welcomes Alexey. "Alexey went up to him, bowed down before him to the ground and wept. Something surged up from his heart, his soul was quivering, he wanted to sob" (263). Zosima calls the young novice to him, to look closely at his face and to remark on the suffering he saw the day before in the face of his brother, Ivan. Alexey asks: "'Father and teacher,' he began with extreme emotion, 'your words are too obscure. . .. What is this suffering in store for him?'" (264). To which Zosima responds: "'Don't inquire. I seemed to see something terrible yesterday... as though his whole future were expressed in his eyes'" (264). Alexey struggles with his teacher's vision of impending disaster.

It is a moment in the student of disorientation, of unclarity and confusion, a part of the teacher-student relationship that is important to note, for not all that one attempts to learn can be grasped; some experiences of learning leave one in confusion that one must reflect on, question, and come to some sense of coherence with, even in its mysterious expression or perhaps because of it.

At this moment Zosima turns to Alexey and sees his future as one living in the world as a monk: "'You will have many enemies, but even your foes will love you. Life will bring you many misfortunes, but you will find your happiness in them, and will bless life and will make others bless it—which is what matters most. Well, that is your character'" (264). He goes on to confess for the first time why Alexey has been so dear to him, for he has reminded Zosima of a lost brother "'who had died before my eyes at seventeen'" (264). Alexey in Zosima's imagination had carried his brother's remembrance and prophecy and, in this capacity, had been a mentor to Zosima: "'Alexey, who has some, though not a great, resemblance in face, seems to me so like him spiritually, that many times I have taken him for that young man, my brother, mysteriously come back to me...as a reminder and an inspiration'" (264).

This admission is crucial for Alexey's own image of himself as a student, for Zosima informs him here that the young monk has also served as *his* inspiration. It seems that no matter the level or abilities of any of our students, we as teachers can learn from them, even be inspired by them, and see more into our role and obligations by means of them. What Zosima is most moved by is the spiritual kinship of his student to his deceased brother. Such a revelation heard by Alexey may be the beginning of his shift from student to teacher in his own imaginative growth.

In sum, his words that live on with fierce force after his death capture the monk's essential teaching that each is responsible for all, that no one remains outside the purview or range of responsibility for anyone else. Assumed in his belief is that there is no important division between people and that individual diversity harbors beneath it a mysterious unity. Living one's life and conducting oneself according to this philosophy is the deepest teaching that Zosima shares with Alexey and the monks; now it is Alexey's destiny to carry it to the next generation and multiply its crucial presence in the imagination of others.

At the same moment, Zosima begins to detach from his student to allow him the space and desire to transition from student to student-teacher, which he has been doing in tutoring some young boys already, then to a full-fledged teacher in his own right and style.

Making a Teacher

Alexey's grief by the coffin of his mentor suggests the death of one relationship with his elder and the birth of himself as perhaps a spiritual extension of Zosima, as the latter already suggested of his brother's spirit above. Perhaps it is possible here that the spirit of Zosima passes more fully into the grieving student; his mentor's death is the occasion for a birthing as well.

In addition, and if any good student is already a teacher in one's ability to learn, inspired by the love of one's teacher, then the death of the latter signals the full birthing of the former. Teacher and learner cannot really be separated, for the teacher who has stopped being a student has also abdicated being a teacher. But one role is played down and the other gains insistence in this coffin scene.

Grieving by his mentor's corpse, Alexey falls asleep and dreams of the miracle of Cana of Galilee. He realizes he is part of the new wine that has been changed by Christ into the best refreshment for the guests, who are impressed that the best drink was saved until the end. Having fallen asleep on his knees, he suddenly awakes and walks quickly to the edge of the coffin. In his dream, which is another form that teaching can take in our lives, he had heard his mentor's voice proclaim the new wine in the story of Christ's first miracle.

We might see the story as a rich metaphor: the new wine as Alexey himself, created or transformed by Father Zosima into a new refreshment that will quench the thirst of the students who come under Alexey's mentorship. The story dreamt may even be, for Alexey, a new way of being mentored.

He now carries this new expansive feeling in his heart out of the monastic cell and into the night air, transformed by the presence of his dead mentor and the vision of a new expansive city: "The vault of heaven, full of soft, shining stars, stretched vast and fathomless above him. The Milky Way ran in two pale streams from the zenith to the horizon. The fresh, motionless, still night enfolded the earth...The silence of earth seemed to melt into the silence of the heavens. . .. Alyosha stood, gazed, and suddenly threw himself down to the earth" (340). A graceful transformation overpowers him, as if all that he had learned and contemplated constellate at one instant into a profound change of heart in this lyric vision, perhaps the highest and deepest consequence of learning.

This moment, occurring soon after his mentor has died, expresses a resurrection of the soul as a result of what Alexey has learned, as if all his knowledge were now in the service of a *metanoia*, or transformation of the heart into a new way of feeling. Such a dramatic transformation, a sustained and enriched vision of himself and his communal place in the world, takes form. Here, nothing will be excluded from his embrace.

Dostoevsky's language captures the powerful effect taken in by remembrance, of memory herself, as a profound teacher; the suggestion is that the memory of Zosima, accompanied by all his words and deeds, gathers in the imagination of the learner, allowing the learner-turned-teacher to extend, but not duplicate, the soul of the teacher's memory. "But with every instant he felt clearly and, as it were, tangibly, that something firm and unshakable as that vault of heaven had entered his soul. It was as though some idea had seized the sovereignty of his mind—and it was for all his life and forever and ever. He had fallen on the earth a weak youth, but he rose up a resolute champion, and he knew and felt it suddenly at the very moment of his ecstasy" (341).

I suggest that the memory of Father Zosima is distinct from his living reality; memories have their own autonomy, and that quality of remembrance has entered Alexey's imagination to renovate his vision of himself and his destiny. Within his transformed understanding, prompted and nurtured by his mentor's image, now preserved and flowering in his memory, he comes into his own authority as a teacher and as a person, resolute, certain, and yielding to his life work; it will not be in the monastic setting but rather in his "sojourn in the world" (341).

The great teachings and active loving of others engaged by Zosima in life lead Alexey, his best student, not to copy the original, but to grow into his own unique self, imprinted, however, with qualities of courage, generosity, self-knowledge, unconditional acceptance, tolerance, and patience, all of which he may have never acquired without first yielding unconditionally to his mentor's vision of "active love" embodied.

Part of the difficulty of some of the characters, like Ivan Karamazov, Madame Holklhakov, and others, is their implicit rejection of the embodied other that they struggled to love; their preference instead was to love humanity in the abstract. Zosima's suffering and death, followed by his stinking corpse, returns us to the embodied nature of our being, infused with spirit. Teaching and learning are embodied, social, and communal actions wherein the body is central to its design.

The unexpected odor of Zosima's decaying body, which creates a scandal in the monastery and fuels his detractors with confirmation that he was not, really, a holy man, preserves the union between spirit anchored in flesh and thus avoids an intellectualism severed or dismembered from the individual's own flesh as well as the world's body. Learning, the good teacher reveals, is an embodied action of the soul, not a fractured mind-centered performance.

In the spirit of Mother Russia, from which Zosima emanated and to whom he returns, the teacher that he was and continues to be knows that losing the body can breed a form of abstracted, alienated relation to the soil, as Ivan's more intellectual ideas have coerced him into. Such a union of soul with flesh originates from the Great Holy Mother Russia herself.

Zosima's presence and his decaying corpse reminds all those who worshipped him and learned from him that embodiment is the vehicle we are given in order to express the spirit of teaching and learning.

As a budding teacher, Alexey shares this generous quality of his mentor with his own young students who gather around to celebrate him as he instills in them love for one another even as they attend to a funeral honoring and burying a young boy they all knew. Yet unformed, the young boys display an eagerness for a mentor, anxious for direction and purpose and in need of a vision of life that they each can build on. Then Alexey collects the youths, all of whom love their young teacher. He does not judge them, but he does ask them to remember what they have done and to reflect on its consequences for each of them.

As a teacher Alexey conveys to the young boys a sense of their own goodness, even beyond what they thought of themselves; this attitude of self-loving and acceptance, even in the face of grief and loss, carries on the legacy of Zosima by instilling in the students a sense of their own worth, and because of it, their capacity to excel beyond themselves. Active love, fully embodied, modulates shame, a form that self-hate assumes, as well as self-torture, self-reprisal, self-demeaning, and self-laceration.

Like *his* teacher, the young man who is the teacher at the novel's end exhorts, acknowledges, and witnesses goodness: "'Let us all be generous and brave like Ilyushechka, clever, brave and generous like Kolya,…and let us all be as bashful but also as clever and sweet as Kartashov'" (734). As a gifted teacher, Alexey passes on a legacy of largesse, of a generous spirit, and the virtue of remembrance that is to "'live forever in our hearts from this time forth!'" (735). Learning is in large measure adapting and integrating a legacy of what must be remembered "eternally" (735). Its sensibility is what the compassionate teacher promotes and instills in his students, as Alexey does here. He has changed the hearts of the young boys for the rest of their lives, and their response, in gratitude, is active love exuberantly returned: "'Hurrah for Karamazov!' Kolya cried once more rapturously and once more all the boys chimed in" (735).

Teaching is not data-processing, although the mania for testing and the rage for accountability may try to convince us otherwise; rather, teaching and learning are actions of the soul, the intellect, and take place in the flesh of the student and the flesh of the world, each with its imperfections and its grandeur. To teach and to learn are among the noblest activities a person can engage; the desire to learn is innate in the soul; so many obstacles can obstruct the clear path of learning and the love as well as joy that can companion such an initiative.

No matter how discouraged we may be, we must remember the powerful role of memory *The Brothers Karamazov* illustrates in the act of teaching and learning. Sometimes what is of value in learning may not descend on us as students for years, even decades. At those moments we find ourselves thanking those teachers who did not give up on us or surrender to the crushing workload or the tendency to give up; they persevered, continuing to love their subject matter as well as our ability as students to co-create it.

For these reasons, teachers must remember themselves into the future and take heart that their full value may not be recognized today or next week, but in the fullness of time.

Works Cited

Dostoevsky, Fyodor. *The Brothers Karamazov*. Trans. Constance Garnett. Norton, 1976.

Palmer, Parker J. *To Know as We Are Known: Education as a Spiritual Journey*. HarperCollins, 1993.

9

OATH-TAKING AS SCAR-MAKING: REMEMBERING THE ORIGINAL WOUND IN HOMER'S *ODYSSEY*[*]

Few books or essays by James Hillman have revealed to me the creative workings of his fertile imagination as the chapter "Puer Wounds and Odysseus' Scar" in *Senex & Puer,* volume 3 of the *Uniform Edition* (214-247). There, the reader can track with both wonder and gratitude the mythopoetic method that outlines and supports Hillman's manner of presence to being wounded and its relation to the two psychological ways of being conscious that emanate from one's suppuration in the figures of senex and puer. Odysseus' famous wound, which scar tissue runs through the twenty-four books of the *Odyssey* and comprises his signature, his brand, and his being in the world. It is one thing to be wounded, Hillman writes; it is another to survive it. Yet we do not get to the hero's wounded nature until we have traveled through two-thirds of the essay (*Senex & Puer* 235).

I have identified ten separate oaths; the first appears in Book II and the last ends Book XXIV. I am going to use the figures and forces of senex and puer to think about oath-making and taking; I cannot rehearse

---

[*] Originally delivered to the 4th Annual James Hillman Symposium at the Dallas Institute of Humanities and Culture, October 16th -17th, 2015, and published in *Conversing with James Hillman: Senex and Puer* in 2016. Used here by permission of the Dallas Institute of Humanities and Culture Publications.

or "reversion" Hillman's delineations of the two; it would take the entire essay to do so. But a few observations are necessary. Most importantly is Hillman's insistence that "imaginal reality informs puer consciousness" (*Senex & Puer* 223). Further, crippling is indispensable for the puer. He has a greater viability through his vulnerability (223). Senex qualities, on the other hand, include "judgment, sobriety, prudence, deviousness, isolation, and suffering . . . yet he has little power" (238).

Odysseus, Hillman argues, is a combination of puer/senex energies, attitudes, and dispositions. Running parallel with him is the series of oaths that run like a through-line in the epic, beginning in Book III and ending the epic in Book XXIV. I believe that the oath itself is a senex-puer creation holding energies of both figures in a tension that allows for peace to be maintained if the terms of the oath are honored by the adversarial parties who agree to it.

By oaths I am also including pacts, truces, cease-fires, and any other form of compromise that allows the tension of opposites and oppositions to sustain a peace through a languaged code or set of agreements. Here resides the contemporary value of Hillman's astonishing insights into the wound (*Senex & Puer* 214-244). The oath is an expression of senex-puer energy that can heal while remembering the original violation, affliction, or wounding. In the service of space, I wish to list a series of observations, many of which were arrived at as I read and contemplated the thirty pages he devotes to chapter 8: "Puer Wounds and Odysseus' Scar."

- Oaths carry both puer and senex energy; every oath carries the shadow of the wound that has been inflicted or may be inflicted further in the absence of an oath. Following Hillman, an oath can parent the wound and the wounded which is so necessary today given the increasingly violent instability, decapitations, and mass murders that assault us. The puer spirit imagines rather than manages (*Senex & Puer* 220). It is to the senex spirit to manage. But first the oath or truce must be imagined with great craft and subtlety.

- An oath can cauterize the bleeding of the puer as he imagines the terms of an oath codified by senex consciousness. An oath is a woven marriage between contrary tensions into a fabricated whole.

- Scars are the memories wound that oaths carry as the scar tissue of conflicts.
- Oaths and their deeper mythic makeup are crucial for any chance of peace today; leaders must gain some understanding of the mythic, not just political or economic implications of these formidable agreements and perhaps their origins in weaving itself.
- An oath or truce is analogous to the scar tissue that knits the wound into a new form. An oath then is always a memory of the original affliction, its origins and terms. Oaths, truces, heal over but do not erase or efface the genesis of the affliction; but the oath as scar does not ooze or suppurate the original affliction as it surely may without the cauterizing of it through oath-taking and sustaining.
- Oaths are adroitly crafted works that combine the energies of *metis,* or craft, with *bie* or force, strength. I understand the puer spirit to be integral to the former, senex spirit to the latter.
- Oaths craft a new reality out of two deeply wounded ones.
- Not only are both Penelope and Odysseus co-conspiring joiners, weavers, of cloth, plots, and purposes, but they are also weavers of restraint, the lexicon of oaths.
- An oath is a gift to both sides of adversity; it has the healing capacity to remove the onus from the wound and opens both sides to a new, crafted future without bloodshed, theft, or destruction.
- Odysseus is a mythic figure who resides between senex consciousness (his father Laertes) and puer consciousness (his son Telemachos) and participates, in his nature, in each. He is a joiner, maker, craftsman, and gushing puer consciousness who struggles repeatedly in the epic to keep his mouth and to restrain his behavior. As a leader coming from the chaos of war, he struggles to merge senex and puer consciousness into his homecoming. Raft and oath here—joining disparate pieces into a new unity.
- With an oath, a new reality comes into the world midway between two potentially or fully formed wounded forces.

- An oath, like a wound as Hillman describes it, can be "a learner and a teacher both and has been compared to a mouth" (*Senex & Puer* 223).

- An oath allows a different imagination to intervene (puer) and then codifies this imaginal form (senex).

- An oath staunches the continually flowing blood shed by creating a new vessel to stabilize and so end the leaking vessel of war's destruction (*Senex & Puer* 228).

- An oath initiates two opposing forces into a third container. The container stops the hemorrhaging. Oath-taking is therefore a compromise that formalizes the sacrifice on both sides of the antagonism needed for the tension of opposites to be set in place. Missing in the puer is a psychic container (*Senex & Puer* 229); missing in the senex is the imaginative vitality needed for oath construction.

- The vessel that an oath is comprised of may be feminine, a womb of sorts (*Senex & Puer* 229) for the senex-puer to gestate, to envision further options. It buys time for a new birthing and gives space to allow energy to be redirected. The vessel fills in "what is fundamentally missing in the puer structure . . . the psychic container for holding in, keeping back, stopping short, the moment of reflection that keeps events within so that they can be realized as psychic facts" (*Senex & Puer* 229).

- The closed or enwombed nature of the oath as vessel offers a habitation for an open raw wound to close, or open wounds from both conflicting sides to heal into a new form of wholeness. Scars will keep the memory alive and visible.

- Odysseus "is not locked into opposites. He does not suffer from one-sidedness" (*Senex & Puer* 237), so he is available to oath-making.

- An oath promotes restraint and moderation; it appeals to the emotional intellect. In its creation blood ceases to flow; life is preserved, and hospitality is reinstated.

- The scar "reminds consciousness of its wobbly uncertainty, the dark vulnerability in the heart of its light" (*Senex & Puer* 238). So too does the oath, like a scar for two contrary forces, serve as a similar reminder.

- An oath is a form of collective therapy. In therapy we 'reversion' the story, "to integrate the symptoms by discovering their inherent necessity' (*Senex & Puer* 240).
- Such an act of reversion "takes us out of story and into image. We see that the wound has been inherent in us all along . . . and we realize that image consciousness heals" (*Senex & Puer* 240). An oath, then, offers both sides of a suppurating conflict an image to grasp onto for its healing properties. An oath moves both sides out of an adversarial narrative into a nurturing of the oath's terms and conditions.

Further, an oath carries the gravity of a pact based on mutual trust, or senex energy and the energy of a new form of relationship: puer power. It pulls something old into a new arrangement, so the oath is composed of a puer-senex conglomerate; each sacrifices so that each gains something. It places the relationship between warring factions on a new level of cooperation, and out of competition for power and control.

An oath is also an attempt to construct a pattern of wholeness; when disparate and conflicting pieces fall into an agreed-on and rightly ordered relation with one another, such that they are transformed from pieces to patterned oneness, there arises a union of opposites that nests a senex-puer consciousness. An oath forms a new story, as a truce, a compact, a binding agreement that grows from arbitration. An oath allows a new pattern to emerge, which may happen only after a certain level and intensity of violation and destruction occurs to reach it.

The voice of Athena as both warrior and voice of persuasion intervenes at the end of Book XXIV to staunch the bloodshed between the families of Ithaca. War, however, is a form of violent persuasion that makes one side the victor; an oath, on the other hand, rests on cooperation that allows both sides to win; but only through mutual sacrifice, not swords, is coherence, cosmos, and continuity for the furtherance of *communitas* inaugurated.

The oath or truce carries the creative high spirit of the puer in line with the gravitas of the senex. In Book XXIV, Zeus is senex energy.

Athene goes to him as a faction of Ithaka puts on armor to fight Odysseus. She pleads with her father: "'Tell me when I ask, what plan of yours is concealed here?'" (*Od.* XXIV, l. 474).

To which Zeus replies, first, that she should have thought out for herself how Odysseus would take vengeance on the suitors through war. He then advises: "'Since godly Odysseus has done vengeance on the suitors, /Let them solemnize an oath that he may always reign./And let us bring about oblivion for the murder/Of their sons and kinsmen. Let them love one another/As before, and let there be abundance wealth and peace'" (*Od.* XXIV, ll. 482-86).

She takes her father's words to heart and admonishes the fighting: "'Ithacans, hold off from war, which is disastrous, /So you may separate without bloodshed'" are the powerful goddesses' words. Then, as the fighting has stopped, she addresses Odysseus directly: "'Hold off and cease from the strife of impartial war, /Lest Zeus, the broad-seeing son of Cronos, in some way get angry'" (XXIV, ll. 542-44). Odysseus, war-weary but knowing no other way to end the conflict, "rejoiced in his heart. Then Pallas Athene, daughter of aegis-bearing Zeus, /Established oaths for the future between both sides, /Likening herself to Mentor in form and in voice" (*Od.* XXIV, ll. 546-48).

The creation of the final oath-taking at epic's end weaves all disparate and conflicting parts of the city's soul into a unity of tolerance through trust. Senex-puer energy is woven into the fabric of the conflict to allow the city to flourish within the tension of the oath, whose tensile strength is trust.

We note that language has achieved a high stature in these exchanges: words now have warrior energy in a new form: the oath. The words of an oath structure a new reality that rests on trust; trust is the core of the truce, not the trauma of war. Like a narrative that has been a central piece throughout the journey, an oath is the achievement of "a structured desire" (*Living Myth* 158), according to D. Stephenson Bond, to find and hold energy patterns that complete us in a unique, creatively substantial, and meaningful way. The oath, if held in a healthy tension between two competing energies and beliefs, allows both sides to individuate.

The oath is then an ongoing wish to remain intact and whole so further development is possible. The oath creates a new living myth from the shards of two previous myths violated, bruised, dismembered, dismantled, and bloody. It brings them into some form of *sophrosyne,* a larger cultural version of the union of Odysseus and his beloved Penelope founded on sweet agreement and accord.

The importance of such brilliant insights by Homer for the contemporary global warring is now more evident. Only on this deeper, mythic level can there be a possibility for reconciliation without total annihilation of one side or the other. Now peace can be both measured and sustained.

Works Cited

Bond, D. Stephenson. *Living Myth: Personal Meaning as a Way of Life.* Shambhala, 1993.

Hillman, James. *Senex & Puer. James Hillman Uniform Edition* 3. Edited and introduced by Glen Slater. Spring Publications, 2005.

Homer, *The Odyssey.* Second Edition. Translated and edited by Albert Cook. Norton, 1993.

10

THE AESTHETICS OF THE CITY: MOMENTS OF ARREST*

Books often surprise us by the way they find a way into our literary and personal lives. Henry A. Giroux's The *Violence of Organized Forgetting: Thinking Beyond America's Disimagination Machine* is first disturbing, but also a complement to James Hillman's perspectives on politics and aesthetics. Giroux writes early in the book of the dissolution of democracy as an ideal in American life since the 1970s; he offers this conclusion: "Schools, libraries, the airwaves, public parks and plazas, and other manifestations of the public sphere have been under siege, viewed as disadvantageous to a market-driven society that considers noncommercial imagination, critical thought, dialogue, and civic engagement a threat to its hierarchy of authoritarian operating systems, ideologies and structures of power, domination and control" (32).

Beside Giroux's commentary in several places that imagination lives and that aesthetics, as Hillman understands it, flourishes, or collapses, is the latter's understanding of *aesthesis* as a critical constituent for cultural flourishing: "The word for perception or sensation in Greek was *aesthesis,* which means at root a breathing in or taking in of the world, the gasp, 'aha,' the 'uh' of the breath in wonder, shock, amazement, an aesthetic

---

* Originally delivered to the 3rd Annual James Hillman Symposium at the Dallas Institute of Humanities and Culture, October 16th-18th, 2014, and published in *Conversing with James Hillman: City & Soul* in 2015. Used here by permission of the Dallas Institute of Humanities and Culture Publications.

response to the image (*eidolon*) presented. In ancient Greek physiology and in biblical psychology the heart was the organ of sensation: it was also the place of imagination" ("Anima Mundi: Return of the Soul to the World" 36). Some of his most insightful writings on aesthetics and its necessity for the health of culture are contained in *City & Soul,* from which the above quote is taken.

In 2009, in fourteen provocative and often witty conversations with Sonu Shamdasani in *The Lament of the Dead: Psychology after Jung's Red Book,* Hillman returns to this major staple of his thought and its close relation to poiesis, to the poetics of soul, to the making or shaping of a life mythically inflected and imaginatively slanted. In a current cultural paralysis that speaks only of one's economic state of being, Hillman insists that we must have the courage to stand up for our "aesthetic sense" as an antibody to the "pall of numbing conformity [which] deadens our language, our food, our work-places and city streets" (*City & Soul* 145). When an individual or an entire population suppresses the aesthetic response, "we leave the world to itself and isolate ourselves from its plight" (149).

World rebuilding cannot occur without a major virtue that aesthetics promotes and undergirds: Trust. To lose trust is to deny or reject the aesthetic response; further, we lose trust in the animal sense of things, the way and intensity of instinct in events, people, and objects in the world that attract or repel us. Blunting such a crucial faculty of culture seems a major intention of the engineering in its intensity and relentless striving taking place today to fashion a new myth, one which denies critical and aesthetic responses as well as the ability to discern and to exercise a sense of taste. In such a condition, the souls of individuals and nation atrophy.

Hillman saw this coming well before many of us even noticed it as a green blip on the screen; he wrote his way towards heading it off before the debacle of disposability that laces today's consumer culture dug into the soul's soil. Noticing, seeing clearly, paying attention to the details and particularities of things, objects, ideas, and images, all italicize an aesthetic presence as well as stimulate a form of awareness that weds once more ethics to aesthetics. Separated, as they are today, both fall into oblivion or are maimed into disuse. United they command; divorced they cripple: "I'm suggesting that all our ethical concerns for justice and fairness, for decency, require as well an aesthetic vision, such as images of the biblical and classical ideals of Jerusalem, the city on the hill, Zion, the restoration of the Temple, the image of Athens and its Acropolis, the cities of the Renaissance like Florence and Venice, images of Paradise, of Eden" (*City & Soul* 152).

Moreover, and coupled with aesthetics and ethics. is language itself in both its eloquent and infirm utterings. Words themselves carry soul; it is part of Hillman's frequent mantra: to develop a poetic basis of mind, which is to speak poetically in a language that enjoys and employs health, stamina, and freshets of phrases. One might look then to the health of language in its freedom from clichéd expressions, worn-out locutions, conventional knee-jerk sentences, soundbites, and unconscious use of anemic metaphors to glean the soul illness of a people, a city, and a civilization.

It is one measure to learn to observe; it is quite another to find renewed language, free from group-speak, up-talk, up-chuck, and the dead mutton of exhausted words that comprise another form of the malady of "psychic numbing," a term Hillman borrows from the cultural historian Robert J. Lifton.

In Chapter 15: "Natural Beauty without Nature," he argues against separating beauty from the quotidian order of things: buildings, fence posts, drinking fountains, fish aquariums, graffiti, and pop music. Placing beauty in nature or in a painting misses the point of the aesthetics that underlies it. He therefore unfurls a series of proposals to help with "disentangling the need for beauty from the need for nature". . . so to cease splitting "the natural from the urban" (*City & Soul* 166).

We sense Hillman's deliteralizing impulse when his imagination deconstructs what we have accepted as formal properties of places like "nature" and "wilderness." By contrast, he envisions beauty occupying an ideal wilderness, as one example among many; this way of imagining "can be fostered by the attitude of walking the world without injury to it, leaving no trace, no leftover actions to be dealt with by others, giving priority to the physical thing over the subjective will" (*City & Soul* 170). We sense here an enactment of beauty, a nascent sense of ethics and political action as ecological awareness all at once.

Also, and not least present, is an attitude of humility, of humus, of humane treatment of the particulars to allow their dignity to flourish. I find most fascinating here and elsewhere his process of seeing down, into, and through as a reclamation of not just an earlier economy but an earlier mythic sensibility toward all things. Ecology then assumes the garment of psychological aesthetics.

He soon opens to lamenting the absence of beauty's discussion in therapy: "and the aesthetic plays no role whatsoever in therapeutic practice, in developmental theory, in transference" (*City & Soul* 174), nor in successful or failed therapy or when it terminates. Moving to a wider lens, Hillman's lament orbits further to embrace the world's condition as it is, as well as the chronic lapse in remembering that beauty attends it in many ways no longer noticed, witnessed, or cultivated. Beauty performs benevolent service as the mucilage of the soul that holds the world together in a particularly organized way.

Ignoring or debasing such a quality or attitude under the mistaken idea that it really does not matter, affects the very way we see matter and make certain elements in our personal lives matter, what he will soon call the world's "inherent radiance," which "lights up more translucently, more intensively within certain events" (178).

His claims grow bolder in the section where he thinks mythologically by homing in on Aphrodite's presence in the world; actually, she is more "a sense of the world" as a form of divine enhancement (179). She brings the world into a kosmos, which Hillman translates as "fitting order, appropriate, right arrangement, so that attention to particulars takes precedence over universals" (*City & Soul* 180).

Hillman's brilliance is in his discerning the benefits in one of the most marginal forms of fear in our society—street gangs—resuscitating not just beauty but its relation to an ethic, a code, a form of behaving that while not accepted by a larger public, works very effectively within the backdrop of gang membership and the streets. "Appreciate the display: the hairstyles, tattoos and piercings, the attention to dress, the value of shoes, of jackets, the rapid transit of fashions. Listen to the beat in the language, watch the dance in the walk, the formalities of greetings, the words that indicate an eye for style, elegance, display. Show for its own sake" (*City & Soul,* 198).

Notice here Hillman's own *aesthesis*: Aphrodite in the specific details, a scent of Helen's beauty in particularities, the poetics of the rhythm of his language. The end-stopped fragment—show for its own sake. The last word, standing defiant by itself: "aesthetics." His poetic genius, his mythopoetic couplings, link the mythology of gangs to their revisioning and reviving aesthetics for the entire culture. Their own brand of *poiesis* is mirrored in Hillman's language describing it. Go to the margins to see the clear outline of things; see the clear reflection in what is rejected.

Reflection in remembrance—seeing from a different window, through a different lens, hearing with different ears, being attuned to the beat of hip-hop, indigenous language, identity through style, fashion, creation, flipping a mass-produced Chevy or Nissan Altima into a stylized low-rider painted with a brilliant lacquer that makes the eyes tear up, displaying a gang's cryptic logo—it all glistens under the lamp of genius. And our imaginations are illuminated thereby.

Works Cited

Giroux, Henry A. *The Violence of Organized Forgetting: Thinking Beyond America's Disimagination Machine*. City Light Books, 2014.

Hillman, James. *City & Soul*. Edited by Robert Leaver. *James Hillman Uniform Edition* Vol. 2. Spring Publications, 2006.

Hillman, James and Sonu Shamdasani. *Lament of the Dead: Psychology After Jung's Red Book*. Norton, 2013.

Slattery, Dennis Patrick. "Toward an Aesthetic Psychology: A Review of James Hillman's *City & Soul*." *Spring Journal*. Winter 2008. Vol. 2, No.1. 49-56.

11

MYTHS MATTER: THEIR UNIVERSAL WISDOM CAN GUIDE US[*]

Ever-so-slowly, a presence of mythic consciousness is returning as a valid way of knowing. But there is still much confusion about the nature and definition of the words "myth" and "mythology." Joseph Campbell, the premier mythologist of the last century (1904-1987) gained prominence with the excellent 7-part series, *The Power of Myth,* a series of interviews with Bill Moyers. It remains the best series that Public Television offers periodically during on-air fundraising.

I had the pleasure of teaching the only exclusive course on Joseph Campbell for sixteen years in the Ph.D. program in Mythological Studies at Pacifica Graduate Institute in Carpinteria, California. I loved the experience and continue to use his writings in workshops and talks in the U.S. and Europe. In addition, I continue to read and to reread his thoughts for inspiration and for the creative possibilities they embody.

Campbell found himself on the literary and cultural map when he published *The Hero with a Thousand Faces* in 1949. It is still a bestseller for those who trip across his name and want to explore his thoughts on myths and stories. The Joseph Campbell Foundation is a vibrant and energetic organization that promotes his work with new publications of earlier works as well as blog posts pushing his thoughts further (JCF.org).

---

[*] Originally presented as "The Heroic and Health" to a group of Parkinson clients in a program directed by Robert Cochran of The University of Las Vegas. March 2020.

In 2017, my colleague Evans Lansing Smith and I read 1400 of Campbell's letters as well as responses to many of them; in 2019 we published a co-edited volume in the *Collected Works* category of the Campbell series entitled *Correspondence: 1927-1987.*

You all know how reading someone's letters can offer fresh angles on that person's history. In them a more personal, less public person surfaces and the insights are often greater than from reading their more formal presentations. So it was with this very relational Irishman. His warmth and humor are a tonic to anyone who enters his rich space of metaphor, myth, and history.

Trained as a medieval literature scholar, he transferred his energies to the mythic realm after being captivated by seeing the same stories repeated in ancient, medieval, and modern literature. He noticed, for instance, how James Joyce took Homer's 8th century BCE epic and revisioned it for his audience at the beginning of the 20th century in *Ulysses,* which has just celebrated its 100-year anniversary this year, 2022.

Campbell found immense delight in focusing on the patterns, the mythic templates, and the deeply interconnected themes that undergirded literary creations globally; such a revelation sent him on his own quest to study and become a comparative mythologist. In the process, he learned to write in a manner that was accessible to any intelligent lay reader interested in pursuing their own myth. Campbell's approach seemed to anger academics, who out of envy condemned him as a lightweight. My own inclination is that their envy corroded their evaluation of his meticulous scholarship.

If you become interested in Campbell's thought, start with *The Power of Myth* (1988) as your launching pad. In this conversational volume with Bill Moyers, Campbell is both relaxed and on fire about the value of developing a mythic consciousness. He was harshly critical toward how America has lost the sense of a mythic infrastructure, which, it has been argued, is directly related to the increased violence in our country. He understood how myths assist individuals and even nations to find a balance, a coherence, and a purpose that are necessary for a life of meaning and value. Myths are value-oriented and surround us daily.

In order for myths to be of assistance, we must develop an affiliation with the imaginal world of metaphors, symbols, figurative language, dreams, and the galaxy of archetypal realities that underlie powerful and universal stories. Campbell sought out and unpacked mythic images in both literature and in the outer trappings of architecture, painting, cave drawings, and other sources that expressed imaginal corridors to life in its deeper complexities.

He offered in both the book and video conversations with Moyers the idea that "myths are stories about the wisdom of life . . . but specialization tends to limit the field of problems that the specialist is concerned with" *(Power of Myth* 9). He also linked myths to one's spiritual life when he responded to Moyers' question that linked myth to religion: "What the myths are for is to bring us into a level of consciousness that is spiritual" (14). But, as spirit is incarnated in matter, a mythic consciousness follows the patterns of nature, as many artists, like Cezanne, called for returning to the natural order to discern its rhythms and frames of reference. Campbell supports this insight when he observes: "We have today to learn to get back into accord with the wisdom of nature and realize again our brotherhood [and sisterhood] with the animals and with the water and the sea" (31).

Here I want to include four points that he makes repeatedly in his writings: the four functions of a myth. "The first is the mystical function . . . to see what a wonder the universe is, and what a wonder you are, and experiencing the awe before the mystery" (*Power of Myth* 31). Far more than other avenues to what cannot be explained, "myth opens the world to the dimension of mystery, to the realization of the mystery that underlies all forms. If you lose that you don't have a mythology. You are always addressing the transcendent mystery through the conditions of your actual world" (31).

The second is a cosmological dimension, one in which science shared. But Campbell understood the difference between myth and science. Contrary to the scientific method, he described this second dimension as "the dimension with which science is concerned—showing you what the shape of the universe is but showing it in such a way that the mystery again comes through" (31). One begins to see that a myth is an attitude, a point of view, a way of valuing something. To reveal something in such a way that what is hidden shines through. That is what each of our personal myths can accomplish: a way of seeing as well as a way of understanding leading to a sense of being itself. Myths point the way but from an oblique angle.

The third function Campbell develops "is a sociological one—supporting and validating a certain social order. And here's where the myths vary enormously from place to place. You can have a whole mythology for polygamy, a whole mythology for monogamy. Either one is okay. It depends on where you are" (31).

This third attribute Campbell believes is out of date and in need of renewal. That is, to my mind, what so much of the rampaging tribalism and culture wars are focused on: whose myth, whose narrative, will dominate; such a dualism bypasses the other alternative, that there is room for accommodating both.

But it requires a much more generous form of imagining. Myths are ways of imagining. I would add that myths are ways the world imagines us in our particular cultural settings.

And then to the last one: "But there is a fourth function of myth, and this is the one that I think everyone must try today to relate to—and that is the pedagogical function, of how to live a human lifetime under any circumstances. Myths can teach you that" (*Power of Myth* 31).

In line with Campbell's thought on the nature and function of myth are two other renowned mythologists, David Feinstein and Stanley Krippner. They offer that a "personal myth is a loom on which we weave the raw materials of daily experience into a coherent story" (*The Mythic Path* 20). Sam Keen and Anne Valley-Fox further extend our understanding of myth by suggesting, "A myth may make a cow sacred in one culture and a hamburger patty in another" (*Your Mythic Journey* xi). Same animal objectively, a different animal mythically. Two different inflections of its meaning—sacred for one people, lunch for another.

We notice in the last quote that a myth establishes a context, as well as a content, through the power of metaphor. The metaphors that individuals choose to align with in an act of fidelity will largely determine what reality they adhere to, what reality they refer to, so that what reference points become sacred also establishes reverence points that one turns to for sustenance and direction, if not coherence. Myths, in short, continue to provide meaning to our lives locally and nationally.

An individual or a culture that loses its seminal story also loses its mythic compass, its belief system that acts as an infrastructure to provide guidance in the terrain of uncertainty and even in periods of disintegration. We note the crucial importance of being aware of what myth and under what terms of that myth guide one's life as well as the life of a nation.

I end with a few notes on the power of metaphor that accompanies the power of mythic consciousness, even a mythic attitude. For the myth we adhere to will shape the attitude we carry both deep into ourselves and out to the world. If we are both conscious and conversant with the myth that informs our consciousness, that even affects the level of conscious awareness we achieve after hard work, we can more clearly discern and deal with our shadow material that is often safely underground in our unconscious. A mythic consciousness can tease the shadow unconsciousness into view to be worked on and through. As myths shadow us, our shadows mythologize us.

"What we reject we project" is an axiom of depth and archetypal psychology. What we find abhorrent and repulsive in others may be what we have not faced in ourselves. A deeper mythic consciousness can bring such shadow material to the surface to be worked with. Connie Zweig and Steve Wolf's excellent study, *Romancing the Shadow*, asserts that "the *cultural shadow* is the larger framework in which the personal shadow develops. It helps to determine on a large scale . . . what is permitted and what is taboo, thereby shaping individual and family personae" (52). I would add that the shadow is part of the mythology of every person and nation. It is a potent universal archetype. Let's return to Joseph Campbell's thought on myth with the shadow in mind.

"Metaphor is the native tongue of myth" is one of Campbell's stout statements that underlies much of his mythic understanding. He describes metaphor as stemming from two words: "Meta=to pass over, to go from one place to another, and *phorein*=to move or carry" (*Thou Art That* xvi). Metaphors carry us from one place to another. They carry us beyond rational knowing; they allow for and even encourage us to cross boundaries otherwise impossible to traverse. Furthermore, they challenge us to risk flying out of our familiar nest into arenas of unknowing and uncertainty. Metaphors are like vessels, Campbell suggests, that carry us deeper into reality's depths. As vehicles of trans-portation, they are also states of mind that invite trans-formation.

Metaphors, like myths, rest on connotations, not denotations; this latter category, for Campbell, represents "the hard, factual, unidimensional casings of their historical reference" (*Thou Art That* xvi). Metaphors excite a polyvalent imagination that does not foreclose on one answer or option; rather they choose where there are many sides and meanings possible to understand the same event. The Hero's Journey is itself a metaphor, not necessarily to be taken as literally. It is an imaginal journey, offering us imaginal, not simply literal presences. We can, for example, be swept away into another terrain of experience in reading, watching a film, or listening to a piece of music or a favorite song. And we have not even left our armchair.

When a myth atrophies so that it no longer serves the organic nature of an individual or a culture, it becomes sclerotic, with little movement or tolerance. My sense is that all ideologies are atrophied mythologies that once nourished but now feed off their hosts in a univocal vision of meaning one thing only. Such rigidity encourages a form of tyranny towards one's own beliefs to the exclusion of all others. Within this calcified coffin, all conversation ceases, and assertions, often without anything sustaining them in the shared, lived world we inhabit, become ascendant through force, delusions, deflections, and lies.

Keep uppermost in mind that myths are belief systems in storied form. Ask yourself: what stories do I tell myself daily? What stories do I share with certain others? What stories do I dare not expose? We know that some stories are meant for certain audiences only. And what, I ask myself when I write in my journal at 4:30 in the morning, did I wonder about yesterday? Where did I see beauty, mystery, or experience a moment that arrested me? It is my way of trying to stay conscious when other forces would prefer that I doze off, become distracted, mindlessly consuming. But the spirit remains starved, even anemic. Myths have the ability to wake us up to grandeur, to integrity, and to compassion for others.

To Joseph Campbell I defer for the last word here: "A mythology may be understood as an organization of metaphorical figures connotative of states of mind that are not finally of this or that location or historical period, even though the figures themselves seem on their surface to suggest such a concrete localization" (*Thou Art That* 6-7). Seeking and expressing the metaphor in matter, the metaphors that matter, is not just the task of the artists and philosophers; it is a duty, an obligation assigned to each of us to remain free of the scourge of literalism that inevitably places us back in that frozen antagonism of Us/Them.

Works Cited

Campbell, Joseph. *Thou Art That: Transforming Religious Metaphor*. New World Library, 2001.

---. *The Power of Myth, With Bill Moyers*. Edited by Betty Sue Flowers. Doubleday, 1988.

Feinstein, David, and Stanley Krippner. *The Mythic Path: Discovering the Guiding Stories of Your Past—Creating a Vision for Your Future*. Jeremy Tarcher/Putnam Books, 1997.

Keen, Sam and Anne Valley-Fox. *Your Mythic Journey: Finding Meaning in Your Life Through Writing and Storytelling*. Jeremy Tarcher/Putnam Books, 1989.

Zweig, Connie, and Steve Wolf. *Romancing the Shadow: Illuminating the Dark Side of the Soul*. Ballantine Books, 1997.

12

Epic Migrations: Ishmael's Weaving the World Anew in Herman Melville's *Moby-Dick**

". . . that it seemed as if this were the Loom of Time, and I myself were a shuttle mechanically weaving and weaving away at the Fates."

~Chapter 47, "The Mat-Maker," in Herman Melville's *Moby-Dick,* 228.

By way of prelude: I recall with great pleasure the seventeen years of taking students whale-watching into the Santa Barbara Channel each spring. Many would bring their children, husbands, wives, or friends. In the spring months we were virtually guaranteed sightings of the following whales: Humpbacks, Minke whales, maybe a stray Grey Whale, and if really blessed, one or two Blues. The latter are frequently 80-100 feet in length and weigh a thousand pounds a foot.

Of course, the Condor Express, the whale-watching boat we boarded, would often witness a hundred and sometimes thousands of bottle-nosed dolphins either charge directly toward us or emerge alongside from the stern and ride the pressure waves created by the boat's

* Originally presented to the participants in "The Epic Tradition" at The MacMillan Summer Institute for Teachers in Dallas, Texas, July 28th, 2022.

plunging or simply slicing the water at the bow. They entertained all of us on board year after year.

But without fail, the whale sightings would transform the atmosphere of all of us on board. While we were some two dozen or smaller in number, the boat could accommodate 100 more passengers. People who were total strangers moments before, found themselves talking to one another, pointing out sightings that the captain may have missed, and sharing what they knew about whales and dolphins. The docents on board were helpful in filling in the blanks to all our questions.

The whales' presence created a social atmosphere of awe among us. The change was almost instant; it extended out to include everyone; many witnessed their first whales. The captain would offer a running commentary on whale life, behaviors, and markings while distinguishing those who were residents of the channel from those who were passing through, pausing to fatten up by devouring the plentiful krill that smeared the waters between the mainland and the several Channel Islands some twenty-three miles from shore.

The whole experience was magical in the way that nature and our human nature coalesced around graceful creatures of the deep. Humpbacks in particular, being the most social of the whale populations, would put on shows to amaze us all. In one instance, a Humpback came up to the bow and began bumping it repeatedly to get our attention. In another, two Humpbacks took turns breaching just yards from the ship and made magnificent water displays. In their presence, the whales wove us together into a temporary but no less grateful community. Such is their draw; such is their texture.

The whales touched something deep within all of us, something that may not have been stirred in just this way before. A deep connection to the natural order was fixed in passengers' own fixations with the sea mammals, sometimes blowing their smelly breaths within yards of the Condor Express. I think the word "awe" is an appropriate way to speak of this charged and delighted bonding of humans and whales; for a moment, no space existed between us.

And yet something more: the whales breached in so many of us a sense of wonder, a connection with Nature that only whales could excite in the imagination. But beware, whalers, of being downwind of their nasty exhalations. I have watched passengers suddenly vomit in response to sniffing the wind of a whale's blowhole within feet of the boat.

I use this illustration to enter Chapters 46-90 of Melville's master-piece, where Ishmael, the poet-whaler, uses the stubbed harpoon of his writing quill to scratch the white surface of his pages in creating the won-der world that is Melville's epic quest; it is also a spiritual quest—to try to paint the whale while it appears only partially but always falling short of the mark.

As narrator, Ishmael is also in the tradition of alchemists seeking the elixir of gold from the grail of life's meaning. These chapters reveal how he sees in matter the movement of spirit; that the subject matter of *Moby-Dick* is the imagination's capacity to remythologize worlds, and how spirit animates matter. Yes, he went to sea to see more deeply into the connec-tive tissue of the cosmos, what epic poetry seeks in varying degrees. Per-haps then, epics offer us inroads as the most abundant seekers, as seers of the invisible realms not accessed through reason alone. Ishmael grasps what the ancient philosopher Heraclitus understood: what is above is also below, and what is without is also within.

One of Ishmael's signal contributions as whaler/writer is that he de-velops an alchemical poetics by pushing language's capacity to express metaphysical realities inherent in matter. Whaling became his "transport vehicle," his energy field, to allow it to happen. His opus is the open seas, where depth contains treasures to imagine anew, including the Bible as well as other texts that Ishmael rejuvenates into new contexts. One of his many tasks as a mythopoet is to remythologize old texts through a careful weaving of history with the contemporary world.

His visionary, epic intelligence offers up the image of a new Moses, a leader of nations, ushering us readers across the wilderness of whale massacres towards the inklings of a new myth, one in which the demo-cratic spirit is reanimated and the natural order, including the beleaguered earth herself, is given a rearranged new order within the spiritual dimen-sions of organic life. Stewarding the earth and its inhabitants is a major impulse driving Ishmael's vision, a steward of language's mystery and power.

As a poet/pilgrim he behaves as a weaver god. His cultural weaving follows the patterns of how nature works. Within the seas of analogies he constructs is an underlying intuition that a new myth is needed if an order of stewardship and communal trust is to birth, develop, and transform the attitude of humanity into stewards of the earth, not its destroyer. That myth has as a central element of its infrastructure one of doubling, of duplication, of mirroring the external world's matter with the interior life of the soul. His story witnesses a new *mythodology,* a new way of myth-making, with the waters of the Bible comprising the essential seas for the Pequod to sail across.

Within Ishmael's epic vision, everything in the world is animated, everything carries its own life form. His quest as epic poet is to dive deep enough in order to see the animated, interdependent qualities of all that exists in a rich fabric of circumstances. His myth rests on the creative act of doubling, of exposing the doubleness of life by identifying how the physical world doubles itself in mind, in imagination, then drawing these correspondences out through poetic animation. That is his central task, it seems to me. We as readers, whom Ishmael addresses frequently, are invited to bring our own imaginations to bear on the voyage. We are active participants in the drama. The epic needs and desires our doubling presence in order to expand its mysterious meanings.

Ishmael taps into his enterprise in Chapter 55, "Of the Monstrous Pictures of Whales." He establishes his intention: "I shall ere long paint to you as well as one can without canvas, something like the true form of the whale as he actually appears to the eye of the whalemen when in his own absolute body, the whale is moored alongside the whaleship so that he can be fairly stepped on there" (279/205),[†] even as he plans to debunk all previous illustrations of the whale as inadequate. "The living whale, in his full majesty and significance, is only to be seen at sea in unfathomable waters; and afloat the vast bulk of him is out of sight. . ." (282/208).

His field of vision is also epic in magnitude, as he reveals in Chapter 57, "Of Whales in Paint." There he fantasies, "Nor when expandingly lifted by your subject, can you fail to trace out great whales in the starry heavens, and boats in pursuit of them, as when long filled with thoughts of war the Eastern nations saw armies locked in battle among the clouds.

[†] The first number in all the quotes of the novel is from the Easton Edition, the second from the Norton 3rd Edition.

. ... With a frigate's anchors for my bridle-bits and fasces of harpoons for spurs, would I could mount that whale and leap the topmost skies, to see whether the fabled heavens, with all their countless tents, really lie encamped beyond my mortal sight!" (291/213). Such an expansive vision seems reserved for the epic poet's destiny.

Always either seeking the visible order behind the phenomenal world, or animating the world's matter in its particularity, Ishmael's epic vision is ample enough to include all. Now let's for a moment twist his *mythodology* smaller, as when he offers us reveries on two kinds of whale lines, the Manilla rope and the more inferior hemp, both of which enjoy cameo appearances as characters in this cast of hundreds in the epic. In Chapter 60, "The Line," he muses: "Of late years the Manilla rope has in the American fishery almost entirely superseded hemp as a material for whale lines . . . (and I will add that there is an aesthetics in all things), is much more handsome and becoming to the boat, than hemp. Hemp is a dusky dark fellow, a sort of Indian; but Manilla is a golden-haired Circassian to behold" (298/217).

The Circassian reference is to the people who lived in the northwestern region of the Caucasus, which saw heavy trading by the ancient Greeks along its coast. By 1875, under Peter the Great, it had become a Russian province (www.britannica.com). Historical referencing and mythmaking are two sides of an alternative way of seeing. As a mythmaker and shaper, Ishmael is rarely far from mythopoetically divining the world in its particulars as part of his epic-shaping vision. In fact, references to "eyes," and to seeing, are rarely absent from any page of his plot to "sea" anew.

I should also mention that in "Loomings," the reference to the myth of Narcissus and Echo offers a clue to reading his tale. I sense it is the myth through which we read the entirety of *Moby-Dick*, through the "isinglass" of this myth of reflection and fixation; when Narcissus, having jettisoned Echo, approaches the virginal waters of a clear, pure lake, he gazes down into its depths and sees below a figure he does not recognize; on further reflection he becomes aware that the figure in the water is none other than himself. Ovid describes this moment powerfully: "He is the seeker and/the sought, the longed-for and the one who longs;/he is the arsonist—and is the scorched" (*The Metamorphosis* Book III, 94).

In Chapter 61, "Stubb Kills a Whale," Ishmael has been standing at the foremost head where he finds himself as one who "idly swayed in what seemed an enchanted air; . . . in that dreamy mood losing all consciousness, at last my soul went out of my body; though my body still continued to sway as a pendulum will, long after the power which first moved it is withdrawn. . .. The waves, too, nodded their indolent crests; and across the wide trance of the sea, east nodded to west, and the sun over all" (302/220). These moments of oneness, of a unity enshrouded in enchantment, occur to Ishmael often on his pilgrimage as moments in which dream and reality coalesce into a single vision.

He is soon awakened, however, by the reality of a whale's presence: "Suddenly bubbles seemed bursting beneath my closed eyes; like vices my hands grasped the shrouds; some invisible, gracious agency preserved me; with a shock I came back to life" (302/220). He becomes aware of the presence of a large Sperm Whale "lolling in the water like a capsized hull of a frigate; his broad, glossy back, of an Ethiopian hue, glistening in the sun's rays like a mirror. . .. The whale looked like a portly burgher smoking his pipe of a warm afternoon. But that pipe, poor whale, was thy last" (303/220). Along with the gracious writing, we note the mirror image, the reflective doubling of one world by means of another, the Narcissistic quality of creation.

Part of Ishmael's epic imagination is top-heavy with likes, as-s, as-ifs, mirrorings, correspondences, and similarities. "What is the whale?" competes with "what does a whale looks like?" reminding us perhaps of the Neoplatonist philosopher and mystic Plotinus' assertion in his *Enneads* that "all learning takes place by likeness" (*Enneads* I, 8, 1). I believe it is a form of seeing double, of seeing one reality set up against the other in a mythic overlay. It sees by force of the analogical imagination, a centerpiece of consciousness itself.

Jungian scholar D. Stephenson Bond asserts that "the function of a myth is to express the outer and inner balance which the psyche continually adjusts even as myth provides the context of our own development" (*Living Myth* 57). Such is the organic living part of Ishmael's epic pilgrimage into the precincts of the world of symbolic correspondences.

In Chapter 68, "The Blanket," Ishmael offers a meditation in reading the whale books he owns through the isinglass, a substance by which "from the unmarred dead body of the whale, you may scrape off with your hand an infinitely thin, transparent substance, somewhat resembling the thinnest shreds of isinglass" (326/234). He uses the dried bits to mark where in his reading of whales he has left off. But they can also be used in their transparency when laid across the printed page: "I have sometimes pleased myself with fancying it exerted a magnifying influence. At any rate, it is pleasant to read about whales through their own spectacles, as you may say" (326/234-35).

Such a doubling stratagem allows the whale at least to be understood skin-deep. The whale here is doubled, as part object to be seen as well as a way of seeing; it offers a new medium of perception. In short, the whale is a mythic image, a content and context that is both the organizing principle of whale hunting as well as its victim.

His pilgrimage to grasp this phantom that is the whale in its blubbery presence as well as its essence continues by getting to the skin, or "the skin of the skin" (326/235), then diving below or beneath it. Our blanket is our sleep skin. To see the words on whales in his whaling texts through the spectacles of the whales' membrane allows Ishmael to imagine Leviathan anew. For the whale becomes a way of seeing through its own transparency. It sees through its own seeing, creating a greater level of complexity in duplication. Whaling indeed duplicates a double business bound in the fluid of water and wounds.

Both reading and writing are part of Ishmael's vision of a new form of epic. In Chapter 63, "The Crotch," he ventures another observation on the doubling of nature to the double nature of writing itself: "Out of the trunk, the branches grow; out of them, the twigs. So, in productive subjects, grow the chapters" (310/224). Thus does the epic grow in Ishmael's own likeness, embellished to be sure by many traditions of writers before him. But as weaver/writer, Ishmael threads the pieces into a new tapestry.

In addition, he reveals another redundancy in whaling by having two harpoons ready in the crotch to hurl in quick succession at the hunted prey. A connection emerges between the lines of his narrative, the lines attached to the harpoons, and the lines of "intimate passages" yet to be finally painted. The narrative, then, is double-lined to convey a second reality below the water line. I believe this is another element or even strategy of mythic consciousness.

I am reminded of literary and cultural critic Louise Cowan's insight that I have been following above, namely, "This establishment of an arena in which the divine and human can come together to work at the task of history, is, as we have indicated, the veritable creation of the epos, the epic word, providing a model for the moral universe within which human beings carry on their lives. . ... They have been allowed to see the physical order as permeated by the spiritual; in a sense, everything is sacred" (*The Epic Cosmos* 12). The world is a permutation of the human imagination in dialogue with the entire created order, through which we as readers catch glimpses of our own doubled nature, divine and human, its nexus, the world soul, *the anima mundi.*

In Chapter 58, "Brit," Ishmael invites us to "consider the subtleness of the sea; how its most dreaded creatures glide under water, unapparent for the most part, and treacherously hidden beneath the loveliest tints of azure. . ... Consider once more, the universal cannibalism of the sea, all whose creatures prey upon each other, carrying on eternal warfare since the world began" (294/215). His orbit of vision continues to expand and deepen to include the sea as its own galaxy, deep beneath the surface teeming with mysterious life forms waging their own eternal wars of eating and being eaten.

Life feeds on life in an endless cycle of birth and death. That is an element of the eternal round that epic intelligence discerns below the surface of the visible world. The pattern is both impersonal and persistent. To go to see on a whaling ship is the corridor of admission to these depths.

He continues to develop this insight in the same chapter by spiraling back to the human heart's knowledge it seeks, perhaps at times unknowingly. When he asks us to consider both the "green gentle and most docile earth" (294/215) in comparison to the sea, "do you not find a strange analogy to something in yourself? For as this appalling ocean surrounds the verdant land, so in the soul of man there lies one insular Tahiti, full of peace and joy, but encompassed by all the horrors of the half-known life. God keep thee! Push not off from that isle, thou canst never return!"

(294/215). His power as a seer and writer is that he can see double—the phenomenal world laced with its own ontology, its own manner of being.

That "insular Tahiti" is a *temenos*, a sacred space, that feeds the soul when it is inhabited; it feeds the hunger for peace and joy but does not shirk from eyeing the surrounding horrors of life as well. I venture that the epic we are reading is a similar *temenos* of the imagination. Described as a temple enclosure of ancient Greece, *temenos* space is a sacred precinct, not unlike the four genres of poetry, each containing its own sacred enclosure, yet it remains a porous vessel, as well as a unique poetic intelligence.

Chapter 64, "Stubb's Supper," offers a comic interlude, when the second mate asks the old black cook, Fleece, to prepare him a whale steak by running a match underneath it, which reflects Stubb's desire for a rare slice of blubber. He further coaxes the old cook to preach to the sharks that create such a riot of feeding frenzy; Stubb insists that Fleece preach moderation to them. But Fleece must seek out the right language, the persuasive rhetoric, the careful word choice, to domesticate their appetites: "'You is sharks, sartin; but if you govern de shark in you, why den you be angel; for all angel is not'ing more dan de shark well governed. . .. Don't be tearin' de blubber out your neighbor's mout, I say'" (314-15/228).

Again, we are invited back to language's central role in the epic enterprise; language itself is one of the central characters of the epic. Our own alphabet has twenty-six characters. The language must fit and elevate the occasion by praising those in need of transformation so they can aspire to a higher calling, even if it is the call to consume. Epics carry within themselves ideals to aspire to; Fleece's sermon to the appetites of nature rests in the belief that self-transformation is possible within nature as within human nature's rapacious appetites for slaying and barreling whales.

The process changes their substance from nature's bounty to culture's commodity. Epic's language has the capacity to raise the natural order to extraordinary heights so it can expose and reverence the ideal inherent in the real. The spiritual and mythic dimensions are elevated as images to aspire to as they eye one another in a complex harmony.

Ishmael's own interior journey discovers analogies in each chapter, as Chapter 69, "The Funeral," illustrates. As the "peeled white body of the beheaded whale flashes like a marble sepulcher . . . it is still colossal. Slowly it floats more and more away, the water round it torn and splashed by the insatiate sharks, and the air above vexed with rapacious flights of screaming fowls" peck at the body. . . . the great mass of death floats on and on, till lost in infinite perspectives" (329/236). Ishmael sees in its "desecrated" body the presence of a vengeful ghost that will haunt this sliver of ocean and remain an invisible presence for years to come. He is quick to chastise outmoded beliefs and traditions that have outlived their organic power yet remain in place like phantom obstacles one must jump across.

Here, as Louise Cowan observes in "Epic as Cosmopoiesis," an old myth is dying off, making room for one that is more vital and consequential to the present. Ishmael employs an accusatory, even mocking tone: "There's your law of precedents; there's your utility of traditions; there's the story of your obstinate survival of old beliefs never bottomed on the earth, and now not hovering in the air! There's orthodoxy. . . . Are you a believer in ghosts, my friend?" (329-30).

These ghosts of the past include an outmoded mythic cosmos that needs the reset button of history to ground it back in the world. Ishmael is not only a mythmaker; he is also a myth-destroyer when he senses that prevailing beliefs have hardened and calcified into a fixed orthodoxy that muffles any deeper understanding it was at one time charged to illuminate.

In "The Sphinx," Chapter 70, Ishmael expands his repertoire to include the tincture of Eastern philosophy in his description of the ship's atmosphere after a sperm whale has been beheaded and butchered: "Silence reigned over the before tumultuous but now deserted deck . . . an intense copper calm, like a universal yellow lotus, was more and more unfolding its noiseless measureless leaves upon the sea" (331-32/237).

We learn from Daniel Herman in his book *Zen and the White Whale: A Buddhist Rendering of Moby-Dick* that Melville was "a voracious reader on esoteric topics, including religion, mythology, history and archaeology, among others." Herman refers to Melville as "a man of outlandish allusions" and that *Moby-Dick* is Melville's "most complete accurate portrayal of Buddhist teachings" (13). These continued references to traditions outside the Western imagination add a texture to the epic and expand its orbit into realms that have their own relations to what is securely established in Western consciousness.

We learn shortly that into this serene calm Ahab appears to prod the head "with Stubbs's long spade" and demand it speak to him. "'Speak mighty head and tell us the secret thing that is in thee. Of all divers, thou has dived the deepest'" (332/238). The scene is reminiscent of a supplicant approaching the figure of the Sybil in hopes of gaining a wisdom from depths unknown and unfathomed. Ahab seeks oracular knowledge; his hunger is for a depth of understanding that he may not be prepared to receive, much less yield to.

Like the wounded king of medieval epics, Ahab seeks any form of healing when he allows himself to seek a cure. And yet, this approach, grounded in the controlling impulses of ego rather than in the openness of self, ensures that he will not grasp what is ungraspable; only later in the Grand Armada chapter will three chosen whalers enter the liminal precinct to gain a knowledge of the forms that underlie and shape the physical world.

Partly in frustration, partly in a moment of illumination, Ahab's language reflects a depth of understanding central to the epic ordeal of seeing through one myth by means of another or entering a reverie of clarity: "'Where unrecorded names and navies rust, and untold hopes and anchors rot; where in her murderous hold this frigate earth is ballasted with bones of millions of the drowned . . . O head! Thou hast seen enough to split the planets and make an infidel of Abraham, and not one syllable is thine'" (332/238).

This insight is what Louise Cowan points to in quoting mythologist Mircea Eliade, who refers to "the terror of history" ("Cosmopoesis" 4), "the forgotten and never known, the unspoken and laid to an uneasy rest in her murderous hold, this frigate earth" (332/238).

Such a dramatic monologue in the depth-inflected, inflicted captain is interrupted by the sighting of a whale, which pulls Ahab towards uttering one of the hallmarks of epic poetry: "'Would now St. Paul would come along that way, and to my breezelessness bring his breeze! O Nature, and O soul of man! How far beyond all utterance are your linked analogies; not the smallest atom stirs or lives on matter, but has its cunning duplicate in mind'" (333/239). Can we think of this revelation as a step towards healing the wounded Fisher King, an impulse he will deny as the Pequod looms closer to the white whale?

Ahab brushes here on an epic paradigm that is also at the heart of mythic consciousness, even, in Cowan's words, "a web wherein insights are captured, a matrix where intuition can dwell from it" ("Cosmopoesis" 10). In addition, if we follow Ralph Waldo Emerson's thinking in his essay "Nature," we read under the heading "Language" that every natural fact is a symbol of some spiritual fact. "Every appearance in nature corresponds to some state of the mind and that state of the mind can only be described by presenting that nature appear as its picture" ("Nature" 32). Was Melville reading Emerson at this stage of creating his epic?

Emerson's reveries on the natural world lead him far and deep into the nature of the entire cosmos. In nature, he suggests, "Things are so strictly related that according to the skill of the eye, from any one object the parts and properties of any other may be predicted" (220). As we remember Ahab's vision above, we follow Emerson a bit further: "The craft with which the world is made runs also into the mind and character of men" (222); and if we keep the epic poet's project in the bow of our mind, we can see further into Emerson's insight that "the poet, the prophet, has a higher value for what he utters than any hearer and therefore it gets spoken" ("Nature" 222).

Emerson finishes his contemplative journey by suggesting, "Nature is the incarnation of a thought, and turns to a thought again, as ice becomes water and gas. The world is mind precipitated. . ... Hence the virtue and pungency of the influence on the mind of natural objects, whether inorganic or organized" (226).

In Chapter 82, "The Honor and Glory of Whaling," Ishmael journeys to the wellsprings of the hunt, the quest, to see its great honorableness and its ancient beginnings: "The more I dive into this matter of whaling . . . the more I find so many great demi-gods and heroes, prophets of all sorts, who one way or other have shed distinction upon it, the more I am transported with the reflection that I myself belong, though but subordinately, to so emblazoned a fraternity. The gallant Perseus, a son of Jupiter, was the first whaleman" (388/272).

His vision here is myth-historical, wherein he places himself at home in such a gathering of gods and mortals and joins the community of epic outliers who see often from the margins what is missed at the center of cultures. Throughout, Ishmael's marginal position raises being marginalized to a position of seeing that may not be available to those more centered in their outlook.

Louise Cowan is helpful here when she writes that when we think of the original divinities of the Greek Pantheon, "we tend to think those ancestral parents safely done away with and forgotten. Might they now, however, in the aggregate of time, still be present to us analogically?" ("Cosmopoesis" 18).

Perhaps then, history itself is redeemed through the power of analogies to weave our present world with that earlier history of antiquity so that we discern with a double vision, as myths tend to articulate. Ishmael's imagination can peer into the matter of history and to the history of matter. There he sees its interior nobility, which elevates meanings to other degrees for further contemplation. "Perseus, St. George, Hercules, Jonah, and Vishnoo! There's a member roll for you! What club but the whaleman's can head off like that?" (389-90/274).

Joining such an elite core, Ismael heals the wounds of his orphaned soul by finding his place in the order of things. By implication, he invites us to find our own order, our own mythic presence in our participatory reading, which links us in community with the millions of who traversed the waters of *Moby-Dick* before us.

As he continues his struggle to achieve some grand measure of his own vision as epic poet, Ishmael runs close to despair in his ability to articulate it with the level of detail he yearns for. In Chapter 86, "The Tail," he plays with the tale he is shaping, sculpting, and painting through language. In the image he creates to describe the whale's fluke—that place on its body that offers a unique design of its uniqueness—a flukeprint of sorts—he returns to the archetypal image of weaving: "The whole bulk of the leviathan is knit over with a warp and woof of muscular fibers and filaments, which passing on either side the loins and running down into the flukes, insensibly blend with them, and largely contribute to their might . . ." (402-03/281).

Here he doubles his tale with the whale's tail, the source of its propulsion and guidance and the body's source for leaving a footprint, or sleek on the surface of the water, the trace of the whale that has already disappeared. I wish we could linger and play with this rich image further. I would only add that "fibrous fictions" comprise our own tales, full of sinewy intricacy, overlaps and filaments woven by a controlling myth's presence. Each thread of these tales wraps around our entire lives from first thread to last yarn. All members of our narrative, I have written elsewhere, "congeal through an overarching plot that encourages our personal myth to breach into view" (*Our Daily Breach* 231).

Our last station is one of the most mystical and spiritual, if not mythic moments in the entire epic: Chapter 87, "The Grand Armada." For a brief instant, we join Ishmael, Queequeg, and Starbuck in their whale boat that is ushered graciously into the circle shaped by whales, with two of them serving as threshold guardians, selecting those who are worthy to enter this aquatic mandala and excluding all others.

The action is occasioned by violence. The three men advance into the herd of whales with their harpoons, but the tightness of the crowding and panicked whales make it impossible to dart any of them: ". . . as we went still further and further from the circumference of commotion, the direful disorders seemed waning. So that . . . we glided between two whales into the innermost heart of the shoal, as if from some mountain torrent we had slid into a serene valley lake. . .. In this central expanse the sea presented that smooth satin-like surface, called a sleek, produced by the subtle moisture thrown off by the whale in his more quiet moods." From chaos to a sublime and almost silent order, Ishmael observes that, "Yes, we were now in that enchanted calm which they say lurks at the heart of every commotion" (414/289).

In such a rich liminal space, a sanctuary in the middle of surrounding chaos and fear aroused by one whale with a mincing spade wrapped around its fluke and wounding so many whales within its range, the three whalemen are offered a vision that rests at the origin of all life. As the young whale cubs approach the edge of their boat, "like household dogs they came snuffing round us, right up to our gunwales, and touching them. . .[as] Queequeg patted their foreheads; Starbuck scratched their backs with his lance, an instrument fashioned for killing that has been transformed as an appendage of affection" (415/289).

Their vision is arresting in exposing two worlds inhabiting one another: "But far beneath this wondrous world upon the surface, another and still stranger would met our eyes as we gazed over the side. For, suspended in those watery vaults, floated the forms of the nursing mothers of the whales. The lake . . . was exceedingly transparent and as human infants while suckling will calmly and fixedly gaze away from the breast, as if leading two different lives at the time; and while yet drawing mortal nourishment, be still spiritually feasting upon some unearthly reminiscence; —even so did the young of these whales seem looking up towards us, but not at us, as if we were but a bit of Gulfweed in their new-born sight" (415/289).

In such a cloister of tranquility and clear vision, "these inscrutable creatures at the centre freely and fearlessly indulge in all peaceful concernments; yes, serenely revealed in dalliance and delight" (416/290). As if infected and inflected by such a dream-like image, the whale appears not as a commodity to be butchered but as a source of mythopoetic knowing where the warp and woof of human beings is woven into the fabric of nature's bounty and largesse.

Ishmael, inspired by the shared nature of this whale wonderment, dreams an analogy to life that all of us can relate to: "But even so, amid the tornadoed Atlantic of my being, do I myself still for ever centrally disport in mute calm; and while ponderous planets of unwaning woe revolve around me, deep down and deep inland I will bathe me in eternal mildness of joy" (416/290).

The scene repeats or doubles the Narcissus myth, in which he gazes into the pond where he has knelt on its shore to refresh himself; there he sees the strange figure looming up at him, that, on reflection, he realizes is a mirror image of himself. The myth is furthered here as the three men gaze into the transparent waters of life itself and find their own natures reflected at them, not in antagonism but in mutual affection. It is also a moment, as Louise Cowan observes, "of a conjunction of masculine and feminine energies sharing a moment that resides deep in their mutual natures" ("Cosmopoesis" 21-22).

I hope that glancing for a few moments at these various scenes is of value to you in contemplating the mystery and wonder of the epic imagination in this, perhaps the riches precinct of the four genres.

Works Cited

Bond, D. Stephenson. *Living Myth: Personal Meaning as a Way of Life.* Shambhala, 1993.

Cowan, Louise. "Introduction: Epic as Cosmopoiesis" *The Epic Cosmos*, edited by Larry Allums. The Dallas Institute Publications, 2000. 1-26.

Emerson, Ralph Waldo. *The Essays of Ralph Waldo Emerson. The First Series and the Second Series.* The Heritage Press, 1934.

Herman, Daniel. *Zen and the White Whale: A Buddhist Rendering of Moby-Dick.* Lehigh UP, 2014.

Melville, Herman. *Moby-Dick, or, The Whale.* The Easton Press, 1977.

Ovid, *The Metamorphosis.* Translated by Allen Mandelbaum. Harcourt, Brace and Company, 1993.

Parker, Herschel, editor. *Moby-Dick. An Authoritative Text. Third Edition.* Norton, 2017.

Plotinus, *The Enneads.* Edited by Lloyd P. Gerson, and translated by George Boys-Stones, John M. Dillon and Lloyd P. Gerson, et al. Cambridge UP, 2018.

Slattery, Dennis Patrick. *Our Daily Breach: Exploring Your Personal Myth Through Herman Melville's Moby-Dick.* Fisher King Press, 2015.

13

LETTING GO OF MATTER TO DISCOVER WHAT MATTERS*

Poets have for millennia served as some of our richest in-depth psychologists. They seem to understand deep in their bones the archetypal realities that propel and guide every one of our life stories. We can, by reading their words in an attitude of deep reflection and meditation, discover lasting insights through analogies that touch most poignantly our personal and collective myths. Out of this rich collaboration arises a deepened and unique form of knowing through the poetic imagination.

In his own life, Leo Tolstoy (1828-1910), one of the greatest 19th century Russian writers, was gripped by a sustained terror of death. His decision to lean into this fear rather than run from it, and to explore it deeply, may be the most cogent reason for his creating the character of a rising, successful Russian Magistrate, based on a historical judge named Ivan Ilych Mechnikov. Ronald Blythe writes in the Introduction to Tolstoy's masterpiece of only 112 pages: "He [Tolstoy] proves how, when it is almost eaten up by disease and frightful to contemplate, and when pain is searching out the breaking point of the intellect, another factor, call it the soul or spirit or the true self, emerges" (*The Death of Ivan Ilyich* 2).

A rich irony undergirds and supports Tolstoy's masterpiece: the life of a man who with great judicial detachment and objectivity for

---

* Originally presented to the annual conference, Jung in Ireland. "Facing Mortality: Fear of the Unknown," April 13th, 2019 in Enniskillen, County Fermanagh, April 8th-13th. Directed by Aryeh Maidenbaum and Diana Ruben.

sentencing, and even condemning others to death, remains completely unconscious of his own sentence. The novella brings to the fore so many of the themes this conference was designed to address. Ivan Ilych's trajectory puts us directly in touch with C.G. Jung's observation that "the gods have become diseases; Zeus no longer rules Olympus but rather the solar plexus and produces curious specimens for the doctor's consulting room" (*CW* 13, para. 54).

One of the story's most powerful images is that of the curtain, the covering, the drapery, the fabric, the surface appearance of life that hides the often distasteful and uncertain reality beneath it. Yet there exist moments where one is forced to spiral down and into the greatest anxiety felt towards death itself, and perhaps more terrifying, one's own unique format for dying. Death itself is another universal form in which the gods appear, as Jung's observation above attests to.

Before his wounding, one that seems so insignificant at first but then blossoms into his illness, Ivan Ilych has enjoyed a life of many successes; he is promoted up the ranks of the Justice Department until he reaches a very prestigious position as court judge hearing cases, deliberating, weighing the evidence and then often passing a death sentence of years of hard labor in the most atrocious conditions, to the many criminals who appear before him. His life is filled with death, but he remains untouched and unscathed by it because his position is his curtain, even his suit of armor, between what sentences he doles out and what the real consequences of them are, which he has heretofore escaped.

His successful insulation from unpleasantness keeps what he does as a Magistrate abstract, disembodied, and safe. He never sees or hears about their embodied sufferings. He never sees any of them loaded onto trains and shipped to Siberia to carry out sentences that will, often, torture them to death.

Ivan Ilych's vocabulary mirrors what is most important in his hierarchy of values: order, arrangement, systematic, agreeable, decorous, pleasant, correct. These words comprise the verbal calculus through which Ivan Ilych adjudicates his own life. Yet, the narrator continually cuts through these conventions in a very understated tone that ramps up the terror hidden in the folds of Ilych's formal life: His life "had been most simple and commonplace—and the most horrifying" (43), Tolstoy writes.

Certainly, a harsh judgment is leveled at him in part because his thoughts and actions have always been inflected towards the world's commodities, including promotions and acquisitions, with little attention paid to the interior life of spirit and the summons of his soul. He has been, in C.G. Jung's words, guided by "the spirit of the times" while "the spirit of the depths" (*Red Book* 119) remained muted. But to be fair, accumulation itself does not lead to alienation from oneself. Something else is afoot here that we must understand: how his minor wounding occurred when he slipped off a ladder while hanging custom curtains in his new, larger home as a result of a major promotion. His new life becomes the originating condition for his dying.

And even further, how such an affliction of his being can be considered a gift, in fact, a most prized possession, because it allows in the last hours of a painfully awakened life, perhaps the single most fully lived moments that he ever experienced. Disease can be a royal, if painful road, to self-discovery. Dis-ease—to be ill-at-ease—out of sorts, where something new can enter, is to be valued.

The act of being wounded, afflicted, dismembered, and set into disease often initiates an archetypal pilgrimage back to one's origins, to the beginning of being, as Ivan Ilych's illness will return him memorially to recapture his innocence as an elementary school student, a time when he recalls through the aperture of his dis-ease, was the happiest period of his life (*Death of Ivan Ilych and Other Stories* 105).

The wound as illness offers what the Greek tragedians, as Francis Ferguson reveals in his Introduction called a "peripety," a turning about, or reversal, and an *anagnorisis,* which is an instance of recognition of one's true identity and character, hidden until this moment of revelation, when one is spun around and sees one's history with new eyes, the eyes of soul itself, through the imaginal gaze of reflection ("Introduction" to Aristotle's *Poetics* 16-17).

Tolstoy's structure of the novella reveals something essential about Ivan Ilych's life and death. The plot begins with *the words* of his death, which his former law colleague, Peter Ivanovich, reads from the obituary column of the daily newspaper to a group of fellow clerks during "an interval in the Melvinski trial: 'Gentlemen, Ivan Ilych has died.'" The story ends with *the action* of his death: "He drew in a breath, in the midst of a sigh, stretched out, and died" (*The Death of Ivan Ilych* 156). From the story's structure we grasp the fact that Ivan Ilych has lived his life backwards.

We learn that he lived through his childhood "without [its] leaving much trace on him" (*The Death of Ivan Ilych* 105), but through the lens of his illness, through its focal length, so to speak, his childhood's ending marked the psychic death knell of any trace of happiness henceforth. As his disease progresses, it unfastens the straps of his imagination, allowing him to envision not just the world of officialdom, which was becoming increasingly dissatisfying, but that of childhood, when the number of divisions and curtains in his life were minimal and when his joy was greatest. Think of a life curtained off again and again as a series of insulations from life's full face and force; it will reveal an individual enwombed in his limitations.

As the demands of professional power and prestige over others increase in the years leading up to his affliction, Ilych's life becomes more fragmented and functional, more concerned with the outer trappings of things and less with any rustlings of interior inklings about his own identity. A curtain is neatly and efficiently drawn between soul and world; this division locates itself within his body. In this condition lies the terribleness of his existence. All his moves are formulaic, all according to a well-constructed template: to move as society dictates with as few interruptions as possible and with as many pleasantries as can be mustered.

To avoid "inconveniences" and to "secure his own independence" are the guiding values of his reason for being, all the while maintaining the illusion of decorous and agreeable behavior as he enlarges his professional power and cordons it off from his family troubles. I don't think we can have it both ways. He neatly and cleverly draws a screen between his home life with his wife, Praskovya Fyodorovna, daughter Liza, and young son Vasya, and his professional world. When unpleasantness at home, which appeared earlier in the form of his new wife's inconvenient pregnancy with their first child collapsed into arguments and strife that ruptured decorum, he drew with great efficiency a blind between domestic troubles and his social life of playing bridge and behaving, as Tolstoy enjoins, "agreeably."

In such a manner, Ilych can exert the illusion of control on his world through the attitudes of technical functioning and efficiency, qualities that cohere his rigid, if not outrightly arthritic mythology. In the process his soul atrophies for want of nourishment.

Depth psychotherapist Robert Romanyshyn suggests that the "mind that is addicted to the literal," which has no room in the imagination for the ambiguous in its striving for purity (100) develops a "habit of mind" that recoils from uncertainty and its attendant fears of the unknown; such is in fact "a self without a shadow, a self, then, which is discarnate" (*Technology as Symptom and Dream* 101). Is this one of the price tags for leading an efficient, unambiguous existence? One loses or abandons one's embodiment and embraces only the body of the world, but on a surface level only.

From such an attitude, Ilych's being is defined by things behind which he hides; the curtain that he hangs in his home signals his striving for decorousness through decoration, so that where he lives, in increasingly luxurious homes, can reflect the banality of normalcy. An exclusively horizontal existence is a horrible way of being, even if the individual is unaware of what is missing.

But he succeeds, Tolstoy observes, only in creating a place that "looked so much like the others that it would never have been noticed, though it all seemed quite exceptional to him" (115). It seems to underscore a "seeing unknowingly," but what is on the other side of the curtain? The horror of what might be there is a driving force in Ilych's need for absolute control.

Then the turn that initiates both a rise and a fall in his neatly arranged life. First though, and after suffering from depression for several months, the consequence of having been passed over in a recent competition for a higher, more prestigious judgeship, Ilych is suddenly rewarded with a lucrative promotion. He immediately buys a new and larger home and fills it with new furniture, curtains, and other lavish possessions, stretching the boundaries of the archetype of the consumer with his rampage of purchases.

He supervises all the placements of the furniture and the drapes, all in the service of shuttling everything into its right place: "when he glanced at the unfinished drawing room he conjured up an image of the fireplace, the screen, the what-not, the little chairs, scattered here and there, the plates and China on the walls and the bronzes, as they would appear when *everything was in place*" (115, my emphasis). A handy but futile attempt to stave off the unknown.

In his preoccupation for managed efficiency, and as he shows the upholsterer how he wants the drapes hung, "he missed a step and fell, but being a strong and agile man, he held on to the ladder and merely banged his side against the knob of the window frame. . ... The bruised place was painful, but the pain soon passed, and he felt particularly bright and well just then" (116). So long as he has things to "adjust," "arrange," and "order," he is happy. But something is now amiss, out of place, rebellious; his contentment is in turn dislodged. It too begins to migrate from its rightful place.

Now, only when things have all found their fixed residence, does he become quickly irritated; he shows annoyance if anything he possesses carries even the slightest impurity, stain, or blemish, the slightest wound or marking from use or abuse; he recoils in anger when they show any deviation from his own successfully designed pristine spotlessness he has put in place for himself and his family.

I call it a rage for purity, for pure certainty, unadorned with any form of pollution. As well, it is a move of the imagination to maintain a naïve innocence in the face of growing ambiguity. They too become symptoms of his dis-ease. In fact, every "disturbance" distresses him, even while he clings to the watchwords that define his existence: "decorous," "pleasant," and "easy."

More on the image of the curtains and window later, but for the moment let's look at the window knob that Ilych falls against as he slips from the ladder and inaugurates the wound, which I am considering as an opening, an orifice into another world. The knob of the window allows it to be opened and closed, both engaging another space and closing it off. The ladder cooperates actively, if disagreeably, in Ilych's fall as it enters a conspiracy with gravity to bring him down, to ground him from his elevated status.

Things are not inanimate in Tolstoy's depiction of Ilych's world. They each possess a life force as well as specific roles to play, as characters would in a story, to further a growing and increasingly terrifying drama in the ordinary.

In this stage action, Ilych slips and is suddenly pulled out of the mainstream of life and into an eddy of quiet suspension. What was hidden before, now in disease, surfaces: things become "distasteful"; he experiences a queer taste in his mouth when he plays bridge, *especially* when he wins. Fearing this displacement by life's accident, he consults a specialist for his constant pain: "The doctor said: such and such indicates that you have such and such, but if an analysis of such and such doesn't not confirm this, then we have to assume you have such and such. On the other hand, if we assume such and such is the case, then. He must assume that and that" (*The Death of Ivan Ilych* 121).

Ilych's response is chagrin that there is not an efficient, easy solution forthcoming; he falls into ambiguity and uncertainty because no two doctors can agree on his "condition." All arrangements and containments are off and Ilych begins to sink deeply into himself, into the underworld of his unlived life through the gap of the wound. Something is out of place, but at this stage unknowable.

We are not able to diagnose Ilych's illness because part of Tolstoy's poetics of dis-ease is to make it nameless, going only so far as to refer to the disease through the pronoun "it," with a purposely vague antecedent. This vague antecedent incites terror in his soul, even as the pronoun "it" grows into an upper case "IT."

The depth psychologist Russell Lockhart's diagnosis of cancer is illuminating here. He writes of the disease as "growth gone wrong" ("Cancer in Myth and Dream" 6), "a response to something of one's psychic and bodily earth that is not allowed to live" (2). Growth gone wrong is an apt description of Ivan Ilych's personal life when the bruise blossoms into disease. Now, to reclaim what is out of place becomes Ilych's central mission. He continues to hope "to adjust what was wrong, to master it and attain success, or make a grand slam. But now every mischance upset him and plunged him into despair." Even more, the disease tears through the psychic curtain Ilych has hung and maintained up to the fall that separates his interior life, heretofore neglected, from his exterior existence, including his family: any "unpleasantness" at home, any "lack of success" at work, or even "bad cards at bridge" make him "acutely sensible" of his disease.

His illness acts like a new gravitational pull in his life, sucking all elements of it into itself. His soul wants its voice to be heard; the disease obliges this request. The disease, in effect, alters and realigns his personal myth. It becomes a rival for the leading character in the novella. Edward Whitmont cites the work of C.A. Meier: "When sickness is vested with such dignity, it has the inestimable advantage that it can be vested with a healing power" (qtd. in *Alchemy of Healing* 1).

The curtain or crust or shell that Ilych has used successfully to protect himself from irritation and annoyance liquifies under the pressured presence of disease and exposes him to his being ill-at-ease, face to face; but the medical model of anatomy and physiology tyrannically pushes everything about his malady into a specialized vessel or container. Containment is more important, in some ways, than cure. When the specialist visits him to take unequivocal charge of the disease, he brings up a question "about a kidney and a caecum that was not behaving properly, and that would soon get a good trouncing from Mikhail Danilovich and the celebrity and *be forced to mend their ways*" (123, my italics).

In other words, Ilych falls victim to the specialist—not unlike how prisoners fell victim to his diagnoses of their crime—who draws a curtain around the body of anatomy and physiology and treats it as Ilych once treated things and people who came before him in court—through management, adjustment, order, and control.

Ilych feels the full power of crisis management leveled against his condition but gains paltry reassurance in this knowledge. He now experiences the weight of another knowing presence deep in his flesh; it becomes more disconcerting for him to listen to its voice. But he must in order to learn the power of analogy, of similarity, of correspondence between one's interior ecology and that of the world he moves within. Such a breakdown through dis-ease will allow him to break through his incubated existence shortly before he draws his last breath.

Yet even in his current condition, death is far too ubiquitous, and refuses, like an obstinate patient, to be isolated; instead, the consciousness of "IT" pours through the opening of his wounded and assumes the face of his disease. As he struggles initially to shape his malady, his disease turns and begins to shape *him*, to remythologize his life; he begins the journey, even a quest, because of the questions that now guide him in his pain, to be refashioned by his illness and through it, his relation to his own life on two levels: His past and his heretofore ignored interior life.

His disease, in other words, is a way of seeing and judging the quality of his existence as well as furnishing the psychic courage to peer into it. Through it, what was critically important for him becomes trivial, and what was insignificant for him takes on a profundity that terrifies. Paradox strikes at the center of his existence.

The formerly comfortable life Ilych lived promoted a natural tendency to reestablish routine and make things pleasant and entertaining; but that life has evaporated with increasing acceleration. The upholstery on the furniture has tattered and unraveled. With his friends in a card game, he makes a grand slam and feels simultaneously the queer taste in his mouth "and under the circumstances it seemed preposterous to him to rejoice in a grand slam" (126). Through his wound, he begins to wonder, and that wondering exposes him to the trivial nature of his existence.

The "game" he has been playing grows less and less satisfactory. The "queer taste in his mouth" may be likened to the alchemists' *prima materia,* the base matter which they would begin with in order to refine it into a more valuable metal. Writing on "The Alchemy of Illness," Kat Duff cites Paracelsus' belief that "each disease 'bears its own remedy within itself. . . .. Health must grow from the same root as disease'" (qtd. in "The Alchemy of Illness" 47).

Russell Lockhart follows the word "cure" in disease to its origin and discovers there that the root *cura* also gives rise to "curious" and "curiosity" ("Cancer in Myth and Dream" 21). He speculates that in patients with terminal diseases, a cure begins when one does not flee from the wound, but "when someone is motivated by curiosity to go into the pathology rather than away from it" (21). This soft spot in Ivan Ilych's side becomes a breach or perhaps even a window into the life of the soul through reflection. The body calls him back in and through the wound.

Writing of wounding in another context, James Hillman suggests wounds have a spiritual quality: a wound "is a learner and a teacher both . . . and has a message" ("Puer Wounds" 108). It is a place, as in other "handicaps" one suffers that "give[s] soul" (109). Suffering has its own eyes and ears that can deepen the one who suffers into mystery and into deeper meaning.

Not a little irony is present here: the disease that unfurls from Ilych's initial wounding may be his most prized possession—bought for a high fee perhaps; it never goes on sale—far surpassing in value all of what he has materially acquired; it was bequeathed to him *through the things he believed he possessed.* It is a gift that wounds, "the gift of a wound" ("Puer Wounds" 107).

I mentioned that one might see Ivan Ilych's pilgrimage from health to sickness as paradoxically a path from sickness to health; both are quests. He begins to question not the terms of his disease but a consciousness that his life was poisoning the lives of others and that poison did not weaken but penetrated more deeply into his core being. His wound as gift begins to parent him, especially since his childhood begins to loom up in his reflections; going deep into himself, which is a journey he never allowed himself when he lived on the surface of his upholstered life, he feels and touches his disease and slowly begins to suffer, that is, in the original meaning of the word, "to bear it" or "bear up" with acceptance.

None of his colleagues at the court come to visit him at home; his family members generally keep their distance from his room where he incubates in solitude in his dark night of the soul. But one of his pantry servants, a young healthy Russian youth by the name of Gerasim, generously aids and guides Ilych in his illness and through the dark night of his awakening; he is the embodiment of service and an emblem of Christian love and sacrifice as his employer continues his tutorial through the disease as well as his own deepening, journeying below the upholstered surface of a superficial life. The introduction of this generous, healthy, and robust servant comes at a moment when Ilych experiences a major realization introduced through his illness.

As his condition worsens, Ilych is more embarrassed by his bodily functions, especially his bowel movements; they become a torture to him, as Tolstoy writes, "a torture because of the filth, the unseemliness, the stench, and the knowledge that another person had to assist in this" (*The Death of Ivan Ilych* 139). But through his shame, he paradoxically gains great comfort for the first time since his illness because the young Gerasim faithfully, even cheerfully, carries out the chamber pot. When he entered, he exuded a "pleasant smell of tar from his heavy boots and of fresh winter air" (139). In his generosity, Gerasim is the only one in the entire household who offers Ilych "the compassion he craved" (135).

As Gerasim is Ilych's guide to the underworld, he embodies the Greek god who leads souls to Hades. a version of Hermes in heavy boots. Ilych senses that he is entering into another realm when he imagines an image of a black sack which he senses he is dropping into. His thoughts at this time, inconceivable before his disease— "that he had not lived the kind of life he should have—might in fact be true" (147) as he contemplates with horror: "'What if my entire life, my entire conscious life, simply *was not the real thing?*'" (147).

With these thoughts, and with the presence and support of Gerasim, Ivan Ilych descends farther into the black sack in a rite of passage that is essential in order for him to recover from his spiritual illness: "It seemed to him that he and his pain were being thrust into a narrow, deep black sack, but though they were pushed further and further in they could not be pushed to the bottom. . ... He struggled but yet co-operated. And suddenly he broke through, fell, and regained consciousness" (147).

The first thing he becomes aware of is Gerasim at the foot of the bed "dozing quietly and patiently" with Ilych's "emaciated stockinged legs resting on the young man's shoulders" that helps to relieve his pain. Gerasim's presence also helps to alleviate his suffering. The young man's presence helps Ilych to redeem and to forgive himself for his soiledness; his life, so devoted to keeping all stains, all impurities, all defects encapsulated and stowed out of sight, now opens to its own inauthenticity, its soiled and ragged condition. Words like "uncleanliness" and "unseemliness" replace the earlier vocabulary of "decorum" and "arrangement."

Another curtain has been rent from Ilych's heretofore fixed imagination so that he can acknowledge that what he thought he had been controlling with a host of antiseptics—life's messy ambiguity and uncertainty, indeed, the shit and the stench that is part of any human life, was a sham.

The wound opens another painful recognition, as he discovers through his now more porous imagination: "'It is as if I had been going downhill while I imagined I was going up. And that is really what it was. I was going up in public opinion . . . but life was ebbing away from me" (148). His recognition reverses, to some degree, the definitions of health and disease themselves; they are both recalibrated and redefined through the orifice of woundedness and, as such, actually parent the dying man. His body of resistance must pass completely through the black sack and into a new attitude, one which is fueled by forgiveness. A new mythology is forming within the womb of the illness to connect him to the true nature of his being where for the first time in his life he has an occasion to befriend himself, then his family.

Wounding has transformed his consciousness by putting him in touch with a life that has been devoured by promotions and possessions. The gift of touch and comfort migrates from the body of Gerasim to Ilych and from the body of Ilych to his son, the only family member who appears to mourn for Ilych's condition as he journeys toward death.

Before the last scene between father and son, however, I want to describe one of the few moments when his wife, Praskovya Fyodorovna, enters the room to check on his condition. After congratulating him on taking holy communion from the priest who visited, she asks plaintively: "'You really do feel better, don't you?'" "'Yes,' he said without looking at her" (146). And then this further recognition: "Her clothes, her figure, the expression of her face, the sound of her voice—all these said to him: 'Not the real thing. Everything you lived by and still live by is a lie, a deception that blinds you from the reality of life and death'" (146). With this realization bearing down on him, he orders her out of the room.

In the closing scene of the story, Ivan Ilych commences three days of prolonged and uninterrupted screaming whose duration ends with his final breath. Except for one instant. While he has taken on the burden of an inauthentic existence—one that is not the real thing—he has a moment of illuminating light: "'I can still make it *the real thing*—I can. But what is the real thing?' Ivan asked himself and suddenly grew quiet, at this instance, toward the end of the third day, an hour before his death" (155).

As if in response, and before he ceased screaming to contemplate the above illumination, his young son enters the room quietly and approaches his bed. As Ilych "screamed desperately and flail[ed] his arms"

(155) he feels someone kissing his hand and looks toward this act of kindness. When he discovers it is his son, "he grieved for him." Then his wife enters, weeping, and approaches his bed: "He grieved for her" (155). He tries to ask for their forgiveness but says instead "Forgo." In his sorrow for them, not himself, he feels something lifting from him that had been oppressing him throughout his illness; "it was vanishing all at once—from two sides, ten sides, all sides. He felt sorry for them; he had to do something to keep from hurting them. To deliver them and himself from this suffering" (155). And even as he feels this liberation from oppression, he realizes that he is no longer in pain. Finally, "He searched for his accustomed fear of death and could not find it. Where was death? What death? There was no fear because there was no death. Instead of death there was light" (155).

At this juncture I want to add something about this moment in Ilych's suffering into death. Alan Watts writes in his classic text, *The Wisdom of Insecurity*: "Death is the epitome of the truth that in each moment we are thrust into the unknown. Here all clinging to security is compelled to cease, and wherever the past is dropped away and safety abandoned, life is renewed. Death is the unknown in which all of us lived before birth. Nothing is more creative than death because it is the whole secret of life. It means the past must be abandoned, that the unknown cannot be avoided, that 'I' cannot continue and that nothing can be ultimately fixed. When man knows this, he lives for the first time in his life. By holding his breath, he loses it. But letting go, he finds it" (117-18).

To return to Ilych's moment of death: all the above happens in an instant; he felt a sense of bliss overcome him, though he was to scream for another two hours. The exterior expression of death was not the authentic one; now it was the inner tranquility that showed on his face when he was laid out in the parlor after he passed. But now he discovers, "'Death is over,' he said to himself. 'There is no more death.' He drew in a breath, broke off in the middle of it, stretched himself out, and died" (155).

This elegant and understated narrative renders mythopoetically the search for wholeness in one soul who in his quest for decorum, propriety, and control of the world's matter, discovers through woundedness and disease the fulfillment of a life when it is directed both deeply into oneself and outward toward the care of others. Being wounded opens him to living fully in his life's last minutes even while it clearly marks the trajectory of his death. We are left to ponder: What is a life well-lived and how might our afflictions mentor us toward that end?

Works Cited

Aristotle. *The Poetics*. Translated by S.H. Butcher. Introduction by Francis Fergusson. Hill and Wang, 1961.

Duff, Kat. "The Alchemy of Illness." *The Parabola Book of Healing*. Continuum, 1994. 45-53.

Hillman, James. "Puer Wounds and Ulysses' Scar." *Puer Papers*. Spring, 1979. 100-128.

---. *Revisioning Psychology*. HarperCollins Publishers, 1975.

Jung, C.G. *The Collected Works of C.G. Jung*. Trans. R.F.C. Hull. Vol. 13. Princeton UP, 1983.

---. *The Red Book. Liber Novus*. Edited and with an introduction by Sonu Shamdasani. Trans. Mark Kyburz, John Peck, and Sonu Shamdasani. W.W. Norton, 2009.

Lockhart, Russell. A. "Cancer in Myth and Dream." *Spring Journal: An Annual of Archetypal Psychology and Jungian Thought*. Spring, 1977. 1-26.

---. *Words as Eggs: Psyche in Language and Clinic*. Spring, 1983.

Romanyshyn, Robert. *Technology as Symptom and Dream*. Routledge, 1989.

Tolstoy, Leo. *The Death of Ivan Ilyich*. Translated by Lynn Solotaroff. Introduction by Ronald Blythe. Bantam Classics. 2004.

Whitmont, Edward C. *The Alchemy of Healing: Psyche and Soma*. North Atlantic Books, 1993.

Watts, Alan. *The Wisdom of Insecurity: A Message for an Age of Anxiety*. Vintage Books, 2011.

PART II

VIGNETTES OF CULTURE

14

WHAT STORY WILL WE CHOOSE TO REMEMBER?*

The second anniversary of the January 6th insurrection is fast approaching. I have thought about what story or stories will surface to express the reality of that day and those leading up to its execution. As in the past, there will be competing narratives, each advancing the events and their meaning to conform with outcomes that may be self-serving.

For several reasons I was drawn to an article in the 2022 December issue of *The Atlantic* entitled "How Germany Remembers the Holocaust and What America Can Learn About Atonement," written by Clint Smith.

As a mythologist I am interested in stories as carriers of values, aspirations, and ideals as well as the shadow side of both personal and collective myths. I also share with many an interest in what motivates some versions of stories to be cultivated and shared while others rise up through the energies of specific interests—political, spiritual, practical, fictional—and by whom?

Stories are vehicles that have as their core a belief or set of beliefs which we choose to adopt or reject in our personal or national life. Their power resides in their ability to shape our thinking as well as the behaviors that emanate from them. Stories are like the infrastructure that supports and maintains our identity. Who we allow, tolerate, or assign authority to in telling our story is a monumental decision because it shapes

---

* Originally published in the *Herald-Zeitung* December 9th, 2022.

our destiny as a people. Today we find ourselves in the tall grass of competing narratives.

We might pay close attention to what kinds of stories are being suppressed today, what is allowed to be taught, what books should be banned, what ideas should be exiled, what values should be marginalized. For stories, more than any other form of expression, are the oldest carriers of our identity of who and what we are committed to.

These narratives grow directly from how we choose to remember our history and what we lean towards surgically removing, including our founding narrative as a Democracy, our shared origin myth.

Unfortunately, there are those in power positions who are making decisions with startling consequences. We must be cautious and vigilant toward those who step forward to proclaim:

The following book titles should be banned from libraries and schools.

- Topics on sexuality, race, and gender should be prohibited to "protect our children." For some age groups, however, this is a good decision.
- Certain truths about our own history of genocide would best be kept under wraps, their identity simply denied.
- Real respectful conversations about our differences should be avoided, deploying instead a series of "d" words: deny, deflect, deceive, deflate, demean, destroy.

Such a "method" for silencing alternative views places in direct jeopardy the most fragile, and seventh "d" word: Democracy.

Much has been written about America's pseudo-innocence, which in its expression has taken up a less-than-nuanced stance towards history, especially our own. Pseudo-innocence prefers to keep the same historical accounts, the stories we wish to remember, frozen, atrophied so that our nation's shadows remain hidden in the basement of our collective consciousness.

Remembering seems unwise. Yet it seems that remembering has its own propriety, its own moral or amoral code feeding it. So what and how we refuse to remember is worthy of our study, and along with it, what fiction we drive into the hard ground of history, will further form, or deform our fragile yet coherent myth.

Clint Smith's illuminating article reveals how Germany today continues to create new rituals to remember the Holocaust; he notes that the movement to remember anew emerged not from government authorities who have their own myth to promote, but "from ordinary people outside the government who pushed the country to be honest about its past." He also delineates places in our country that have begun such efforts of honest reclamation of our story through memorials.

His final words will be mine: "It is the very act of attempting to remember that becomes the most powerful memorial of all."

15

WHAT DRAWS US TO WONDER?*

Who has not occasionally paused to wonder about something or some-one, some circumstance, some situation, that gathers mystery around it? For over thirty years I have written in my journal most mornings. As a prompt, I write about what wishes to be remembered from yesterday. It takes only a few seconds, after I have brewed coffee, lit a candle in my study at 4:30 a.m. and sat with that question, that the remembered line up. At the end of each morning's writing, I ask myself: "What did you wonder about or become curious about yesterday?" Sometimes no an-swer steps up; other mornings two or three emerge, vying for attention.

I sense that wonder has its own way of knowing. A deeper form of learning is often evoked through wonder. Not seeking the right answer but paying attention to the questions that grow naturally from wondering, like the fruit that emerges from a well-tended seed that blossoms into a plant. That is wonder's pathway.

Curiosity is also a form of wondering. So can questioning what we believe, value, and even what we sense might be time to discard from our lives. In one of his *Dialogues,* the Greek philosopher Socrates questioned his student on what he thought was the nature of knowledge. When his student grows dizzy trying to answer this question because it sets him wondering, his teacher salutes him: "This sense of wonder is the mark of the philosopher," namely, the love of wisdom (Philo-Sophia). I sense that it grows directly from being curious.

---

* Originally published in the *Herald-Zeitung,* November 19th, 2022.

Mythologist Joseph Campbell suggested that one of the primary functions of myth is to stir in the individual a sense of awe and mystery. I don't think we have to travel any farther than what is valued in an ordinary day; but there is no such thing as ordinary, especially when events in our lives encourage or provoke wonder.

Wonder gains traction when it emanates from the heart, not the head. One experiences something or someone that is heart-felt. Wonder does not seek the right answer, the fixed fact; it is more nuanced than that, more pliable, more oblique. It does not deflect ambiguity but welcomes it.

In wondering, we run the risk of touching what is mysterious in life, what gravitates toward a sense of awe. It brushes against what is both ineffable and sacred. In the words of Rabbi Abraham Joshua Heschel in his book *I Asked For Wonder,* he writes, "What we cannot comprehend by analysis we become aware of in awe."

As an example: In these blessedly cooler mornings, my wife and I step out early, before daylight, and gaze for a few moments at the stars that appear so brilliantly against a black sky. There, in the stillness of 4:30 a.m., we stand for a moment in silence. If the moon is visible, we salute her glowing presence.

Gazing up at the night sky full of brilliant lights, we are inevitably drawn to wonder what this new day will bring, how it will both shape itself and be shaped in part by our plans, our schedules, and our obligations. Wonder seems to dissolve under the weight of duty.

In this moment, however, we sense the power of wonder implicit in the ordinary. Wonder coaxes what we call "ordinary"—a word so inadequate to our experience, so we remain for another moment, silent in the immensity of the early morning sky before it dissolves into the day's birthing sunrise.

In the cool dark air of the morning, we don't stop to think; we stop thinking. For wonder seems more intimate with a felt sense of what is real *and* mysterious. In wonder we are allowed to exist in that slender hyphen between them.

I sense that such fleeting moments are what poets and artists seek through their creative imaginations: to capture the beauty exposed by wonder and how, for instance, the moon's shadows will spread across another day, shaping itself, already, from darkness into light.

I end by wondering if these moments of closeness with the natural world serve as bridges to the ineffable mystery of a sacred presence, suddenly there in front of us, if we open ourselves to its terms, not ours.

16

TROUT FISHING IS NOT ABOUT THE FISH*

> Many men go fishing all of their lives without knowing that
> it is not fish they are after.
> ~Henry David Thoreau

We have been fishing for rainbow trout in the Missouri Ozarks for 30 years. It is an annual pilgrimage from San Antonio to a rural fishing lodge in southwest Missouri, 1600 miles round trip. We recently returned from our journey with reflections to share.

Over these three decades our friendship has strengthened on each excursion to the point that we now admit the week together is not about fly rods, reels, dry flies, and nymphs. Nor is it about the fish we hook.

So, if the trip is not primarily about the mechanics of fishing, then what is the throughline of this adventure? We now realize that fishing has become a rich metaphor for what matters in our lives.

It is about camaraderie and friendship, undertaken in one of the most ancient of human activities, the journey, and what we discover each time we enter this vessel of adventure.

---

* Originally published in *The San Antonio Express*-News October 26th, 2022. Co-authored by Roger C. Barnes and Dennis Patrick Slattery.

In our younger days we fished early in the morning, then again late in the afternoon for hours on end. No longer. Our time on the stream has shortened considerably.

Our pilgrimage has assumed a more contemplative, less active rhythm; the fish play a smaller role than they once did. Emphasis has shifted comfortably from the fish and the size of the catches to our shared friendship.

Catching three fish per day, not eight, is more than satisfying. Something more valuable is caught now in the nets of our imaginations, like a return to the value of an ordinary day and the treasures which invite a sustained feeling of gratitude.

Preparing and enjoying our meals together in the house we rent has become a sacred ritual.

Now, it is about sitting on the porch and feeling dusk descend. We enjoy hearing the crickets and other critters that stir in the thickening shadows, creating a chorus of sounds as the day curls into its own darkness.

Our time of stepping out of the regular rhythms of our lives allows for remembrances by giving story form to memories of previous trips and to our lives more broadly.

Now in our 70s, we fish for stories to pull from the deep waters of memory. The stories allow their shiny, colorful hues, like those of the trout jumping into sunlight, to illuminate our present identity.

We have become more conscious of the reality that where the water runs most swiftly, and especially in the shadows of the stream, is where the invisible trout frequently cluster.

It has become our way of reconnecting to the natural order, with its own wondrous rhythms and shadings.

Our fishing excursions bring much of our individual lives to the surface. Our life events are for a moment fixed in the telling, which is itself one of the richest elements in a long and sustained friendship.

Our fly lines have, over time, morphed into our story lines. We read more now on our outings and fish less. It has become a shift in awareness where we now sense there are bigger fish to fry.

It is a time for rich conversations about what we have read or films we've watched or music we enjoy. We are now at our age casting our attention at the meaning of life itself. These trips are now occasions for taking stock of the bigger questions that life poses.

A shift in our collective attitude is itself a migration from quantity to quality; an important observation to consider because it includes the very journey of life itself in its constant flow, eddies, and currents that attend our lives.

What we now grasp is the importance of connecting our stories. They are the mythic underpinnings of our lives, offering us coherence, cohesion, and camaraderie.

But to be clear about the trout we do catch: Yes, we take them home and we eat 'em!

17

— • —

ATTEMPTED SCAM IS A LESSON ON FRAUD*

My goal was simple: to cancel a rental car in another city because I no longer needed it. When I called the number that I assumed would connect me with those who could assist in my canceling the rental car, I had no idea what a vortex of fraud I was to enter.

I cannot relate here the intricacies of those who professed to be employees of the car rental company, but who in fact were scammers, skilled in how to disarm their victims by encouraging trust in them and their deep concern for quickly refunding to my checking account money I had spent for the car. While the plan to extort had begun, I was initially deaf to its shape and pattern.

The upshot of such a slick scheme was that my bank, smelling something foul about a request for funds from the scammers, sent me a notice while I was still on the phone, growing only slightly suspicious of their propaganda. I told the scammer that I wanted to call my bank first before seeking the refund further. A bank employee asserted that our accounts were to be shut down immediately and that my wife and I should come in to begin the process of opening new accounts. The old ones were frozen.

Everyone who my wife or I have talked to about our close encounter of the fiendish kind, almost without exception, was eager to share their

---

* Originally published in the *Herald Zeitung*, May 21st-22nd, 2022.

own story of facing fraud without knowing it, and how stupid, even ashamed, they felt afterward. I do not believe it has anything to do with being stupid. But I do sense that there is something pornographic about fraud. Its intention is to play off a person's basic sense of trust as well as their generosity, when they fall victim to helping someone they know who needs financial assistance, which is a false claim by scammers. Such a violation of these human virtues takes the strategy of bilking individuals of their savings.

The most current *AARP Bulletin* was devoted primarily to "The Bad Guys: Who They Are and How to Stop Them." Immensely helpful. And painful to read for many of us who see in their reporting the very scam patterns leveled at us. Its main article begins with a quote from the classic text *The Art of War* by Sun-Tzu: "Know the enemy and know yourself; in a hundred battles, you will never be defeated." A tall order given the intricate, sophisticated, and well-practiced fraud schemes that have netted those in the counterfeit game hundreds of millions of dollars from unsuspecting victims. Those of us sixty years or older are particularly vulnerable.

The large caution for all of us is to be wary of divulging any information to solicitors by phone, email, or other vehicles of transmission. *The Bulletin* goes on to outline the eight most prevalent "fraud pitches" being used in accelerating numbers across the US—and suggestions for how to avoid their quicksand pitches.

Over 700 years ago the Italian poet Dante Alighieri outlined in his *Divine Comedy* in the first cantica, *Inferno,* the face of fraud: "Behold the beast who bears the pointed tail. . . /Behold the one whose stench fills all the world." And then to fraud's visage: "The face he wore was that of a just man, /so gracious was his features' outer semblance; and all his trunk, the body of a serpent; . . . And all his tail was quivering in the void/while twisting upward its envenomed fork."

His figure is an unnatural amalgam of a stinging scorpion with an innocent human face. Be aware that such an appetite for wealth, driven by deceit, is only a telephone call or email away.

18

WHY WRITE? IT CAN BE HEALING*

For the past thirty-five years I have kept journals and written in them at least five days a week. I have always felt it sometimes soothing, sometimes painful but always valuable when I home in on topics that go beyond simply recording my days; my expressions go deeper, bearing down on losses, challenges, financial and physical limitations, as well as hopes for a productive and purposeful future.

When I write more intensely about what conveys in my life a sense of bliss as well as what events have sprouted blisters that needed more attention, I gain new levels of understanding. Experiences deepen into insights to cultivate.

But in my readings of late, I am discovering how medicinal writing can be about discomforts, challenges, or places where life has entered to hijack my best plans. Several books have attracted me to this topic, but none more grippingly than James W. Pennebaker and Joshua Smyth's *Opening Up by Writing it Down: How Expressive Writing Improves Health and Eases Emotional Pain.* It has been out since 2010 and is currently in its third edition.

I have frequently experienced such a healing quality to my journaling, but now I see from these psychologists, whose research has revealed with various groups how the immune system is boosted, how memory improves, how clutter in our often traffic-jammed mind can be lessened, how understanding can be gained on a deeper level of awareness, and

---

* Originally published in the *Herald-Zeitung,* April 9th-10th, 2022.

how a new focus to our lives can be installed—all through what they call "Expressive Writing."

Their method is as uncomplicated as it is profound. Essentially, they call for remembering an event such as a loss, a failure, an unexpected turn in the road of our life's journey, or any impediment that stops one short; we know these incidents because we feel their power to arrest us, to swallow us, and often to force us into reassessing what our true purpose in life is.

Pennebaker and Smyth suggest not writing about it immediately, but letting some time pass. When we are ready, write about it for fifteen minutes a day for three or four days to allow it to unfold. But he also cautions that self-reflection in writing is not the same thing as self-absorption; the latter takes over when we simply relive the experience repeatedly to the point of madness.

Instead, they encourage writing about the event *in detail* from a detached point of view, where we can see ourselves with some objectivity. In this expressive writing, we ask how we felt at the time of the event (critically important) and how we feel now in writing about it.

When, after research trials with large numbers of writers following this simple but effective way of understanding what happens to us from a writer's point of view, he asked them months later what they had gained. A common response was, "It helped me think about what I felt during those times. I never realized how it affected me before." Another: "Writing deeply and thoughtfully about what happened to me and the feelings that accompanied it, I was able for the first time to let it go completely."

Expressive writing can also include a persistent story we tell about ourselves that can be either demeaning or uplifting. In the former case, we may want to edit and revise those stories that shame or belittle us, and create a contrary version that can change the emotional terrain we live by.

19

◆ ● ◆

MEDITATION HAS LASTING BENEFITS*

Meditation practices are growing in our country. They are being used to increase consciousness, to improve health and vitality, to deepen one's spiritual life, and to offer a counter way of being conscious of our everyday experiences.

I think it is also being evoked by more individuals pausing in their lives to ask: What kind of world is being shaped and insisting we enter its terms, values, assumptions, and prejudices as well as its beliefs, all of which can indoctrinate us into a worldview that we may not agree with?

If we fail to pay attention to these often-subtle changes and shifts, we can become victims of the illusion of freedom. Pausing less to analyze, which is often ego-driven, one-sided, and reductionistic, and more to meditate, which is more holistic, we are drawn closer to our most authentic selves and to the implicit holiness of the ordinary.

Meditation draws us into a greater depth of understanding that goes beyond information; it gravitates more toward an authentic transformation of consciousness.

To cultivate a practice of meditating opens us to experience the daily round of our lives in greater depth. Each day we are asked by a variety of sources—news outlets, shows, movies, advertising, political maneuvering,

---

* Originally published in the *Herald-Zeitung*, September 6th, 2022.

friends, and family, to remember and accept certain circumstances and conditions, while forgetting others. We can then in this din of forces fall asleep to what is truly remarkable. I have discovered that meditating can cultivate a different, more embracing attitude as well as a fuller way of imagining the world's ordinary particulars as tinged with the sacred quality of life.

In contrast to egoic, one-sided thinking. in which power is often accumulated under the guise of analysis, meditation is more holistic; it does not explain, it illuminates understanding. Meditation leans toward recognizing the interrelatedness of all elements of what at first glance may seem so diverse, even antithetical to one another. Meditation allows, even welcomes, paradox, complexity, and ambiguity as part of the fabric of life; it is closer to the image of weaving, of creating a tapestry rather than reinforcing the independence of life's texture absent an underlying unity.

One of meditation's most important qualities is that it can lead us to wonder, that is, to envision the ordinary happenings of each day—a brief contact with a stranger, an act of courtesy, a moment of self-forgiveness or forgiving another, the sounds that gather around one during a morning walk—as instances that evoke gratefulness for what had once been labeled and catalogued as trivial. Meditating slows us down, even for the space of twenty minutes, if we choose to find time each day for silence and solitude. Even taking a moment to become aware of our breathing, and to notice how often each day we move breathlessly from one task to another, is a gift to oneself.

Meditating awakens us to the beauty of our heart and to our sense of being embodied. It reveals how we might take in the world we inhabit at a single moment, with all our senses. Meditating can also reveal where our lives are only half-lived or possibly needing renewal and revision. We may imagine how our inner life is disconnected from the outer social world we move in daily.

It can also assist us during times of illness, misfortune, loss, and grief by finding a place for such suffering within the larger fabric of who we are and to what we are destined. A meditative practice can shift us from skating across the surface of possessions, distractions, and future plans and promotions by reminding us of what we all possess in common: this very moment of vulnerability and promise. We can be present only to the

present. That itself is a gift worth acknowledging in meditations of gratitude.

20

Journey Into Space and the Mythic Imagination*

Human beings possess a deep hunger to explore, to leave the known world and reach out to mystery, to what is uncertain, and to gain new insights that deepen our understanding of who we are. Myths have revealed this for millennia.

With NASA's announcement of a new series of eight exploits called Artemis, the mythic dimension is once again front and center. The moon will serve as destination and way station in the Artemis program, whose goal is to eventually reach Mars.

The Apollo program is no more. Next in line is Apollo's divine sister—Artemis—who is associated with the moon and her illumination, as well as with nature, especially animals. Her favorite was the bear. As a huntress, she possessed, like her brother, deadly accuracy with her arrows, especially as they traveled long distances. And like her brother, she was a divinity of strife but also of ambition, excitement, and drive.

Mythologist Joseph Campbell reminded us that myths use the language of metaphor for their energy and durability. Based on two words—*meta*, across or beyond; and *phorein*, to carry—a metaphor, like a myth, is "a transport vehicle" that encourages us to move out of the boundaries of the known and familiar into unknown worlds. By introducing the

---

* Originally published in the *San Antonio Express-News*, September 16th, 2022.

goddess Artemis, NASA adopted a new metaphor, a new mythic figure, for such a transport.

This is a healthy sign mythically and imaginally. It complements the earlier masculine presence of Apollo to establish a greater presence of feminine energy in space travel. I sense in the "Artemis" naming for the next eight space flights—which includes the goals of sending a woman and a woman of color to walk on the moon's surface—a mythic expression of integration with the masculine in the service of a greater wholeness and completeness.

 Her name is no small matter for our national imagination. A new analogy ripens with her presence; Apollo and Artemis are known in the wisdom tradition of myth for their healing powers. As curative presences, they promote healing wounds of infection, strife, dissension, and disorder.

Mythic thinking has a strong poetic element, and NASA rises in our imagination as a witness to this presence. Mythic—or mythopoetic thinking—rests on the power of analogy in creating a new story by reviving an old narrative and fabricating it in modern clothing. The space program is once again the launchpad for the imagination; it allows us to see ourselves within a larger cosmic frame.

The power of myth is then twofold: First, to see ourselves anew within the frame of an epic and vast terrain; the space program yields to something far greater and grander than us, yet includes our greatness as a species. Second, to see and imagine from a double perspective by retrieving from ancient history, as filmmakers Steven Spielberg and George Lucas have done, stories and figures of earlier wisdom traditions, and reinstating them within our cosmic dreams.

The ancient past, then, coalesces with our dreams of a distant future. Such is the power of mythic imagination. We all need the mythic world to refresh us as we gaze skyward. Let Artemis show us the way as our new guide, joining the constellation of earlier figures on our trajectory deeper into the universe and into our knowledge of ourselves.

21

WORDS DEFINE OR DESTROY OUR COUNTRY'S DEMOCRACY*

Some 30 years ago I developed a habit of rising early to write in my journal. I sit quietly after lighting a candle and invite from yesterday what wishes to be remembered. The language I deploy to record yesterday's events leads me into what significance they had and how they may shape my life today.

On a national level, we recently remembered a historical event, recorded as it unfolded: the January 6th, 2021 insurrection. The unprecedented invasion grew out of a grievance that was unmoored from any historical facts—that the national presidential election was somehow stolen and that only a violent response could right such a fantasized wrong. Words alone, absent any historical referents, provoked a vicious violation of the Constitution's instructions for the peaceful transfer of power.

Words were also used by competing factions to shape what we saw. We were exposed to fiction on one hand, and on the other hand to the facts recorded by many news outlets. The insurrection revealed an invasion of the written document that defines us as a nation. Carefully worded by the Founding Fathers, but still open to interpretation, the Constitution expresses a method of governing that installs the will of the people in their most prominent position: the center of an experiment in

---

* Originally published in the *San Antonio Express-News*, January 16th, 2022.

democracy. In such a revolt, language itself was attacked as a carrier of what was true and installed in its place the fantasies of one man.

We proclaim to be a nation founded by words that we agreed to as a people to further what democracy is and can be. When Alexis de Tocqueville visited the United States from France in 1831 at age twenty-five to observe this experiment, he noted the rights of the people were linked to virtue. "The idea of rights is nothing but the conception of virtue applied to the world of politics," Tocqueville wrote in *Democracy in America.*

And while he praised the new nation for linking virtue to rights, he readily admitted, "Nothing is harder than freedom's apprenticeship. The same is not true of despotism" which has a sinister intention; it "often presents itself as the repairer of all the ills suffered, the support of just rights, defender of the oppressed, and founder of order."

His observation intimates that democracy will always be in jeopardy of being undermined by words that promise the opposite of their actions. Democracy, nested in the language of the Constitution, is always vulnerable to an invasion by hordes of words that disguise insidious intentions. Words conveying "a stolen election," and promoted by nothing more than a desire for power, led to the January 6th attack, reinforced by an army of laws to suppress voting. Yet each citizen's vote is an expression of the larger language of the people's will.

The rights of the governed face accelerated erosion today by words that shape laws to steal the voice of citizens. Words have the power to orient or disorient us, to shape our thoughts and behavior, as well as distort our perceptions and beliefs. Acts of violence are promoted as justified responses.

In *On Tyranny*, Timothy Snyder explores the power of words in the section "Be kind to our language." He encourages us to read more and watch news outlets less; avoid using clichés that deaden ideas and fresh thinking; and develop our own way of speaking to avoid the sinkholes of media-speak in order "to define the shape and significance of events." He promotes shared conversation over angry confrontation because it encourages a more critical attitude toward what we hear.

Democracy flourishes when challenged; it falters when our words atrophy into convenient bromides that mute more challenging cthat ground us in a shared reality.

22

TRUST'S PRESENCE OR ABSENCE WILL MAKE ALL THE DIFFERENCE*

Many will remember Ronald Reagan's famous and oft-repeated mantra, "Trust but Verify." He was taught this Russian proverb by an American scholar, liked it, and made it a signature slogan in many of his talks. Trust is a virtue worth exploring at a historical moment of its corrosive weakening. "In God We Trust" is printed on our currency. In money's circulation Trust is also shared and exchanged. We see the word in "Boards of Trustees," in "Bank and Trust" logos, in setting up a "Trust Fund," or in *entrusting* what we value to another.

Security and good faith underpin many formats of Trust in our society; it is verification that something or someone is in good hands.

I think of Trust as the heartbeat of any authentic relationship. In our exchanges with others, a fundamental question we might and should ask is less, "Is this person loyal?" but more deeply, "Is this person trustworthy?" From the response to this central question, all other elements of that relationship ripple out. Along with the virtues practiced by many—Faith, Hope, and Love—I would add Trust as the fourth term in a virtuous life.

Trust is also no stranger to Truth; they are intimate first cousins. Truth suffers a hit when Trust is attacked or dismantled. When Trust is

---

* Originally published in the *Herald-Zeitung*, February 19th-20th, 2022.

beaten down, we may at first gasp, then grasp for certainty anywhere it appears available.

Further, Trust is also sacramental; it creates a sacred way of being with ourselves and others, including our social and political institutions. Belief too shares with Trust a sacred partnership; what and who I Trust I can believe in. They are mutually supportive and nourishing. Without Trust, a host of demons can invade the gap opened by Trust's absence. Here are a few that come to mind:

- Suspicion of others
- Lust for power
- Uncertainty that breeds fear and anxiety
- Extreme obsession with safety and security
- Tribalism
- Rigid us/them splits
- Magnified inequities towards Others pushed to the margins
- Intolerance
- Rigid control
- Extremism
- Self-doubt

In Trust's absence our horizons may narrow, suffering severe constrictions. Without Trust, generosity loses its vitality as largesse and courage diminishes. Without Trust, relationships suffer malnourishment and anemia, their vital affection suffocated.

Trust is a compilation of all the above and more as they assemble a worldview, a life perspective, a way of being. Seeing the world through the lens of Trust offers a differently textured world than one envisioned through the filter of Distrust.

When the very young French visitor, Alexis de Tocqueville, visited the United States in 1830, he observed and wrote deeply and thoughtfully about our way of life, the role of citizens within our political institutions, and other cultural topics. His insights about the nature of our government remain poignantly relevant today.

In his massive *Democracy in America*, he observed, "The will of a democracy is changeable, its agents rough, its laws imperfect . . . But if it is true that there will soon be nothing intermediate between the sway of democracy and the yoke of a single man, should we not rather steer toward the former than voluntarily submit to the latter?"

He concludes his chapter on "Maintaining a Democratic Republic" by asking us to consider this question: "And if we must finally reach a state of complete equality, is it not better to let ourselves be leveled down by freedom rather than by a despot?" Despotism creates a formidable opponent of Democracy; what separates the two rests on the vital and vigorous presence of Trust; when mutual Trust is organic, and robust, Despotism scuttles into the shadows.

Retrieving mutual Trust could inaugurate a lasting national and international Peace by first admitting what is true from fabrications engineered by self-serving despots.

23

THE THEFT OF A NATIONAL NARRATIVE HARMS US ALL*

There is an Irish saying my friend Phil Cousineau includes in his book *The Oldest Story in the World:* any journey one takes is not complete until one tells a story about their adventure. So, the story about the voyage is as crucial to its meaning as the adventure itself.

In mythologist Joseph Campbell's classic work of 1949, *The Hero with a Thousand Faces,* he illustrates three "moments" of a journey: 1. Departure from the normal and familiar; 2. Meeting with both adversaries as well as helping companions; 3. A return home with "the boon" or the story of what one has learned during their quest.

The boon or story surveys the knowledge and perhaps the wisdom that expands and deepens the storyteller's vision of themselves and the world traversed. When shared with others, the story may deepen the level of their self-and-world knowledge; stories look both within one and outside to the world they inhabit. Many of you know that 12-Step Recovery Programs are guided in large measure by stories, personal narratives told to and received by others. Some healing power emerges in narratives that one can experience imaginally, not simply literally.

We can connect with strangers and friends more deeply when we share our tales with them, which is to share our identity, our history, and

---

* Originally published in the *Herald-Zeitung*, July 23rd-24th, 2022.

our aspirations. Telling our narratives and listening to others' plots satisfies a deep hunger in both speaker and listener. Our stories voiced is one of our most creative acts; sharing our stories can be a generous way of relating deeply to ourselves and others on a level far more profound than those offered by statistics, surveys, and other forms of facts that don't reveal the contours of a coherent narrative on a deeper level. One's myth remains hidden.

When someone asks who we are, our response often takes the form of a story. Each story we tell or hear carries a mythic resonance. We remember that the word "mythos" means *story*.

When we identify deeply with our own story, we tap into closely held beliefs, prejudices, shadows, values, assumptions, and aspirations. In a sense, we language ourselves into our present being through the stories we tell. Narrating ourselves in the world seems to be essential to our nature as a species. This deep hunger reveals the impulse to present ourselves both *as* a story and *in* a story.

Storyteller Richard Kearney observes in his book *On Stories* that "each nation discovers it is at heart an 'imaginal community,' a narrative construction to be reoriented and reconstructed repeatedly." Forgetting one's narrative origins, he goes on, is dangerous, because it can lead to "self-oblivion" when the disease of a community takes itself for granted or becomes so narcissistic it believes it is the center of the world and therefore entitled to assert itself, to the detriment or the silencing of others.

In this light, Democracy is less a noun, more a verb; it is a story in motion. However imperfectly, an origin myth or story embodies shared values and stabilizing meanings that promote the following in the collective imagination: 1. participation, 2. Integration, and 3. aspiration. It shapes our past into formed memories that guide us as a people.

I am therefore more concerned with the theft today of our origin story, our founding narrative, that largely defines who we are and wish to become as a people sharing a communal narrative that aspires to benefit all its citizens.

Such a theft—to be replaced by a groundless fiction that is self-serving and just shy of self-serving wish-fulfillment—is felonious. If we allow our founding narrative to be eclipsed by a story-as-scam, we lose something that sustains our identity as a people. Such corrosion unmoors us from a shared history and more painfully, perhaps, from one another. A nation orphaned from its founding narrative opens the door to despots and other self-serving demagogues.

24

BETTING ON FANTASY: A MODERN ALLEGORY*

Not long ago I bought five lottery tickets for a total of five dollars. When I realized that the date was 6/22/22, my fantasy thinking kicked in and I made the investment. I *believed* the date had special significance conducive to my ability to win. So long as I didn't run the lottery numbers through the machine at a local Pit Stop, I could maintain my belief that I might have won. Thus far I have side-stepped the "reality machine" waiting to read my ticket.

My desire to win, as well as my belief that I might have won, joined forces to allow me to sustain the myth of being a winner. So long as I don't expose my numbers to the "reality" machine that will reveal whether I am a winner or a loser, I am able to sustain the fantasy of having won.

However, when I finally run my ticket through the "reality check" and it reveals those dreaded words, "Not a Winner," I have the option of rebuffing the machine's fact by accusing it of malfunctioning and that I did in fact win. The accusation allows me to sustain my magical thinking.

I can further accuse and so deflect the fact that I lost by accusing the store employees of rigging the machine so they could profit from my "winning ticket" that my own fantasy thinking had manufactured. I can

* Originally published in the *Herald-Zeitung*, July 9th-10th, 2022.

then override what had been called by D. Stephenson Bond "directed thinking" in his book, *Living Myth,* which is rooted in facts, in what can be proven, to maintain my magical belief.

An important shift in interpreting experience enters here. "I bet I won" subtly shifts into "I believe I won," so now my magical belief is the new subject matter, not *the fact* that I lost.

When we live in a myth, writes Bond, we encounter experiences through culturally formed ways. If enough people can be persuaded to replace the "myth of fact" with the "myth of fiction," then an empirical reality we once shared is dismantled under the mythic pressure of a new belief system—an alternative universe—a galaxy far away from the grounded reality that once prevailed that proven facts provide. They hold us together, like a bonding agent, so that while there is space for differences, there is an infrastructure that we collectively believe in and share.

When what Bond calls "a functional adaptation to our cultural environment" is ruptured, becomes dysfunctional, and our connection to a shared empirical world "is thwarted," chaos rushes in to fill the vacuum. No one escapes the infection of this maladaptation. Myths die when their balancing tendencies are disturbed, deflected, and dismantled. Then dissociation may soon lead to fear, anger, and violent disruptions in some of its participants.

Myths, both personal and collective, are formed in just this way. This new myth can keep the "winner/loser" disoriented and disassociated from the truth of directed thinking. Perhaps, I think, I can persuade others that I have won so they too purchase my winner fantasy with their own "buy-in" belief that I did really win.

For the time being, I will continue to carry my lottery tickets in my possession. Each morning I wake a winner in my mind's eye. I also suspect that all our beliefs ultimately return to the original myth fanning life into them, be they rooted in reality or fantasy. Someday soon, however, I need to face the "reality machine" at Pit Stop to close out my fantasy. Or collect my winnings?!

25

PRESERVING OUR INNOCENCE: AT WHAT COST?*

Democracies thrive on the presence of diversity, plurality of thought, and competing points of view. The aim here is not about power complexes but on cooperation to ascertain what benefits the common good.

Tyranny, on the other hand, thrives on mass conformity and on renouncing questioning assumptions and beliefs that promote a democratic imagination, which honors differences in the messiness of competing points of view.

I am responding to Fort Worth Senator Matt Krause's task as chair of the Texas House's General Investigating Committee, and candidate for attorney general, to "ensure no child is exposed to pornography or other inappropriate content in a Texas public school." Now "Inappropriate" is a slippery political word. Equally incredulous is language that promises to shield any student who feels uneasy or uncomfortable by what they read.

Krause's fantasy must be addressed, if not directly challenged. He has amassed some 850 titles that he believes are dangerous to today's students. The list is available online. I must ask, Mr. Krause: How many of these titles have you actually read?

---

* Originally published in the *Herald-Zeitung,* January 8th-9th, 2022.

As an educator for over fifty-four years, I have taught elementary grades 1-5 of Special Education students through high school, undergrads in college, as well as graduate students. Shaping the learning environment by purging discomfort requires a closer look, for such a move is a distortion of learning itself.

History reveals a pattern in the nascent stages of tyranny's message: "I/we can protect you from others" or "I alone can protect you," which can lull an entire population into a sense of false security with such a promise. Such a seduction is embedded in a false "benevolence." What concerns me here is the presence in our history of the myth of innocence, which hosts of historians have carefully explored. Innocence can be a terrible force for arresting differences by exiling beliefs not held by a few, especially those in power positions.

This myth may be exploited in the promise of purging books-that-discomfort by promising to keep outside forces, contrary ideas, assumptions, and prejudices outside the compound of thought for security reasons. None of us desires to have our younger people exposed to hard-core pornography, but that is finally not the issue here.

As cultural critic Susan Griffin informs us in *Pornography and Silence,* when the pornographic imagination silences voices of dissent, "Language ceases to describe reality. Words lose their direct relationship with actuality." Fictions can be easily confused with, and chosen, over facts. Pornography, she asserts later, is always about control and domination. It is a form that tyranny takes to suppress Otherness.

Purging book titles on topics that surround and perhaps unnerve us, is primarily why this exiling of ideas contrary to our baked-in beliefs is both fallacious and salacious. Innocence becomes a trap, an enclosure based on a fantasy of preserving the status quo and promoting its egregious distortions.

When students enter the emotional field of unease or feeling uncomfortable, suppressing topics that may incite such discomfort is actually an opportunity and an invitation for authentic learning to begin. Learning to cope with what makes us squeamish is one of the fruits of real learning because where authentic dialogue prevails, delusions can become places of entry to learning tolerance.

What if we at least considered another route than purging, censoring, and suffocating topics that disconcert and create dis-ease? What if we considered instead opportunities for authentic conversation? I think here of the award-winning novelist and cultural critic, Toni Morrison, who wrote in *The Origin of Others* toward the end of her life, "Narrative fiction provides a controlled wilderness, an opportunity to be and to become the Other. The stranger. With sympathy, clarity, and the risk of self-examination."

Literature that brings into consciousness topics of race, gender identity, economics, disparities of wealth and privilege, migrants, haves and have-nots, should not be purged but promoted within a context that does not breed feuds; rather, it can cultivate students' abilities to articulate their perspectives while learning to listen to contrary worldviews and to refrain from condemning them because they are different.

Moments of unease or discomfort should not be the standard for suppressing other voices. Let them be heard in those instances where a "controlled wilderness" can lead to deeper, more reflective listening, accompanied by a more generous tolerance.

26

FLIRTING WITH AUTHORITARIANISM IN AMERICA*

In our personal and cultural lives, trying to understand what events mean becomes more difficult when not informed by an historical context. In 2017, Yale history professor Timothy Snyder published a tiny book with a massive title—*On Tyranny*—in which he laid out "Twenty Lessons from the Twentieth Century." Each one deserves our contemplation to make visible the deep mythic patterns surrounding, if not engulfing, us today.

Now, gratefully, Snyder has teamed up with artist Nora Krug, author and illustrator, to reissue the book in an expanded edition that includes these same twenty lessons in magnificent graphic art, inviting further meditations. The twenty insights include: 1: Do not obey in advance; 6: Be wary of paramilitaries; 10: Believe in truth; 18: Be calm when the unthinkable arrives.

Each discussion is securely nested in historical antecedents so we can ponder them within a fact-based landscape. The one, however, that called most forcefully to me is 9: Be kind to our language. Snyder makes clear that those who hold and control the public vocabulary, in large measure, control reality. Tyranny resides, then, in coercing a population to adopt ideas couched in words, slogans, and cliches that are created more out of desire and self-interest than proven facts. Ideologies are created in just

---

* Originally published in the *San Antonio Express-News,* November 5th, 2021.

this way. Snyder suggests opposing this growing trend, which in George Orwell's dystopian novel, *1984*, reveals how "visual media is highly constrained" to discourage thought, contemplation, and fidelity to the truth.

Snyder encourages each of us to "develop our own way of thinking," which is difficult if our main sources of information stem exclusively from television or computer screens, which can shrink vocabularies and encourage repeating prepackaged prose that pretends to offer, but often fails to express, nuance and complexity. "When we repeat the same words and phrases that appear in the daily media, we accept the absence of a larger framework." One major way to challenge this trend toward oblivion in thought is to read: read books, lengthy articles, essays that, yes, can also deceive, but can engage complexities that propaganda's repetition shies away from as too risky.

In addition, as electronic media moves at electric speed, interspersed with commercials that fracture sustained thought and pull us from the context of a particular content, reading books is a proven way to think through complexity. It sharpens discernment and helps to build arguments and points of view that cultivate both subtlety, even paradox, which is most often sacrificed in electronic presentations of what has now become a constant wave of "Breaking News."

Snyder suggests that "the effort to define the shape and significance of events requires words and concepts that elude us when we are entranced by visual stimuli."

As an antidote, the historian also promotes reading classic works of fiction: "Any good novel enlivens our ability to think about ambiguous situations and judge the intentions of others." He names, for instance, *The Unbearable Lightness of Being* by Milan Kundera, *It Can't Happen Here* by Sinclair Lewis, and *Harry Potter and the Deathly Hallows* by J.K. Rowling. Several of his nonfiction recommendations include *The Language of the Third Reich* by Victor Klemperer, *The Origins of Totalitarianism* by Hannah Arendt, and *The Power of the Powerless* by Vaclav Havel.

In this new rendering of his bestselling original, image and language congeal to expose the monstrous underpinnings of tyranny-in-the-making. We must all learn to read the signs of disease and then become resistance forces to slow its rise.

27

• • •

ENGAGING AGING AS SPIRITUAL PRACTICE*

I never really imagined what aging would be like or how aging might feel.

Yes, an older body subject to disease and limits, a memory that needed kick-starting more often than when I was younger. Perhaps less mobility and more a sedentary life as my default position each day. Would my attitude gravitate toward what South Wales poet Dylan Thomas cautioned in his poem, "Do Not Go Gentle Into That Good Night," which I read as an undergraduate? Would I rage against death, as in his defiant refrain that ends each of the stanzas? But here I am, at seventy-seven, continuing to teach a variety of audiences, writing, publishing books, traveling, taking painting classes, and enjoying family and friends. I am not alone. We are in an unprecedented era of an entire population living longer than ever before in human history. How are people using that extended time to refresh and deepen what purpose their lives are calling them to?

But there is another entire galaxy of interior possibilities, as retired psychotherapist Connie Zweig eloquently expresses in her new book, *The Inner Work of Age: Shifting from Role to Soul.* I recently heard her on a Zoom talk on the book's central features describing how nuanced and complex

---

* Originally published in the *San Antonio Express-News*, October 2nd, 2021.

aging can be. It is a time for new discoveries of one's central myth, namely, the core values and aspirations that give our lives coherence, meaning, and purpose.

She believes, for instance, that aging is a spiritual practice, inviting a deepening into our interior worlds. And far from an individual suffering a midlife crisis, she suggests that as a therapist she witnessed a "late-life crisis" in those she worked with. So, what paths may open within our aging journey? For her, aging into elderhood is an opportunity to awaken to deeper dimensions of ourselves.

Many books on aging and retirement stress new tasks, like volunteering, painting, or dance classes—all admirable activities. But Zweig takes a different tack: "What do you long for in your aging?" "What is your promised land?" as she recalls the end of Moses' life after leading his people to the edge of that famous landscape of milk and honey. "What is falling away from your life that you may have clung to for decades?" She believes our dream life as we age can offer wisdom if we are willing to explore its deeper psychic roots.

As a practicing Buddhist, Zweig offers that cultivating the art of meditation can be a life-preserver, slowing brain degeneration. Citing a University of California, Los Angeles neurologist's studies, she reports, "On average, the brains of long-term practitioners appeared to be seven and a half years younger at the age of fifty than the brains of non-meditators."

Finally, as author/editor of two very popular books on the shadow in our psychological life, Zweig believes that as we move in age to the sage within, we would benefit from engaging the shadow, which is "our personal unconscious, that part of our mind that is behind or beneath our conscious awareness." "The shadow holds the key to removing the inner obstacles that block us from finding the treasures of late life," she observes.

Readers will find in her book many case studies from her practice that provide a host of narratives to further ground her observations and insights about not raging against death, but rather welcoming and connecting with the shaded terrains of our aging pilgrimage.

In moonlight, for instance, our perceptions soften to a less sharply chiseled world; we may then rejoice in the knowledge that a life that honors the shadows of our being can complement all that we have become and achieved as well as dream of what lies ahead.

28

---•---

FROM ACT YOUR AGE TO THINK YOUR AGE*

Unfortunately, most images of aging citizens thrust at us in our youth-propelled culture are outer-directed. They advise us on what to take and what to do to maintain some semblances of youth at a time in our lives when letting those images go honors our aging processes and our emerging Elderhood.

Little, however, is offered to our population on the inner work of aging because our extraverted culture scarcely recognizes honoring the inner life. A new book seeks to address this imbalance: *The Inner Work of Age: Shifting from Role to Soul* by retired Jungian analyst Connie Zweig.

Her book contains dozens of stories from her practice dealing with individuals who feel lost in the often-uncharted territory of aging from within. I will focus on her suggestions about moving into Elderhood. Her claim is that little is offered to the aging population to help us transition from aging to eldering wherein we are invited to pass our wisdom from a well-lived life on to the next generation. Having recently celebrated my 77th birthday, I was open and receptive to learning from her own wisdom on this process from which none can avoid.

Eldering is a natural impulse arising as we age, but she points out that while someone fifty-five can be considered an Elder, someone eighty-

---

* Originally published in the *Herald-Zeitung,* October 26th, 2021.

five may not be. Eldering must be cultivated consciously and with a receptivity to one's own process of aging. Eldering is both a noun and a verb. But the seminal question is: what is an Elder? In Part III of her book devoted to this presence that wants to be recognized in our lives, and because there are innumerable faces an Elder can assume, "We must take care not to define Elder too tightly," the author cautions.

An Elder is one who has let go of old patterns of thinking and being that have held them hostage in life, preferring instead to seek a greater, deeper sense of self-awareness in their inner lives. An Elder transitions from the role of the heroic ego, which invests in doing, achieving, striving, working, and grasping, but "whose mission is over," Zweig asserts. As Elder, one cultivates a more nuanced, quieter, more reflective attitude towards life. Being takes precedence over doing, but that does not eliminate continued becoming who one is meant to be, no matter one's age.

Further, an Elder "knows how to listen because we know how to quiet our minds and be present." An Elder turns one's attitude towards their remaining days to include feeling "committed to life in the face of immanent death," she writes. Like the heroic ideal that called to us earlier, an Elder's reality calls to us later in life; an Elder lives in the contours of gratitude, generosity, a deeper spiritual and emotional life, a lessening of being right and an acceptance *of what is* that we align ourselves to, while not rejecting *what might be*.

The author is also clear about what an Elder is *not*: "an Elder does not resist change or impermanence" and does not "live in the past or an anxious future, denying the portal of presence"; "an Elder is not shame-based nor succumbs to cynicism, bitterness, or resignation." Neither does an Elder "avoid facing fear, suffering, and loss. . . by losing connection to shadow awareness," which tries to discourage us from our continued deepening into our unique selves.

Connie cautions her readers to beware of "the inner ageist," who scolds us for wanting to live our unlived life, by announcing prohibitions like, "You can't do that" or "You're too old to try that" or "You've lived your life, now stay home."

Aging happens on its own; but within that matrix Eldering can open new corridors, new interests, and new risks that continue to give life meaning and purpose.

29

AGING IN BODY, ELDERING IN SPIRIT*

I had previously written here about a new book on aging: *The Inner Work of Age: Shifting from Role to Soul* by retired therapist Connie Zweig. Seldom is it an easy task to rethink and revision a paradigm or set of beliefs that have guided our thinking and behavior for decades. But her book does just that.

Through reflection, writing suggestions, and attending to the guiding patterns of our journey, we can become more aware of our progress towards embracing the "Spiritual Elder" in us.

The core of her thinking is that we can continue to evolve spiritually later in life by shifting our focal length so to "see ourselves in relation to a larger system," open to others' points of view, and allowing our own needs "to be relativized." This spiritual awakening includes muting our ego-driven wants and desires so that a fuller sense of our self can be heard, nurtured, and shared.

At the heart of such a shift is a continual impulse to "expand our awareness and bring that awareness into the larger culture." My sense is that our culture is hungry for voices of Elders to share their wisdom with us, to counter the fierce energy of adolescent flames that insists on "my" and "me" to the exclusion of "us" and "we."

---

* Originally published in the *Herald-Zeitung*, November 9th, 2021.

Connie identifies the qualities of a Spiritual Elder: "inclusion, holism, harmony, interconnection and a non-literal spirituality." Another strength of her study is the rich array of interviews she conducts with Spiritual Elders like Ken Wilber, who offered, "Growing old is an opportunity to reset our priorities, a continuing chance to drop things that aren't important." Easier said than done when we each have our own shadow figures haunting us to keep everything in place. Rather than surrender to them, we can find ways to befriend them, for they have their own wisdom to teach us.

When she asked another Spiritual Elder, Michael Meade, how one can identify oneself as an Elder, he responded, "When someone sees you that way, you become an Elder." He states a truth that each of us might accept regarding our internal wisdom: "All Elders have medicine—physical, emotional, musical, story. Let's give our unique medicine to the world."

Each of us is called to a destiny, to a life that only we can live; if we deflect it, the world will never experience just that specific possibility. This call later in life is grounded in what Connie calls "a holy longing." It may take the form of "Elder Activism." For instance, any number of volunteer avenues, adding one's voice in reading groups, or serving the community's food bank or other organizations "that help the helpless, the marginal."

If we are so fortunate, we may engage in "Conscious Grandparenting," a form that my wife and I enjoy immensely with our three granddaughters. In this way we extend our borders to larger pools of both curiosity and need. Grandparents have perspectives and angles of wisdom that may be unique to them; if we don't share them with our grandchildren, that part of their life will be left malnourished. Simply having conversations with our children's children while throwing the frisbee in the front yard after a meal or reading something together can be rich moments of intimacy between two other generations.

Spiritual activism is one rich avenue of encouraging awakening to the larger story that informs all of us. Perhaps just making space for silent time as a rich field for meditative reading and journaling can deepen our conscious awakening. The point of aging is not to be trapped by what one can no longer do, but to notice where there are openings to further affirm and express a life well-lived. We owe it to our younger generations to illustrate how a rich life does not end with aging.

30

DO WE VALUE SPECTACLE OVER SUBSTANCE?*

When we take a well-earned break from the onslaught of news that bombards us daily, we might wonder, as we should, how fantasies of reality have gained such strength and support in these past years and seem to coagulate today with greater concentration.

I returned to a book I had read in 2012, published in 2009 by a foreign correspondent of twenty years and a *New York Times* writer for fifteen. Chris Hedges' perceptive study, *Empire of Illusion: The End of Literacy and the Triumph of Spectacle,* offers a series of cultural diagnoses that have become more accurate with time.

On the inside dust jacket is a pair of steely sentences: "A culture that cannot distinguish between reality and illusion dies. And we are dying." His book then details carefully and with abundant supporting sources how this stark diagnosis can be grasped. His bibliography carries a cargo of 120 sources.

I chose just a few of his insights to share in this article.

1. "We are a culture that has been denied or has passively given up, the linguistic and intellectual tools to cope with complexity, to separate illusion from reality." As an educator of fifty-five years,

---

* Originally published in the *San Antonio Express-News*, July 14th, 2021.

I have found the most challenging and rewarding task with students is to encourage and foster critical and imaginal levels of discernment with and through the material we study together. Reading and thinking with discernment are both challenging and rewarding gifts to ourselves, to be cultivated in life-long learning.

2.   In the vacuum created by #1 above, "Television has become a medium built around the skillful manipulating of images, ones that can overpower reality." It is not only our primary form of mass communication, it is more: a large segment of the audience receives not just their news from television, but their sense of what is real as well. Each network vies for our submission.

3.   In the engineered new power center of our culture, "Propaganda has become a substitute for ideas and ideology." For many, Hedges continues, "it is the final arbitrator for what matters in life." Anyone who knows and enjoys the rewards of reading understands the often-pale representation of television over the written word, where one can pause, consider, not be told what to think, and draw conclusions from a baseline of the material read.

4.   "My feelings" become the acid test of what is real and true. But we might ask if one's feelings are in fact largely composed of one's assumptions, fears, prejudices, and fantasies that create a virtual Parliament of emotions that one construes as not only true but not to be questioned. So we wind up marinating in a private brew of fantasies, fetishes, and apprehensions.

5.   Hedges proposes that "it is style and story, not content and fact, that inform mass politics." He goes on to cite another writer's term, "junk politics," a phrase that "personalizes and moralizes issues rather than clarifying them." Again, the emphasis is on the private feelings and baked-in beliefs that largely have as their end security and safety, whatever that might cost.

Such a posture can shield one from the ambiguous and unknown future as well as insulate one from the past, from history, from the wisdom of our ancestors, and from a more panoramic view of one's present reality. Such a condition can be reinforced, Hedges argues, by those seeking power and self-interest to create an appearance of intimacy with one's supporters while not actually possessing the qualities they boast about possessing.

Lastly, an important question for any of us thinking critically about these issues to ask: Who in fact is creating or recreating our "public mythology"—Hedges' term—and for what ends?

31

SPEECH CAPTURES TIES BETWEEN LIES AND VIOLENCE: ALEXANDER SOLZHENITSYN*

One of the many values of knowing history is that it often reveals how the present can be a close iteration, even a repetition, of the past. History also gives us a perspective on our current social challenges that we might think are happening for the first time. History helps us shake off our naïve "in-the-moment" perspective so we can widen our vision to discern larger patterns that we mortals repeat with consistent fidelity.

In 1970 a Russian novelist and dissident, Alexander Solzhenitsyn (1918-2008), was awarded the Nobel Peace Prize for his unwavering study of and contributions to the tradition of Russian Literature. He sent his speech to Stockholm to be read, fearing that if he left the Soviet Union, he would not be allowed to return to his country and family.

His idea in the speech was to promote what artists and writers of a culture could contribute to the social and political realms of their time. Artists are the ones, Solzhenitsyn writes, who offer us old truths that endure and that can aid us in understanding "the modern world." "And when the old truth is told us again," he affirms, "we do not remember that we once possessed it." So, like history itself, classic works of literature return our memories to us, both nationally and internationally; they allow us to see ourselves through evocative prisms of what has gone before and to see through a moral valence of what is most valued.

---

* Originally published in the *Herald-Zeitung*, June 12th-13th, 2021.

His speech is rich in its variety and in its depth. However, I was particularly interested in his insights at his speech's beginning and end, on the relation of violence to lies. In contrast to the truths of art, "a political speech, a hasty newspaper comment, a social program can . . . as far as appearances are concerned, be built smoothly and consistently on an error or a lie; and what is concealed and distorted will not be immediately clear."

Art reaches in the other direction, towards what our American writer William Faulkner called those "eternal verities" that inform us of the ways the human heart is often in open conflict with itself.

Towards the end of his thoughtful analysis of the truth of art and the forces that work as lies pretending to be true, he asks us to consider: "What can literature do against the pitiless onslaught of naked violence?" Not an easy question, but he asks us to consider the following: "Let us not forget that violence does not and cannot flourish by itself; it is inevitably intertwined with Lying."

Solzhenitsyn's comparison leads him to this insight: "Nothing screens violence except lies, and the only way lies can hold out is by violence." They are, within his personal Russian history, in which he spent eight years in the Gulag for speaking out against the purges of Stalin, then three more years in exile, intimately related. He ends his speech by offering a tighter coalition between lying and violence. "Whoever has once announced violence as his METHOD, must inexorably choose lying as his PRINCIPLE."

Perhaps many forms of violence, he muses, especially if they are to be sustained, "cannot go on without befogging themselves in lies, coating itself with lying's sugary oratory." Then, by an indirect move, violence may not move in a straight line, but by indirection: "usually it demands of its victims only allegiance to the lie, only complicity in the lie." The place and power of the arts, including writing but not limited to it, is that they have the power "to vanquish lies."

To dispel lies is at the same time to curtail or eliminate violence; they are inseparable in gaining traction; both could be dispelled or modified if we invite the wisdom of our artists into the conversation.

32

THE RIGHT STUFF FOR LIFE'S WRONG TERMS*

The effect of the successful adventure of the hero is the unlocking
and release again of the flow of life into the body of the world.
~Joseph Campbell, *The Hero with a Thousand Faces*

When I was invited by a faculty member at my graduate institute in California to volunteer to teach a correspondence course with inmates from a California state prison, I responded with a course on personal mythology using mythologist Joseph Campbell's classic text, *The Hero with a Thousand Faces*. A notice to the inmates went out and five signed on. Now, eighteen months later, I am grateful that I did not refuse my colleague's call.

In reading the student inmates' essays, I discovered that one shared experience they chose to write about was influenced by Campbell's mythic narratives as well as his own reflections in *Hero*. They learned that he had given them a story in which to place their own woundedness within a larger frame. One student was attracted to Campbell before we began working together, by viewing Bill Moyers' series of interviews with Campbell in *The Power of Myth*. The course offering, he said, created an opportunity to explore Campbell further through guidance from the

* Originally published in the *San Antonio Express-News*, May 18th, 2021.

course's structure and my writing meditations prompts they responded to. But more importantly, many wrote about how they sought a purpose in prison that the *Hero,* as well as other courses, encouraged and helped shape them.

Resentment, hostility, a sustained anger, and feeling out of control— all emotions that placed some of my students in prison initially—yielded to a search for meaning through rekindling a spiritual life they had left behind or never had, or exploring the practice of Buddhism, or attending recovery programs on addiction.

In their essays they related how Campbell's stages in the hero's journey illuminated their own histories wherein they either refused an earlier calling or had listened to and assented to their revised summons within the confines of prison life. Readings in the *Hero* volume validated many of their choices and added others.

One student wrote of how his inability to forgive himself and others who misled him in life resulted in his imprisonment. He used the language of being turned into a monster through his unforgiving attitude. Reading Campbell, he explored with increased clarity his life path and realized that he could reauthor the plot of his story by using the stages of the hero's journey: Departure, Initiation and Return. This template tempered his behavior and moderated his outbursts in prison.

Most dramatic, however, were those who admitted that Campbell's authentic and compassionate prose softened them and taught them to write more deeply about their own self-annihilation and recovery. They also found meaningful parallels between the 12-step programs of recovery and Campbell's stages of the hero's journey. One student phrased it this way: "Working with the 12-step program and Buddhist teachings, along with Campbell's insights, helped me understand myself better and to live in a more peaceful, healthy direction."

In one assignment I asked: "Where in your own life have you found yourself following the pattern Campbell outlined in 'Departure, Initiation, and Return?'" Their profound, insightful, and authentic responses to this mythical pattern opened each of them to their own personal myth. In a word that Campbell uses often in his writing, they discovered "correspondences" with their own story.

I in turn realized more fully how myths can be aspirational by offering students an ancient narrative that they grasped as universal but lived out with authentic personal particularity. Some mentioned that they were learning to write with more clarity as a result of studying Campbell's own writing style, made more poignant by his humanity that connected to their own stories of woundedness.

Writing on the hero archetype consistently affirmed their change in life direction and reinforced their transformed life's purpose. Two of them wrote that initially they reluctantly attended an Alcoholics Anonymous meeting. Now they host them. One discovered that he had talents as an artist; he sent me one of his paintings to share this newly-found form of personal expression. It hangs on our living room wall.

From this rich set of experiences, assisted directly by Campbell's classic text, I became more aware of the power of myth to incite explorations into one's own venture. I have also noticed that, yes, they are incarcerated—some for life—but they are no longer imprisoned. By this I mean that imprisonment feeds the victim archetype, but within incarceration, they located a level of freedom that sustains them. Incarceration is physical while imprisonment is psychological and mythic.

Through reading and writing on sections of the *Hero* image, they envisioned their own narratives in a different, more complex light. Some remarked that in prison they found a level of freedom never experienced before, in part because they felt they had reclaimed parts of themselves heretofore buried.

While meditating on their personal myth prompted by Campbell's insights, they expressed how they discovered their basic goodness, that the mistakes they made, often accompanied by substance abuse, no longer defined them. They ceased totalizing their identity with their crime. Several admitted that assisting others in prison has gifted their lives with joy and a more generous feeling for the suffering of others.

The *Hero*'s journey affirmed and further supported their own life's direction, a greater self-awareness, and the value of being in service to others. Incarcerated, they nonetheless stepped out of their cocoon of self-imprisonment in anger and resentment. One student admitted that he began once more to love who he is and to connect with others in similar compassionate ways.

This latter growth of a soul towards compassion may be the most valuable journey in their development; several faces of the hero's thousand visages found instrumental appearances as each student achieved greater self-acceptance.

Now that our work is finished, I miss and pray for each of them.

33

THE WHITE WHALE AND THE SPIRIT OF EQUALITY*

As fictional creations, classics of literature may afford a whaleship load of insights into the human condition if we read them with an open and receptive mind. And if we reread them later in life, more insights will breach from their depths.

One of these American classics, *Moby-Dick, or, The Whale,* most have heard of or read at some point: Herman Melville's classic tale of a dismembered Captain Ahab, wounded and crazed by his encounter with the white whale, gathers his crew to redress his deep narcissistic wound to slay his dismemberer.

But listen to Ishmael, the whaleman and writer of this epic—for he is the narrator, not Melville—in the first of two chapters titled "Knights and Squires": "Men may seem detestable as joint stock-stock companies and nations; knaves, fools, and murderers there may be; man may have mean and meagre faces; but, man in the ideal, is so noble and so sparkling, such a grand and glowing creature. . .. That immaculate manliness we feel within ourselves. . .."

Hardly the subject matter of a fierce hunt to destroy a white whale that has been made, in Ahab's heated and afflicted imagination, into a scapegoat for his agony. But Melville is also, throughout this grand epic, published in 1851 when he was only thirty-two, exploring the deeper

* Originally published in the *Herald-Zeitung,* August 5th, 2021.

American myth with its attendant aspirations and goals—that of democracy itself.

His interest is less what we are and more what we aspire to be in our best moments. A fierce abolitionist who often wrote of the evils of slavery, Melville was also an equally fierce defender of democracy as both an ideal and a reality.

His keenest and most eloquent, even lofty writing occurs at the end of Chapter 26; for not in the leaders but in the common man does he reserve his praises for; he realizes "an august dignity" that is "not that of kings and robes." "Thou shalt see it shining," he intones, "in the arm that wields a pick or drives a spike; that democratic dignity which, on all hands, radiates without end from God; Himself! The great God absolute! The center and circumference of all democracy! His omnipresence our divine equality!"

What a packed freight of insights and gleanings of the relationship between democracy, the dignity of the common man's noble labors, and the Almighty who reflects "divine equality."

He goes on to raise the common person to grand, epic proportions as embodiments of nobility: "Bear me out in it, thou just Spirit of Equality, what has spread one royal mantle of humanity over all my kind! Bear me out in it, thou great democratic God!"

In an age in which multiple Ahabs abound—those wounded, sometimes howling voices of overstuffed, often counterfeit grievances, coupled often with a sense of victimhood or pandemic surges of self-justifications that tack towards the illusory, Melville's whale of a tale—no fluke intended—calls us back to the ideals from which democracy is not the cause but the effect of an attitude that all people, common and privileged, experience at the heart of democratic energies.

Democracy and divinity complement one another; the God to whom one does not pay lip service but rather one who is incarnated in our actions, preserves a divine union between us mortals and the Godhead.

Of course, the Pequod, the whale ship named after a Native American tribe in the northeastern United States, sails on the waters of the Hebrew Bible and the New Testament. They are the most constant strands that hold Melville's epic weaves together, even as the democratic ideal is the mucilage that knits the entire enterprise of humanity into a coherent whole, a worthy goal to both yearn for and gesture towards.

34

REPLACING THE MYTH OF GROWTH[*]

We owe a debt of gratitude for Mark Friesenhahn's Guest Column, "Water Shortages Must be Addressed" that appeared in Saturday's *Herald-Zeitung* (April 17th-18th). While he does not use the word explicitly, he is speaking about the myth of growth and the dangers of its excesses, especially population growth in our area of New Braunfels, Texas.

Two qualities seem to accompany a myth:

1. They often operate unrecognized and the power they contain is underestimated.
2. They can, over time, grow into the appearance of facts so not to be questioned.

Both are dangerous for an individual's myth as well as for a community or region's infrastructure of Beliefs. Mark's cautions resonate out to a larger, more global dilemma, including the need to make crucial choices. In a recent documentary, "Extinction: The Facts,"[†] narrator David Attenborough takes a panoramic view of the way the earth herself is suffering exhaustion, scarcity, and a pandemic that has become a global COVID infection.

One of the people Attenborough interviews asks this fundamental question regarding over-fishing in the world's oceans. "Do you want

---

[*] Originally published in the *Herald-Zeitung,* May 6th, 2021.
[†] https://www.pbs.org/video/extinction-the-facts-8dbqlc/

enormous catches over a short time, or more modest and sustainable catches over a long time?"

That decision is being made for us by commercial fisheries and law-makers. Myths, as belief systems, offer different narratives; those in control of power positions will reinforce the story they believe most closely aligns with their own views and ambitions, be they excessive or distorted. I believe that locally we are attempting to be persuaded by the narrative that there is plenty of water to go around, regardless of our explosion of growth.

Lost or disregarded in this mythic exuberance is a more global myth of planetary scarcity becoming more of a stable reality than an occasional aberration. Given little or no voice, however, is yet another myth: the interconnectedness of all parts of social and natural segments that form a cohesive whole. Not affirming this interrelatedness of all parts will blindside us in ways we cannot yet imagine.

Every part of nature and culture is interconnected, webbed into a cohesive whole, interdependent; they incorporate us all. Any decision by those who hold power that does not imagine such an interdependency is operating out of a fractured myth and with blurred vision.

No real change or compromise will occur, no laws of consequence will be enacted—though Mark rightly calls for just such action by asking us to contact our representatives—because the underlying beliefs driving the current mythology of growth/expansion/development is stuck in place.

It is necessary to adopt an alternative myth which is the infrastructure that truly powers change. For myths, as much as anything, are attitudes; without a shift in attitude, nothing significant will alter. An alternative myth to the current fixation on growth would include:

• A myth of sustainability
• A series of reappraisals of current growth patterns which underlie a deeper myth: the myth of economics.
• A responsible use of the power of elected officials and those wielding influence in the private sector, to see the longer vision far into the future for our area.

- Modifying the frenetic addiction to growth patterns that are currently self-destructive.

I believe we all have a civic duty to pay close attention and to vote for those who are running for city council and other positions of influence locally. Who is voicing authentic concerns about the limits of our resources and who are at least considering actions to address this most consequential of crises?

The crisis of growth itself is an outdated myth that needs massive editing to promote sustainability. Thank you again, Mark Friesenhahn.

35

WE CAN FIND WONDER IN FRIENDSHIPS*

Now past my mid-70s, I find myself reflecting on many things that I had taken for granted as simply part of life's fabric. But lately I have become curious about friendships that I enjoy and like to nurture.

A friendship is a mysterious, marvelous spirit in human beings. Many of my closest friendships are sources of hope, and they often surprise me. I guess I enjoy being surprised by friendship. A deep friendship allows us to see and become more of who we are. They refresh us and we hope the influence is reciprocal.

I was surprised in discovering many years ago that the woman I have been married to for fifty-three years is hands-down my best friend. What a treasure: to be married to one's soul mate. Through her I catch glimpses of my strongest gifts and my prickly disabilities—those places in my interior life where I must excavate further.

When I befriend someone new, further dimensions of myself, perhaps never explored before, rise to the surface. It is as if in learning of another's stories, where their deepest identity resides, I re-story my own life; the plot does indeed both thicken and broaden. Differences are not deflected, but similarities are highlighted to the benefit of both in a friendship.

---

* Originally published in the *San Antonio Express-News*, December 11th-12th, 2021.

Friendships can also soften some of the hard edges of our sacred opinions, prejudices, and unfounded assertions; a real friend will not be timid about challenging us as much as agreeing with us. Through friends we may gain or become aware of a world larger than our own interior compound has allowed entry.

Certain friends can reveal to us models of thought, beliefs, and models of behavior; on occasion they even serve as Elders to guide us on our life's pilgrimage. They can, in effect, alter the existential syntax that shapes us.

On occasion, a friend can model for us learning how to forgive ourselves and others; a friend can deepen one's capacity for compassion and console us when we are challenged by a life circumstance—loss, illness, a change in fortune, a betrayal—that faced alone, might overwhelm us. Now while we don't want to turn our friends into our therapists, nonetheless, a friend who has learned the art of listening can be a healing presence when our wounds again begin to suppurate.

A friend's warmth can also expose the stranger in us to a relationship that can heal where those persistent afflictions reside. Quite possibly, the stranger in us can, in some instances, be the wound that guards us against becoming vulnerable to new registers of understanding.

I say this because a true friend has the resilience not to surrender their authentic self when it contrasts or competes with ours. Their very authenticity can reveal to us where we may have harbored an inauthentic self whose time to be exposed and expunged or modified is overdue.

All this is to suggest that perhaps our friends have been given to us as gifts that embody a divine presence before us and a spiritual reality gesturing within us. Yes, a friend may be the source of offering a helping hand; but more: a faithful friend may be the one who extends to us a hopeful heart. And, as a friend, we accept a moral responsibility to be available to the suffering and the joys of another.

A deep and abiding friendship always implies some risk, even a faith, that one does not betray the confidences or conflicts of the other. True friends both agree to nurture and cultivate the same cooperative bond of respect in the sense that each extends their own life's richness to the other in a spirit of generosity and trust.

36

<hr/>

A MYTHIC CROSSROADS: WHICH SHALL WE CHOOSE?*

So many of us are trying to make sense of what has ensued after the election, but little of the discussion has implicated what a mythic shift in consciousness is taking place. Think for a moment of the power of myth in this illustration by mythologist Sam Keen in *Your Mythic Journey: Finding Meaning in Your Life Through Writing and Storytelling*: "A myth can make a cow sacred in one culture and hamburger meat in another." Same animal, yet very different beliefs surrounding our bovine friends. What beliefs we hold shape our perception of what we see as well as who we are.

In this sense, democracy is a myth, namely, not a lie, as some claim, but rather a set of values and beliefs and attitudes that express a relationship between the individual, the society one lives within, and the larger environment, including the sacred qualities of life. Simply put, a myth is what we choose to believe in that gives our life coherence, if not meaning and purpose. A life without a myth is a life without meaning.

But the myth we live in often remains underground, out of sight, and as such exerts a formidable power in shaping what we think and what we do. Until the myth is challenged, attacked, or attempted to be erased. That is where we are today.

<hr/>

* Originally published in the *Herald-Zeitung*, December 12th-13th, 2020.

Our myth of a democratic society is shaped by three documents: *The Constitution, The Preamble* to *The Declaration of Independence* and *The Declaration* itself, which is our most forceful mythic statement. These documents state the myth that shaped our democracy. Within them are listed a set of "rights" but with these rights are also present certain responsibilities. One without the other is ineffectual if one wishes to maintain and defend the myth.

As with personal myths held by each of us, there is this larger national myth that breeds coherence, a sense of unity and belonging, and national purpose. If we treasure the myth that reflects us, we will each do our part to maintain it. If we fracture and divide into camps, the myth will lose its cohering power.

The written documents that grew originally from its inception gave shape and form to our nationally shared myth. It also connects us to history—so an intimate correlation exists between history and mythology; they are partners that collaborate to strengthen our beliefs.

As mythologist Joseph Campbell asserts, myths grow from the imagination itself; they offer inklings of latent energies: "Myths are clues to the spiritual potentialities of the human life," he suggests in *The Power of Myth*. Myths are organizing principles: "They're stories about the wisdom of life, they really are" (9). I think his observation is valid on both individual and collective levels. They put us in touch with what is beyond us, what we aspire to, even as they instill in us the energy needed to approximate their wisdom. Voting, for example, is a ritual, by which we embody and act on the myth that has defined us.

But today it seems that the myth of democracy, with its mysterious and fragile core element of human freedom, is being challenged by the myth of individualism and illusory facts. Campbell believes this latter myth of individualism can become its own worldview. People can then lose sight of how they represent something bigger than themselves.

Rituals take the individual out of the equation as central and place them as "agents" of something far bigger: "Joining the army, putting on a uniform, is another. You're giving up your personal life and accepting a socially determined manner of life in the service of society. . ." (12).

The point here is that any political figure, especially, is a representative of some ideal or vision beyond themselves. When that collapses in a democracy, then any person who has been elected by the people for the best interests of the people may turn inward and abuse their position to satisfy personal appetites; under such stress, the democratic myth may need a respirator to survive.

Such personal appetites violate the myth that put them in office to serve something well beyond themselves, something transcendent—most especially the life principle of the people who elected them. What myth each of us chooses to abide by will have repercussions throughout society.

We want to choose our guiding myth carefully and then breathe life into it so it may sustain us when our beliefs are challenged by violence and other acts of tyrannous aggression.

37

---•---

DOES ALL LEARNING HAVE TO BE USEFUL?*

Two of our particularly American myths are: the economic myth and the myth of utility or usefulness. The conventional, and largely inadequate belief, is that students enroll in higher education programs with the aim of finding suitable employment. Such an attitude, such a mythic understanding of "learning for the sake of earning" has been imbedded deeply into our belief system. But learning was not always inflected along such a narrow, utilitarian corridor, however useful it can be.

A recent publication challenges these baked-in beliefs: *Lost in Thought: The Hidden Pleasures of an Intellectual Life* (2020) which is certain to stir controversy. It is one signal of the success of a book if it can do so. Its author, Zena Hitz, winner of The Hiett Prize offered by the Dallas Institute of Humanities and Culture for promising young scholars in the humanities, teaches in the Great Books program at St. John's College in Annapolis, Maryland.

At one point she became so disillusioned with higher education that she retreated from it and entered a monastery for three years. There she carefully reevaluated her thinking about the deeper values of why we learn, beyond job acquisition and earning a living.

In one of her chapters, "Learning, Leisure, and Happiness," Zena poses two fundamental questions asked by few: "What does learning look like, stripped of its trappings of fame, prestige, fortune, and social use?

---

* Originally published in the *Herald-Zeitung*, November 21st-22nd, 2020.

In other words, how is it good for its own sake, because of its effect on the learner rather than because of its outward results?"

Reading insightful, thoughtful books in many fields, from the ancients' exploration of what makes us human in all our complexity, to more contemporary works in philosophy, theology, mathematics, literature, and politics, can open us to the deeper dimensions of who we are as unique human beings. Such an attitude of learning can resist forces in a culture that is more comfortable with consuming, striving for more and greater, and seeking the new and latest for a variety of reasons. In the process, reflection, thoughtful conversations, and questioning the status quo can be sidelined.

Not many educators I have known or read have made the claim offered by Zena; she unabashedly claims that learning, which is one of the deepest instincts in our species, has the capacity to generate joy. To learn is to learn to enjoy being ourselves, being human, and most importantly, learning the art of reflection on our life's journey.

One condition that helps to promote these features is, of course, being willing for brief periods of time to be in solitude, which is not the same as being alone or lonely. Being busy often keeps this tendency or need at a safe distance. In my own life, embracing solitude is the only place from which I can think and write. Then, being with others is more, not less, joyful.

Chapter 3, "The Uses of Uselessness," offers a counter-myth when so much in our lives is measured and valued to the degree that it has "use." Here she addresses a modern trend—the idea that learning for its own sake and joy has "been traded for learning for social utility, for the sake of 'making a difference.'"

Yet, not without irony, the notion of learning as useless carries with it a use: "The value of intellectual life lies in its broadening and deepening of our humanity. . . [which] begins in the readers' or the inquirers' deep engagement with learning, their assumption of their responsibility of being transformed by what they learn, ..."

Zena's inspiring study resists the threadbare slogan in academe that studying the humanities promotes critical thinking. While not wrong, it is too anemic. Zena suggests that learning can transform the individual, which is itself a form of social activism, so that learning more deeply about who one truly is can have profound and positive effects on society at large. We sense the paradox in her discussion: that what might look outwardly as "useless," is actually intensely useful, but on a register not often surveyed by those whose discernment needs a make-over.

ACKNOWLEDGMENTS

Rather than comment on those who have assisted me with this volume of meditations on the cultural imagination, I prefer to list those who have helped me over the decades to reach the rich life I savor today. Each, in his or her own way, has led me to an abundant life of writing, teaching, and other creative ways of living a fulfilling life. I place them in alphabetical order and salute each of their talents they shared with me as guides to a life I have treasured. Their presence at various moments of my pilgrimage have been treasures that one cannot search for; they are given in grace.

Stephen Aizenstat, Larry Allums, Roger Barnes, Clay Boykin, Joseph Cambray, Reverend Barbara Child, Pema Chodron, Michael Conforti, Phil Cousineau, Donald Cowan, Louise Cowan, Don Carlson, Dan Canalos, Toni D'Anca, Tim Donohue, Christine Downing, James Hillman, James Hollis, Linda Calvert Jacobson, Martha Anne Kirk, Akke-Jean Klerk, Machiel Klerk, Will Linn, Phil Lynch, Claudia MacMillan, Patrick Mahaffey, Aryeh Maidenbaum, Maureen Murdock, Bradley Olson, Deborah Anne Quibell, Robert Romanyshyn, Diana Ruben, Jennifer Leigh Selig, Sandy Slattery, Joanne Stroud, Mary Beth Swofford, Marshal Terry, Dianne Travis-Teague, Mary Watkins, Dana White, Willow Young, and Connie Zweig.

I am also grateful to Dr. Seemee Ali, President of the Dallas Institute of Humanities and Culture, for giving me permission to use four of the essays in this collection that, in slightly altered form, appeared in the Dallas Institute Publications.

I also thank poet Timothy J. Donohue for permission to quote lines from his poem, "At A Graveyard by an Orchard" that introduce Chapter 2.

ABOUT THE AUTHOR

Dennis Patrick Slattery, Ph.D., has been teaching for fifty-three years, the last twenty-seven in the Mythological Studies Program at Pacifica Graduate Institute in Carpinteria, California. He is the author, co-author, editor, or co-editor of thirty-two volumes, including seven volumes of poetry: *Casting the Shadows: Selected Poems*; *Just Below the Water Line: Selected Poems*; *Twisted Sky: Selected Poems*; *The Beauty Between Words: Selected Poems of Dennis Patrick Slattery and Chris Paris*; *Feathered Ladder: Selected Poems* with Brian Landis; *Road, Frame Window: A Poetics of Seeing. Selected Poetry of Timothy J. Donohue, Donald Carlson and Dennis Patrick Slattery*; and *Leaves from the World Tree: Selected Poems of Craig Deininger and Dennis Patrick Slattery*. He has co-authored one novel, *Simon's Crossing*, with Charles Asher. Other titles include *The Idiot: Dostoevsky's Fantastic Prince. A Phenomenological Approach*; *The Wounded Body: Remembering the Markings of Flesh*; *Creases in Culture: Essays Toward a Poetics of Depth*; and *Bridge Work: Essays on Mythology, Literature and Psychology*. With Lionel Corbett he has co-edited and contributed to *Psychology at the Threshold* and *Depth Psychology: Meditations in the Field*; with Glen Slater he has co-edited and contributed to *Varieties of Mythic Experience: Essays on Religion, Psyche and Culture*; and *A Limbo of Shards: Essays on Memory, Myth and Metaphor*. His more recent books include *Our Daily Breach: Exploring Your Personal Myth through Herman Melville's Moby-Dick; Day-to-Day Dante: Exploring Personal Myth Through the Divine Comedy*; and *Riting Myth, Mythic Writing: Plotting Your Personal Story*. With Jennifer Leigh Selig, he has coedited and contributed to *Re-Ensouling Education: Essays on the Importance of the Humanities in Schooling the Soul,* and *Reimagining Education: Essays on Reviving the Soul of Learning*. With Deborah Anne Quibell and Jennifer Leigh Selig he has co-authored a book awarded a Nautilus Book First Place Prize for best book on Inspiration and Creativity in 2020: *Deep Creativity: Seven Ways to Spark Your Creative*

Spirit, with Evans Lansing Smith he has co-edited *Correspondence: 1927-1987* on the letters of Joseph Campbell. He has also authored over 200 essays and reviews in books, magazines, newspapers, and on-line journals. His most current publications include *From War to Wonder: Recovering Your Personal Myth Through Homer's Odyssey* and *An Obscure Order: Reflections on Cultural Mythologies*.

He offers riting retreats both in-person and on Zoom in the United States and Europe on exploring one's personal myth through the works of Joseph Campbell and C. G. Jung's *Red Book* as well as on topics of creativity, the mythology of belief and the nature of stories and personal identity.

For recreation he takes classes painting mythic themes in both water-color and acrylic. He also enjoys riding his Harley-Davidson motorcycle with his two sons, Matt and Steve, through the Hill Country roads of Texas. He enjoys being a grandfather to three sweet young women: Kris, Eleanor and Siena.

For more about Dennis, visit www.dennispatrickslattery.com.

www.ingramcontent.com/pod-product-compliance
Lightning Source LLC
Chambersburg PA
CBHW031425270326
41930CB00007B/581